DATE DUE

Whose Child?

Children's Rights, Parental Authority, and State Power

Whose Child?

Children's Rights, Parental Authority, and State Power

edited by
WILLIAM AIKEN
and
HUGH LaFOLLETTE

ROWMAN AND LITTLEFIELD
Totowa   New Jersey

For Rachel, Timothy, and Travis

Library edition first published in the United States of America, 1980, by Rowman and Littlefield, Totowa, New Jersey, 07512

Library of Congress Cataloging in Publication Data
Main entry under title:

Whose child?

  Bibliography: p.
  1. Children's rights—United States—Addresses, essays, lectures. 2. Parent and child—Addresses, essays, lectures. 3. Children—Legal status, laws, etc.—United States—Addresses, essays, lectures.
I. Aiken, William, 1947-   II. LaFollette, Hugh, 1948-
HQ792.U5W48 1980b   305.2′3   79-27577
ISBN 0-8476-6282-9

Printed in the United States of America

Table of Contents

General Introduction

"Children are the most valuable resource of mankind," we are often told. If that is so, we have peculiar ways of treating them. Furthermore, our thoughts about how we *should* treat them are profoundly confused. While some advocate freedom for children to do whatever they please, others scorn this permissiveness. While the United States Supreme Court upholds the use of stiff corporal punishment in the schools, the Swedish parliment outlaws all corporal punishment of children, not only in the schools but also in the home. While advocates clamor for recognition of children's rights, others belittle these claims and reaffirm the "time-honored values" of the nuclear family and respect for parents.

In short, there are no settled views about rearing, treating, or relating to children. At least this is so in our Western culture. In fact, most people rarely think about child rearing. When they do, it is seldom careful and systematic. Instead most of us just "muddle through", leaving the future of our children largely to fate.

We want to remedy this tragic deficiency. As a small step, we have brought together diverse writings about our treatment of children to spur more frequent and insightful discussions about preferred ways of rearing and relating to children. But how can someone even begin to profitably discuss this issue—there are so many diverse and seemingly unrelated questions? To get a handle on this issue one needs to find a general framework. We suggest that questions about our treatment of children be seen as arising from the three way relationship among the child, the parent, and the state. At first glance, many of the questions seem to focus on the relationships between only two of these parties. For example, child abuse concerns the parent-child relationship while the juvenile justice system primarily concerns the child-state relations. Still, even in these cases the other member of the three way relationship plays some role—even if it is just a background role. The state, for example, lurks in the shadows as a force which can punish child abusers. And while parents are not directly involved in juvenile court proceedings, they will clearly exert some influence, at least by providing the court with an alternative to institutionalization. So as you can see, the child, the parent, and the state are intricately interconnected.

The general questions which essays in this anthology will address illustrate this relationship: what rights, if any, do children have against their parents or the state? Do parents have legitimate authority over their children? If so, why, and how extensive is it? Finally, what authority does the state have to intervene in the family—either to alter it by removing children from the home or to restrict parental authority? These are the questions which motivate this book and will be addressed by the selections. More importantly, these are the questions which we all need to ask and to attempt to answer if we are to do justice to "the most valuable resource of mankind."

THE SCOPE AND STRUCTURE OF THE ANTHOLOGY

This anthology is divided into three sections. The first section presents selections culled from the current popular debate about the proper treatment of children. These brief selections from magazines, newspapers, books, and court decisions were selected to acquaint the reader with the scope and complexity of the issues. As an aid to the reader, we will include before each entry, a brief summary of the entry as well as some suggestions or questions to encourage further thought.

The second section is a transition essay designed to serve as a bridge between the popular essays and the philosophical essays which will follow. This essay serves two important functions. First, it will explain what philosophical analysis can add to the popular debate. In particular, it shows how the issues raised in the debate demand the philosopher's systematic approach. Secondly, to assist the non-philosophically trained reader, we will briefly describe some of the concepts used by philosophers to debate these issues.

The third section contains philosophical essays. Some of these are difficult to read. But they are all important since they provide the necessary systematic examination of questions about our treatment of children, for example: How, if at all can children, particularly infants, have rights? Even if children do have rights is it wise to recognize them? What does it mean when a parent or the state claims "to protect a child's interests"? What responsibility do parents have to their children? What responsibility do other adults, say teachers, have to children? Do parents have the legitimate authority to force their children to quit school or hand out religious literature? Can the state coerce parents to protect their children's interests? The philosophers' discussions of these questions are not intended to offer precise, mechanical solutions to specific issues raised in the popular debate. Nonetheless they do help us think more clearly, consistently, and coherently about them. In this section, as in the first, we will include introductory summaries and questions and will also point out certain interconnections between the various philosophical essays.

Part I
The Popular Debate

Peter and Judith DeCourcy

A Case History of Child Abuse

*The essay begins with an officer's report of a severe case
of child abuse; the report is followed by a description of
the subsequent judicial proceedings. Despite the actual
outcome in this case, the proper verdict is apparent: the
children should have been removed from the home. But
decisions about dealing with abuse can be difficult. What
happens, for example, if the child is abused only once—
even if the abuse is severe? Should the child automatically
be removed from the home? How does one tell if a child
has been abused or simply had an accident? Should we
step up efforts to identify abusive parents, even if it means
that many parents will be falsely investigated, accused, or
convicted of abuse?*

DEPARTMENT OF PUBLIC SAFETY
BUREAU OF POLICE
Officer's Report

At approximately 5:45 PM I received a phone call from a Mrs. Ann
Mills who stated that she lived at 6644 N. Octavia St. and that a girl who
appeared to be eight or nine years old had been sitting on the curb in
front of her house crying and that a neighbor had gone out and talked to
the girl and had brought the girl into the house where she was sitting
crying. She would not say who she was and they wished a police officer
to come to the home.

Necessary information was given to Radio Div. and a car was

dispatched. Julie Maxwell, the girl, was brought to the Children's Place of Detention at approx. 6:30 PM, date, by Officer Ray, Badge #980, Car 7. Julie was very upset, and though she had told Officer Ray her name, she would not tell the truth about her phone number, or address or who her parents were. She stated that she didn't want to ever go home again because her father beat her all the time. She said that she hurt because she had not cleaned the house right last night and her father had whipped her.

Approx. 6:40 PM Mr. Maxwell phoned in. He said he had talked to a lot of people in the police department, and he was tired of being run around and asked if we had his daughter, Julie, in custody. He was advised that we were talking to the girl as a result of a citizen's report. He became very irate and started screaming over the telephone at me and demanded to know why I hadn't told him where his daughter was. He was informed that Julie had given us no information and that we were unable to find out her father's name or where she lived. He was also told that she had only been here in custody for ten minutes. After this he calmed down and stated that he wanted to come down here. He was told that Julie was upset and did not wish to return home and that I would probably call him back after I had a chance to talk further to her.

At this time we raised the girl's dress to inspect her legs and found that there were extensive bruises on her mid-section. These started at approximately her waist and went to about her knees. These bruises were very purple, and some of them appeared to be infected, open sores. We asked Julie what had happened, and she stated that her father had beaten her with the belt the night before, that this happened all the time, that the sores never healed, and that she did not want to go home. At this time a formal statement was taken from Julie which reads as follows:

"My name is Julie Maxwell. The policemen have told me that I do not have to say anything. My name used to be Groot until my dad changed it to Maxwell. My dad is my step-dad. Me and my brother cleaned the house last night, and then we had to go to bed. My dad came home from work after a while and got us kids up. Then we got a talking to and then we got in trouble. We got in trouble because we didn't sweep the stairs right and didn't wash the dishes right. I did wrong and my brother did wrong, but if two do wrong, then everybody gets punished. So dad and mom got all of us kids up, my two brothers, my sister and me. We all got a spanking with a belt. Then he told us that if the house wasn't cleaned up right this coming weekend, that he wouldn't feed us any more. A week ago he tied me to the bed with a rope, but I got loose and he hit me in the nose with his fist. I don't remember exactly what this was for. A little more than a week ago he tied me to the bed another time, and I don't remember what for, but he hit me with a belt and with the belt buckle. There are two sores on my right leg between my knee and my tummy from when he hit me this time. About a week ago I think he also got me on the floor and put one foot on my head and another foot on my leg and took the belt to me. We all got spankings two times a week if we needed them."

/S/ Julie Maxwell

After this statement was taken Mr. Maxwell was advised by phone that the girl would be held in protective custody and that he should be at the Juvenile Affairs Bureau Monday morning at which time there would be a hearing about the entire matter. He asked what the charges were and was told that Julie was being taken into protective custody due to the bruises on her legs. He was told that we felt that these bruises were serious enough that the matter should be handled by the Juvenile Court. Mr. Maxwell became very angry and shouted, "You mean to tell me I can't spank my own children?" He was told that we did not mean to tell him any such thing, but we felt that the discipline had been much too severe. At this time he stated, "Well, I just took my belt off and beat the devil out of her." At this point Mr. Maxwell was told to say nothing more, and he was advised of his rights. He was told that he did not have to say anything to me, and anything he said could be used against him in court. He was also told that he could have any attorney, and if he didn't have the money, an attorney would be appointed for him. Mr. Maxwell was asked if he understood these rights, and he stated that he did. He was again advised to be at the 10 AM hearing, Monday, August 4.

Officer Lucas from Identification Division was contacted and the girl was taken to Identification for pictures. Two colored Polaroid pictures were taken of the bruises on her leg and body. At approximately 8:15 PM Julie was transported to the Juvenile Affairs Bureau Wilson Shelter for Children.

At approximately 8:30 PM Mr. Maxwell phoned again and demanded to know what he should do to get his daughter back. We again advised him that there was nothing he could do until the hearing on Monday morning. He then asked if it would be all right if he came into the office to talk about the situation. He was told that if he wanted to, he certainly could come. He asked if he would be arrested if he came in and was told not at this time, but that charges might be placed against him in the future. He said he would be down very shortly.

Detectives who were available were contacted and asked to assist with the interview. At approximately 9:45 PM Mr. and Mrs. Maxwell and three children arrived. Mrs. Maxwell was extremely upset and irrational the whole time she was here. She screamed at me and the other officers and attempted to hit one and called us several wild names. She also threatened to kill us if we tried to take her children away from her. She finally became so upset that she was taken into custody and removed to the psychiatric ward of the County Hospital.

Subsequent to these events Ruth Maxwell bent over to tie her shoelace and bruises were observed on her leg. Further examination revealed that she had extensive bruises on the inside of her right thigh and a few on her buttocks. She stated that these were inflicted last night by her father. The other children were then examined and it was discovered that Paul had extensive bruises on his right thigh and buttocks which he stated were inflicted last night by his father. His penis was bruised and the flesh of the foreskin was scarred and torn. He attributed this to previous beatings inflicted upon him by his father. Michael appeared to have suffered the most serious injuries. He had bruises and open cuts across his upper and lower back, his buttocks and both thighs. He had an extremely large bruise under his scrotum and his penis was cut and bruised.

The degree of cuts and bruises on these children was unbelievable, and Identification was again called and arrangements were made to photograph these injuries. It was noticed that the children behaved almost like little soldiers. They were very well behaved almost to the point of being trained. When they were asked a question, they replied ''yes ma'am'' or ''yes sir'' immediately. They all said that they loved their stepfather; however, it is hard to believe that they know what love means. It was felt that they had been told to say that they loved their stepfather rather than having real affection for him. Julie was the only one who said that she did not like her stepfather, and she was the one who ran away. We believe that these children have been terribly damaged, psychologically as well as physically and request that a petition be prepared on all the children so that the parents may not gain control of them.

Following the examination of the children Mr. Maxwell was advised that all of the children would be taken into protective custody. He stated that he believed he was doing his duty as a stepfather by hitting the children with his belt and that his wife agreed with his treatment. He then became extremely agitated and stated that he knew the police department was interested in persecuting his family. He made what he termed a "formal" request that the police take their vengeance on him and lock him up for the rest of his life or crucify him rather than taking their vengeance on his wife and his children. Consideration was given to holding this man for psychiatric evaluation, but he did eventually become quiet, left the station, and returned to his home.

/S/ John H. Turnau
Badge No. 361
1st Nite Relief

10:45 PM 8-1-69

The case was assigned to the docket of Judge Chester Beshaw, an elderly man with deep religious convictions. He was a member of a fundamentalist sect and had held a variety of lay offices in his congregation. He had acquired a moderate degree of notoriety by his frequent appearances at school board meetings throughout the county to vigorously denounce various academic courses which he termed "Godless."

The first witness was Jane Grace, M.D., a resident internist at the County Hospital. Dr. Grace testified as to the physical and mental condition of the Maxwell children.

The Maxwell's daughter had cryptogenic epilepsy with a long history of seizures. Mr. Maxwell had opposed any treatment for this condition, advised Dr. Grace that "it was the will of God," and had further expressed the opinion that Ruth would "outgrow it." Dr. Grace testified that Ruth's back, buttocks, and thighs had extensive scar tissue as well as cuts and contusions. She stated that these injuries were compatible with a hypothesis that the girl had been severely beaten over an extended period of time. The psychiatric findings were that Ruth was of normal intelligence, but that she was an extremely shy, inhibited child who was forced to rely on a rich fantasy life for the gratification of her emotional needs. It was suggested that unless her environment was modified, a schizophrenic process might possibly ensue.

Dr. Grace's testimony suggested that neither Paul nor Michael suffered from any physical abnormalities other than scar tissue and evidence of recent trauma which was suggestive of repeated beatings. Like Ruth, they were found to be extremely inhibited, but apparently they had made friends with children of their own age, which enabled them to fulfill many of their emotional needs.

The physical examination of Julie revealed that her tongue was badly scarred and that there were large amounts of scar tissue on the inner mouth. Dr. Grace testified that Mr. Maxwell advised her that these scars were the results of burns caused by Julie's childhood habit of licking electrical outlets. Julie told the doctor that the burns had been caused several years earlier by her father, who put live electric plugs in her mouth. It was also found that Julie had suffered meningitis in infancy, which had caused moderate brain damage. Her present level of intellectual functioning was seen as being in the borderline range of mental retardation. The psychiatric evaluation also indicated that she was not capable of suppressing her desires for immediate gratification of her needs, and that when she was thwarted or frustrated, she tended to develop many explosive tendencies.

Testimony as to Mr. Maxwell's emotional state was given by Samuel Douglas, Ph.D., a psychologist on the staff of the County Mental Health Out-Patient Clinic. He described the various tests and diagnostic tools that had been used and stated that Mr. Maxwell was highly intelligent, but that he was psychotic. He was found to be quite egocentric, authoritarian, and resentful. He believed that he had a special relationship with God and that he was acting as God's agent on earth. He appeared to believe sincerely that the Devil could physically enter the bodies of the children and cause them to misbehave, and that when he beat the children, he was, in fact, beating the Devil and helping the children by driving the Devil, who had possessed them, from their bodies. In view of this delusional thinking, Dr. Douglas expressed the firm opinion that Mr. Maxwell would be a continuing threat to his stepchildren if they remained in his custody. The tentative diagnosis was Schizophrenia, Paranoid Type, and Mr. Maxwell's recovery was highly unlikely.

Testimony on Mrs. Maxwell's mental status was given by

Phillip Gossen, M.D., a psychiatric resident at the County Hospital. He stated that Mrs. Maxwell was mentally retarded, with an IQ of 69. It was his opinion that her impaired intellectual functioning, coupled with developmental and environmental factors, had so crippled Mrs. Maxwell's personality that she was unable to react to stress in any adaptive way. She was excitable, emotionally unstable, and attention-seeking. His diagnosis was Hysterical Personality with borderline mental retardation. It was his opinion that little could be done to effect improvement in Mrs. Maxwell's coping mechanisms.

Mrs. Gardner of the Welfare Department offered testimony in which she described her investigation of the Maxwell family. She stated that none of the neighbors had been aware of any unusual events in the Maxwell home, and that the Maxwells were generally regarded as moral, hard-working, desirable neighbors. However, various school personnel reported that the children often appeared exhausted during the school day and that both Ruth and Paul Maxwell had begged their teachers never to send any adverse reports to their father, stating that if he discovered that their behavior and academic achievement was less than excellent, they would be severely punished. She further stated that following the preliminary hearing Mr. and Mrs. Maxwell had made two supervised visits to their children. During these visits the parents were extremely hostile toward the children and condemned them for complaining about receiving punishment that they rightfully deserved. On one occasion Mr. Maxwell told the children that they would all "roast in Hell."

Detective Sgt. Halbert of the Police Department testified that neither Mr. nor Mrs. Maxwell had a criminal record and that neither of them had been arrested or charged with any crime. He further stated that he had been unable to discover any adverse information about the couple in the community except that Mr. Maxwell's fellow employees characterized him as a "religious nut."

The defense attorney, Paul Heiser, presented 23 witnesses, including the pastors of two churches, neighbors, and relatives.

These witnesses strongly stated their opinions that the Maxwell children were well clothed, well fed, well housed, and well behaved. Both Mr. and Mrs. Maxwell were described as being frugal, industrious, well behaved, and highly moralistic. Several of the witnesses, including the two pastors, expressed indignation at the notion that Mr. and Mrs. Maxwell were considered anything but highly suitable parents.

The decision of the court was given on September 3, 1969.

NOW THEREFORE IT IS HEREBY ADJUDGED
AND ORDERED:

Based upon the testimony offered the Court finds that the Maxwells are concerned and competent parents, but that on occasion their concern has resulted in excessive physical punishment.

It is further found that it is in the best interest of the children that they be returned to the custody of their parents, and the parents are ordered to refrain from employing physical punishment as a method of correcting or disciplining their children.

Dated this *3rd* day of *September 1969.*

                              /S/ Chester Beshaw
                              Judge

Those of use who are not lawyers or judges are astonished at how rapidly their behavior changes when they leave a courtroom. All signs of legal aloofness usually disappear and the anger or irritation displayed in the court is replaced by easy camaraderie. Not so with Judge Beshaw.

After he had given a decision in the Maxwell case and the court was adjourned, Beshaw was extremely angry. He addressed a tirade to Raymond Hazel, the Deputy District Attorney.

"You and the police are getting too nosey," he said. "You're sticking your noses into everything. And those doctors and psychologists—all that stuff they try to pull. I was going to be a doctor until I found I had to study a lot of algebra and physics. Tell me, in God's good name, what does a doctor need with algebra? You might as well know I'll *never* take children away from good, God-fearing people like these Maxwells. You heard what those two preachers said; they knew what they were talking about. The Maxwells are all right. Maybe they just try too hard to do what's right."

On September 23, 1969 Julie Maxwell was found wandering on a city street, badly beaten. She had cuts and bruises about her head and neck, and her jaw was fractured. Her buttocks and thighs were covered with cuts and bruises. She was hospitalized, and when she was able to talk, she was questioned by the police. She appeared to be terrified and incoherent, and refused to say who had beaten her, stating that "if I say my dad did it, he will kill me." No formal charges were placed against Mr. and Mrs. Maxwell because it could not be shown that they were the ones who injured Julie. However, they consented to have Julie placed in a boarding school for retarded children.

No further reports were received about this family until January 7, 1970, when Paul's school reported that he was unable to sit in class because of injuries at the base of his spine. The Juvenile Affairs Bureau took him into protective custody and a physical examination revealed cuts and bruises on his upper and lower back, a large bruise at the base of his spine, cuts and bruises on his inner thighs and genitals. He was extremely frightened and stated over and over, "I don't know what happened. My dad didn't do it."

An informal hearing was held on January 9, with Judge Beshaw again presiding. Mr. and Mrs. Maxwell, their attorney, and a representative of the Juvenile Affairs Bureau were present. Paul refused to say how he had gotten his injuries. Both Mr. and Mrs. Maxwell denied any knowledge of the injuries, claiming that he must have had a fight with another boy. A request by the representative of the Juvenile Affairs Bureau that the other children be placed in their custody and given physical examinations was denied. The judge ruled that since it could not be shown that Mr. or Mrs. Maxwell had abused Paul, no action should be taken.

Mr. and Mrs. Maxwell now have full custody of their children who apparently are so terrorized that they will not testify against their parents. Both the police and the Juvenile Affairs Bureau believe that in view of the attitude of the courts, they are powerless to take effective action. Hence, this extremely deviant couple are at liberty to continue their physical and emotional torture of their children.

Ted Patrick
Tom Dulak

A Defense of Deprogramming

Ted Patrick is a rather controversial figure who kidnaps young people who have joined religious cults and attempts to "deprogram" them, that is, he tries to "convince" the person that he/she should leave the cult and rejoin mainstream society. Patrick claims these drastic measures are necessary to rescue these people from the brainwashing of the cults. As you read Patrick's defense of his methods, ask yourself: Do parents have special rights to kidnap (rescue?) their children? Why shouldn't just any concerned citizen kidnap them? Better yet, why shouldn't the cults be closed down? If you think they should not be, then why condone the kidnapping in the first place? Or what should happen if the parents are members of these sects? Would someone else, say a grandparent or a friend, be justified in kidnapping and deprogramming these young people?

Deprogramming, I think, is widely misunderstood—I mean, what I do, what goes on. To read some of the accounts that have been written by reporters who have never witnessed a deprogramming, you would think it was a cross between the Spanish Inquisition and an orgy sponsored by the Marquis de Sade. It's nothing of the kind. Essentially it's just talk. I talk to the victim, for as long as I have to. I don't deny that that's the catch for

From *Let Our Children Go* by Ted Patrick and Tom Dulack. Copyright © 1976 by Ted Patrick and Tom Dulack. Reprinted by permission of the publisher, E. P. Dutton.

many people—"for as long as I have to." Yes, in some cases that means restraint. Yes, it also means the victim may not be free to leave when he wants to. When a victim is exceptionally vigorous, it may even mean a measure of physical restraint.

But let me say this. The techniques I employ do not in any way approximate or parallel the psychological kidnapping and mind control that the cults employ. The cults strike at random; they will approach anyone anywhere, without regard to the person's age, background, sex, or occupation. When they go out into the streets to witness—which is their dressed-up term for proselytizing (which is only another dressed-up word, in this instance, for psychological kidnapping)—they attempt to snare people indiscriminately. The Children of God, for example, have attempted to recruit children as young as nine years old. Once they get a victim, they consciously and deliberately set about to destroy every normal pattern of living the victim has known; he is separated from his friends, he is turned against his family, he is led to renounce his education, his career, his responsibilities. He is literally robbed of whatever financial assets he may possess, and his parents are as a matter of course blackmailed into contributing large sums of money to the cult merely in order to be occasionally permitted to see their child. He is physically abused and often expected to work as much as twenty hours a day fund-raising for the group. He is frequently undernourished and psychologically manipulated to the degree that he cannot distinguish reality and the grotesque fantasies and illusions the cult fosters. He is programmatically turned against his country, taught that patriotism is sinful, the system Satanic. He is urged to become a revolutionary, to destroy the institutions of society in the name of David Berg or some other phony god. Discord, division, hatred, grief—those are what the cults bestow.

Against that, the deprogramming method is first of all very selective. I don't go into a commune and indiscriminately grab the first person I see, as, in effect, the cults do when they are witnessing on the street. The parents of a young person will contact me—usually after months of deliberation, fear and uncertainty. When we take the person into custody he is, admittedly, held against his will. But it's arguable whether at that stage of his indoctrination he can be said to *have* a will, any will, let alone free will in the sense that we normally use that term. Regardless, the child is rarely held in custody by the parents and me for longer than three days. Usually it takes me less than one day to deprogram a person. I've managed to do it on occasion in an hour.

The important things to remember here are how the cults treated the individual, what their motives were, and how we treat him, what our motives are. The child is with his family throughout the process. He is well-fed. While I admit that limiting his sleep is a basic element in deprogramming, he sleeps at least as much as he did in the cult, almost all of which use fatigue as a strategic weapon. I do not brainwash. I ask questions, basically, and I try to show the victim how he has been deceived. Whereas, in the cult indoctrination, everything possible is done to prevent the person from thinking, in deprogramming I do everything I know how to start him thinking.

All deprogramming is is talk—a lot of talk. It only lasts two or three days. Not thirty or forty days as when a person joins a cult. Not three or four years of constant indoctrination and slave labor. I'm critized for holding these children against their will. But once you go into the Children of God, or the Unification Church, or the Hare Krishna movement, you are not, practically speaking, free to leave either. Now, that seems to suggest I'm fighting fire with fire—or that, at best, I'm no better in my methods than the cults.

But let's look at motives. I do not make money off the deprogrammed person. His parents pay for my travel and living expenses, and whatever other expenses are incurred during the snatch and deprogramming. He certainly does not become a follower of mine, selling plastic flowers in the streets to support me in a life of great luxury. I do not seek to implant in him any dogma, any preconceived or manufactured view or philosophy of life. Once he is deprogrammed he is absolutely free to do whatever he wants to do. Go to school, go to work, lie on a beach and look at the clouds. Whatever. That's none of my business. All I want and all I do is to return to them their ability to think for themselves, to exercise their free will, which the cults have put into cold storage. I thaw them out, and once they're free of the cult, with very few exceptions they begin again to lead productive lives—and not necessarily conformist lives. Deprogrammed people are as various and individualistic as any group in the society. Motives *are* important. The cults' motives are destructive—this can be demonstrated. My motives, I hope I have demonstrated here, have nothing in common with those of the spiritual gangsters who populate outfits like the Children of God.

Wallace v. Labrenz

104 NE 2nd 769
(March 20, 1952)

In Wallace v. Labrenz *the court held, as it frequently has, that a child in need of life-saving medical treatment can be given that treatment even if the child's parents refuse the treatment on religious grounds. Most people find this decision laudable. Yet how far can the state legitimately go in medical matters? Should they be able to force parents to surgically repair a cleft palate, cosmetically alter an unsightly birthmark, or provide braces?*

SCHAEFER, Justice.

After a hearing upon a petition filed in the circuit court of Cook County, an order was entered finding that Cheryl Linn Labrenz, an infant then eight days old, was a dependent child whose life was endangered by the refusal of her parents to consent to a necessary blood transfusion. The court appointed a guardian for the child and authorized the guardian to consent to a blood transfusion. The propriety of that action is challenged here upon a writ of error raising constitutional issues.

The petition was filed on April 17, 1951. It alleged that Cheryl Linn Labrenz was born on April 11, 1951, that she was then in a hospital in Chicago, and that her parents, Darrell and Rhoda Labrenz, were wholly unwilling to care for and protect her, so that she had become a dependent child. The petition prayed that the child be taken from its parents and placed under the guardianship of a suitable person to be appointed by the court.

At the hearing which was had on this petition on April 18, 1951, the evidence showed that the child suffered from erythrobastosis fetalis (commonly called the RH blood condition,) a

17

disease in which the red blood cells are destroyed by antibodies, or poisons. Hospital records and medical testimony established that the child's blood count had been dropping steadily since her birth; that the normal blood count of a child of her age was about 5,000,000 whereas her blood count was 1,950,000; that antibodies in the baby's blood stream were gradually destroying all of the red blood cells; that her blood-supplying system was unable to furnish a supply of its own blood adequate to overcome the condition, and that a blood transfusion was necessary.

Three doctors testified. Two were certain that the child would die unless a transfusion was administered. The third doctor testified that the child had a slim chance to live without a transfusion, but that even if she did live, without a transfusion her brain would probably be so injured that she would be mentally impaired for life. The medical testimony also dealt with the degree of risk involved in a blood transfusion. One doctor testified that there would be no more hazard in a transfusion than in taking an aspirin. While all three doctors testified that there would be risks involved if diseased or mistyped blood was used in the transfusion, all of them agreed that such risk as existed was due to the impossibility of eliminating completely the chance of human error, and that, properly conducted, a transfusion would not involve any serious hazard.

The parents of the child testified that their refusal to consent to a transfusion was based upon religious grounds. Darrell Labrenz, the child's father, testified: "it is my belief that the commandment given us in Genesis, Chapter 9, Verse 4, and subsequent commandment of Leviticus, Chapter 17, Verse 14, and also in the testimony after Christ's time and recorded in Acts, 15th Chapter, it is my opinion that any use of the blood is prohibited whether it be for food or whether it be for, as modern medical science puts it, for injections into the blood stream and as such I object to it. The life is in the blood and the life belongs to our father, Jehovah, and it is only his to give or take; it isn't ours, and as such I object to the using of the blood in connection with this case."

Rhoda Labrenz, the mother, testified that "we believe it would be breaking God's commandment to take away blood which he told us to eat of the flesh but should not take of the blood into our systems. The life is in the blood and blood should not be drained out. We feel that we would be breaking God's commandment, also destroying the baby's life for the future, not only this life, in case the baby should die and breaks the commandment, not only destroys our chances but also the baby's chances for future life. We feel it is more important than this life."

At the conclusion of the evidence offered on behalf of the State, and again at the conclusion of all the evidence, a motion to dismiss the petition was overruled. The court appointed its chief probation officer to be guardian of the person of Cheryl Linn Labrenz, directed him to consent to a blood transfusion, and retained jurisdiction for the purpose of making further orders for the welfare of the child. On May 4, 1951, the guardian reported to the court that a transfusion had been administered on April 18, 1951, and that the child's health had greatly improved. The court then ordered that the child be relased from the hospital and returned to the custody of her parents but refused to discharge the guardian because it found that further periodic medical examinations would be necessary to determine the need for additional transfusions. On June 15, 1951, the court discharged the guardian, released the child to her parents, and ordered that the proceeding be dismissed.

[1–3] Before we reach the merits, we meet the State's contention that the case is now moot and should be dismissed because the blood transfusion has been administered, the guardian discharged, and the proceeding dismissed. Because the function of courts is to decide controverted issues in adversary proceedings, moot cases which do not present live issues are not ordinarily entertained. "The general rule is that when a reviewing court has notice of facts which show that only moot questions or mere abstract propositions are involved or where the substantial questions involved in the trial court no longer exist, it will dismiss the appeal or writ of error." People v. Redlich, 402 Ill. 270, 279, 83 N.E. 2d 736, 741.

But when the issue presented is of substantial public interest, a well-recognized exception exists to the general rule that a case which has become moot will be dismissed upon appeal. See cases collected in 132 A.L.R. 1185. Among the criteria considered in determining the existence of the requisite degree of public interest are the public or private nature of the question presented, the desirability of an authoritative determination for the future guidance of public officers, and the likelihood of future recurrence of the question.

Applying these criteria, we find that the present case falls within that highly sensitive area in which governmental action comes into contact with the religious beliefs of individual citizens. Both the construction of the statute under which the trial court acted and its validity are challenged. In situations like this one, public authorities must act promptly if their action is to be effective, and although the precise limits of authorized conduct cannot be fixed in advance, no greater uncertainty should exist than the nature of the problems makes inevitable. In addition, the very urgency which presses for prompt action by public officials makes it probable that any similar case arising in the future will likewise become moot by ordinary standards before it can be determined by this court. For these reasons the case should not be dismissed as moot.

As an additional reason for retaining the case for decision, plaintiffs in error suggest that the determination below, even though standing unreviewed, would nevertheless bar a subsequent action to recover damages for a violation of the rights of the parents or of the child. So far as we have been able to ascertain, the effect, as *res judicata,* of a judgment which could not be reviewed because intervening circumstances made the case moot, has not been settled in this State. Such authority as exists elsewhere is not in agreement. See Am.Law Inst. Restatement, Judgments, sec. 69(2); cf. United States v. Munsingwear, Inc., 340 U.S. 36, 71 S.Ct. 104, 95 L.Ed. 36; see cases collected in 147 A.L.R. 1038. Because we hold that the public interest requires that the case be retained for decision, we do not decide this issue.

[4] Turning now to the merits of the case, plaintiffs in error

first argue that the court below lacked jurisdiction because the child was not a "neglected" or "dependent" child within the meaning of the statute. The jurisdiction which was exercised in this case stems from the responsibility of government, in its character as *parens patriae,* to care for infants within its jurisdiction and to protect them from neglect, abuse and fraud. Witter v. Cook County Com'rs, 256 Ill. 616, 622, 100 N.E. 148. Historically exercised by courts of chancery, In re Petition of Ferrier, 103 Ill. 367, it is "of ancient origin." Cowles v. Cowles, 3 Gilman 435. That ancient equitable jurisdiction was codified in our Juvenile Court Act, which expressly authorizes the court, if circumstances warrant, to remove the child from the custody of its parents and award its custody to an appointed guardian. Ill.Rev.Stat.1949, chap. 23, pars. 190–220.

[5, 6] So far as here pertinent, the statute defines a dependent or neglected child as one which "has not proper parental care." (Ill.Rev.Stat.1949, chap. 23, par. 190). The record contains no suggestion of any improper conduct on the part of the parents except in their refusal to consent to a blood transfusion. And it is argued that this refusal on the part of the parents does not show neglect, or a lack of parental care. Neglect, however, is the failure to exercise the care that the circumstances justly demand. It embraces wilful as well as unintentional disregard of duty. It is not a term of fixed and measured meaning. It takes its content always from specific circumstances, and its meaning varies as the context of surrounding circumstances changes. The question here is whether a child whose parents refuse to permit a blood transfusion, when lack of a transfusion means that the child will almost certainly die or at best will be mentally impaired for life, is a neglected child. In answering that question it is of no consequence that the parents have not failed in their duty in other respects. We entertain no doubt that this child, whose parents were deliberately depriving it of life or subjecting it to permanent mental impairment, was a neglected child within the meaning of the statute. The circuit court did not lack jurisdiction.

[7] Plaintiffs in error argue that they merely exercised their right to avoid the risk of a proposed hazardous operation—the

transfusion—and that such a choice does not indicate a lack of proper parental care. The short answer is that the facts here disclose no such perilous undertaking, but, on the contrary, an urgently needed transfusion—virtually certain of success if given in time—with only such attendant risk as is inescapable in all of the affairs of life. The argument, based upon such cases as In re Hudson, 13 Wash.2d 673, 126 P.2d 765, and In re Tuttendario, 21 Pa.Dist.R. 561, which deal with operations involving substantial risk of life, is obviously not in point.

[8, 9] It is next contended that if the Juvenile Court Act is held to be applicable, it deprives the parents of freedom of religion, and of their rights as parents, in violation of the fourteenth amendment to the constitution of the United States and of section 3 of article II of the constitution of Illinois, S.H.A. This contention is based upon the parents' objection to the transfusion because of their belief that blood transfusions are forbidden by the Scriptures. Because the governing principles are well settled, this argument requires no extensive discussion. Concededly, freedom of religion and the right of parents to the care and training of their children are to be accorded the highest possible respect in our basic scheme. West Virginia State Board of Education v. Barnette, 319 U.S. 624, 63 S.Ct. 1178, 87 L.Ed. 1628; Meyer v. Nebraska, 262 U.S. 390, 43 S.Ct. 625, 67 L.Ed. 1042; Pierce v. Society of Sisters, 268 U.S. 510, 45 S.Ct. 571, 69 L.Ed. 1070. But "neither rights of religion or rights of parenthood are beyond limitation." Prince v. Massachusetts, 321 U.S. 158, 167, 64 S.Ct. 438, 88 L.Ed. 645; see: Reynolds v. United States, 98 U.S. 145, 25 L.Ed. 244; Jacobson v. Massachusetts, 197 U.S. 11, 25 S.Ct. 358, 49 L.Ed. 643.

Indeed, the early decision in the Reynolds case, upholding a Mormon's conviction for bigamy against the defense of interference with religious freedom as guaranteed in the first amendment, leaves no doubt about the validity of the action here taken. The following language of that opinion is of particular interest, 98 U.S. at page 166: "Laws are made for the government of actions, and while they cannot interfere with mere religious belief and opinions, they may with practices. Suppose one believed that human sacrifices were a necessary part of religious worship, would it be seriously contended that the civil government under which he lived could not interfere to prevent a sacrifice? Or if a wife religiously believed it was her duty to burn herself upon the funeral pile of her dead husband, would it be beyond the power of the civil government to prevent her carrying her belief into practice?''

The recent Prince decision reinforces that conclusion. The court there held that a State, acting to safeguard the general interest in the well-being of its youth, could prohibit a Jehovah's Witness child from distributing religious pamphlets on the street even though the child was accompanied by her adult guardian. Obviously, the facts before us present a far stronger case for State intervention. Further, the court observed in reaching its conclusion in the Prince case, 321 U.S. at pages 166, 170, 64 S.Ct. at pages 442, 444: "The right to practice religion freely does not include liberty to expose the community or child to communicable disease or the latter to ill health or death. Parents may be free to become martyrs themselves. But it does not follow they are free, in identical circumstances, to make martyrs of their children before they have reached the age of full and legal discretion when they can make that choice for themselves.''

We hold, therefore, that neither the statute nor the action of the court pursuant to the statute violated the constitutional rights of plaintiffs in error.

[10] The final contention is that the trial court committed prejudicial error in excluding from evidence the religious magazine, Awake. The contention is without merit. Except as it might bear upon the good faith of the parents' belief in the Scriptural prohibition against blood transfusion, it was inadmissible as hearsay. And since the sincerity of the parents' religious beliefs was not questioned, the exclusion of the magazine was not error.

The judgment of the circuit court of Cook County is affirmed.

Judgment affirmed.

Sibling "Consents" to Bone Marrow Transplant

This newspaper article chronicles a heart-rending story of a baby, suffering from a fatal bone marrow disease, who is to be "saved" by a painful and somewhat risky transplant from his sister. It sounds laudable, but is it? Can the two year old sister really understand the sacrifice she claims she wants to make? If not, do the parents have the authority to allow her to undergo the transplant? What would your reaction be if she did not want to help her baby brother? Could her parents legitimately force her to participate in the transplant?

The amount donated to the J.J. Altenbach Fund has reached $1,981. And that's only in five days!

Kind-hearted *Express* readers contributed $1,299 over the weekend. The first total, reported Friday, was $682.

"I can't believe it. It can't be true. That's unbelievable," Mrs. Walter J. Altenbach of Wilson said when notified of the fund total Monday night. And then she broke down, half in tears and half in smiles.

The 9-month-old boy has a dreaded and rare disease called Wiskott-Aldrich Syndrome. Only a bone-marrow transplant can save the lad. His sister Beth Ann, 2, will donate the bone marrow during an operation at Children's Hospital in Philadelphia.

The family already owes so much for treatment, and the cost

From *The Express* (Easton, Pa.) on June 19, 1979. Reprinted by permission of *The Express*.

to come will be so great that generous doctors and kind officials of Hahnemann and Children's hospitals have advised the Altenbachs not to worry about money.

But Altenbach, who is a bus maintenance laborer, and his wife, who worked until recently, do have other money worries. They worry about money for J.J.'s special diet and medicine and ordinary family expenses—there are two other children—and their car. Their unreliable and unsafe car which has broken down several times when J.J. was being taken for medical tests in Philadelphia.

With great generosity, sympathy and grace, people of *The Express* area have come forward. They have donated sums small and large for J.J.'s cause.

Organizations are coming forward, too. One of the first is the Red, White, and Blue CB Radio Club of Phillipsburg, which has sent $100. The club has given thousands of dollars to local charities. Its generosity is a byword. So is that of another $100 donor group, Easton P.O.S. of A. Camp Washington.

The names of the donors are being listed in *The Express*. They can't all be singled out.

The messages which many sent are touching. "In memory of my son Tommy," says one. Another very aptly calls J.J. "sweetheart." Many donors write that their gifts are not large enough, but are all they can afford.

And there is a special note, with a gift of just $3 in cash and a million dollars (at least) in love. It says, "God bless this family."

Parham v. J.L. and J.R.

47 USLW 4740
(June 19, 1979)

In Parham v. J. L. and J. R. the Supreme Court ruled that parents could seek state administered institutional mental health care for their child without an advisory hearing prior to commitment. What we find significant about this opinion is not just the specific issue at stake, but the general considerations the judges raised in making the decision. For example, the decision is, at least in large part, founded on the conviction that the family unit is important and that parents have "broad authority over minor children." But why should parents have such broad authority? Does the presumption that parents do an adequate job rearing children in everyday affairs justify the belief that parents can make wise and unbiased judgments about matters as serious as institutionalization in a mental hospital?

MR. CHIEF JUSTICE BURGER delivered the opinion of the Court.

The question presented in this appeal is what process is constitutionally due a minor child whose parents or guardian seek state administered institutional mental health care for the child and specifically whether an adversary proceeding is required prior to or after the commitment. . . .

J. L., a plaintiff before the District Court who is now deceased, was admitted in 1970 at the age of six years to Central State Regional Hospital in Milledgeville, Ga. Prior to his admission, J. L. had received out-patient treatment at the hospital for over two months. J. L.'s mother then requested the hospital to admit him indefinitely.

The admitting physician interviewed J. L. and his parents. He learned that J. L.'s natural parents had divorced and his mother had remarried. He also learned that J. L. had been expelled from school because he was uncontrollable. He accepted the parents' representation that the boy had been extremely aggressive and diagnosed the child as having a "hyperkinetic reaction to childhood."

J. L.'s mother and stepfather agreed to participate in family therapy during the time their son was hospitalized. Under this program J. L. was permitted to go home for short stays. Apparently his behavior during these visits was erratic. After several months the parents requested discontinuance of the program.

In 1972, the child was returned to his mother and stepfather on a furlough basis, *i. e.*, he would live at home but go to school at the hospital. The parents found they were unable to control J. L. to their satisfaction which created family stress. Within two months they requested his readmission to Central State. J. L.'s parents relinquished their parental rights to the county in 1974.

Although several hospital employees recommended that J. L. should be placed in a special foster home with "a warm, supported, truly involved couple," the Department of Family and Children Services was unable to place him in such a setting. On October 24, 1975, J. L. filed this suit requesting an order of the court placing him in a less drastic environment suitable to his needs.

•   •   •

(a) It is not disputed that a child, in common with adults, has a substantial liberty interest in not being confined unnecessarily for medical treatment and that the State's involvement in the commitment decision constitutes state action under the Fourteenth Amendment. See *Addington* v. *Texas,* No. 77–5992, at 7 (Apr. 30, 1979); *In re Gault,* 387 U. S. 1, 27 (1967); *Specht* v. *Patterson,* 386 U. S. 605 (1967). We also recognize that commitment sometimes produces adverse social consequences for the child because of the reaction of some to the discovery that the child has received psychiatric care. Cf. *Addington* v. *Texas, supra,* at 7.

This reaction, however, need not be equated with the community response resulting from being labeled by the state as deliquent, criminal, or mentally ill and possibly dangerous. See *ibid; In re Gault, supra,* at 23; *Paul* v. *Davis,* 424 U. S. 693, 711–712 (1976). The state through its voluntary commitment procedures does not "label" the child; it provides a diagnosis and treatment that medical specialists conclude the child requires. In terms of public reaction, the child who exhibits abnormal behavior may be seriously injured by an erroneous decision not to commit. Appellees overlook a significant source of the public reaction to the mentally ill, for what is truly "stigmatizing" is the symptomatology of a mental or emotional illness. *Addington* v. *Texas, supra,* at 10. See also Schwartz, Myers & Astrachan, Psychiatric Labeling and the Rehabilitation of the Mental Patient, 31 Archives of General Psychiatry 329 (1974). The pattern of untreated, abnormal behavior—even if nondangerous—arouses at least as much negative reaction as treatment that becomes public knowledge. A person needing, but not receiving, appropriate medical care may well face even greater social ostracism resulting from the observable symptoms of an untreated disorder.

However, we need not decide what effect these factors might have in a different case. For purposes of this decision, we assume that a child has a protectible interest not only in being free of unnecessary bodily restraints but also in not being labeled erroneously by some because of an improper decision by the state hospital superintendent.

(b) We next deal with the interests of the parents who have decided, on the basis of their observations and independent professional recommendations, that their child needs institutional care. Appellees argue that the constitutional rights of the child are of such magnitude and the likelihood of parental abuse is so great that the parents' traditional interests in and responsibility for the upbringing of their child must be subordinated at least to the extent of providing a formal adversary hearing prior to a voluntary commitment.

Our jurisprudence historically has reflected Western Civilization concepts of the family as a unit with broad parental authority over minor children. Our cases have consistently followed that course; our constitutional system long ago rejected any notion that a child is "the mere creature of the State" and, on the contrary, asserted that parents generally "have the right, coupled with the high duty, to recognize and prepare [their children] for additional obligations." *Pierce* v. *Society of Sisters*, 268 U. S. 510 535 (1924). See also *Wisconsin* v. *Yoder*, 406 U. S. 205, 213 (1972); *Prince* v. *Massachusetts*, 321 U. S. 158, 166 (1944); *Meyer* v. *Nebraska*. 262 U. S. 390, 400 (1923). Surely, this includes a "high duty" to recognize symptoms of illness and to seek and follow medical advice. The law's concept of the family rests on a presumption that parents possess what a child lacks in maturity, experience, and capacity for judgment required for making life's difficult decisions. More important, historically it has recognized that natural bonds of affection lead parents to act in the best interests of their children. 1 W. Blackstone, Commentaries 447; 2 Kent, Commentaries on American Law 190.

As with so many other legal presumptions, experience and reality may rebut what the law accepts as a starting point; the incidence of child neglect and abuse cases attests to this. That some parents "may at times be acting against the interests of their child" as was stated in *Bartley* v. *Kremens*, 402 F. Supp. 1039, 1047–1048 (ED Pa. 1975), vacated, 431 U.S. 119 (1977), creates a basis for caution, but is hardly a reason to discard wholesale those pages of human experience that teach that parents generally do act in the child's best interests. See Rolfe & MacClintock 348–349. The statist notion that governmental power should supersede parental authority in all cases because *some* parents abuse and neglect children is repugnant to American tradition. . . .

Nonetheless, we have recognized that a state is not without constitutional control over parental discretion in dealing with children when their physical or mental health is jeopardized. See *Wisconsin* v. *Yoder, supra*, at 230; *Prince* v. *Massachusetts, supra*, at 166. Moreover, the Court recently declared unconstitutional a state statue that granted parents an absolute veto over a minor child's decision to have an abortion. *Planned Parenthood of Missouri* v. *Danforth,* 428 U.S. 52 (1976). Appellees urge that these precedents limiting the traditional rights of parents, if viewed in the context of the liberty interest of the child and the likelihood of parental abuse, require us to hold that the parents' decision to have a child admitted to a mental hospital must be subjected to an exacting constitutional scrutiny, including a formal, adversary, pre-admission hearing.

Appellees' argument, however, sweeps too broadly. Simply because the decision of a parent is not agreeable to a child or because it involves risks does not automatically transfer the power to make that decision from the parents to some agency or officer of the state. The same characterizations can be made for a tonsillectomy, appendectomy or other medical procedure. Most children, even in adolescence, simply are not able to make sound judgments concerning many decisions, including their need for medical care or treatment. Parents can and must make those judgments. . . .

In defining the respective rights and prerogatives of the child and parent in the voluntary commitment setting, we conclude that our precedents permit the parents to retain a substantial, if not the dominant, role in the decision, absent a finding of neglect or abuse, and that the traditional presumption that the parents act in the best interests of their child should apply. We also conclude, however, that the child's rights and the nature of the commitment decision are such that parents cannot always have absolute and unreviewable discretion to decide whether to have a child institutionalized. They, of course, retain plenary authority to seek such care for their children, subject to a physician's independent examination and medical judgment.

The State in performing its voluntarily assumed mission also has a significant interest in not imposing unnecessary procedural obstacles that may discourage the mentally ill or their families from seeking needed psychiatric assistance. The *parens patriae* interest in helping parents care for the mental health of their children cannot be fulfilled if the parents are unwilling to take advantage of the opportunities because the admission process is too onerous, too embarrassing or too contentious. It is surely not idle to speculate as to how many parents who believe thay are acting in good faith would forego state-provided hospital care if such care is contingent on participation in an adversary proceeding designed to probe their motives and other private family matters in seeking the voluntary admission.

The State also has a genuine interest in allocating priority to the diagnosis and treatment of patients as soon as they are admitted to a hospital rather than to time-consuming procedural minuets before the admission. One factor that must be considered is the utilization of the time of psychiatrists, psychologists and other behavioral specialists in preparing for and participating in hearings rather than performing the task for which their special training has fitted them. Behavioral experts in courtrooms and hearings are of little help to patients. . . .

We conclude that the risk of error inherent in the parental decision to have a child institutionalized for mental health care is sufficiently great that some kind of inquiry should be made by a "neutral factfinder" to determine whether the statutory requirements for admission are satisfied. See *Goldberg* v. *Kelly,* 397 U.S. 254, 271 (1970); *Morrissey* v. *Brewer,* 408 U.S. 471 489 (1972). That inquiry must carefully probe the child's background using all available sources, including, but not limited to, parents, schools and other social agencies, Of course, the review must also include an interview with the child. It is necessary that the decisionmaker have the authority to refuse to admit any child who does not satisfy the medical standards for admission. Finally, it is necessary that the child's continuing need for commitment be reviewed periodically by a similarly independent procedure.

We are satisfied that such procedures will protect the child from an erroneous admission decision in a way that neither unduly burdens the states nor inhibits parental decisions to seek state help. . . .

It is not necessary that the deciding physician conduct a

formal or quasi-formal hearing. A state is free to require such a hearing, but due process is not violated by use of informal, traditional medical investigative techniques. Since well-established medical procedures already exist, we do not undertake to outline with specificity precisely what this investigation must involve. The mode and procedure of medical diagnostic procedures is not the business of judges. What is best for a child is an individual medical decision that must be left to the judgment of physicians in each case. . . .

Although we acknowledge the fallibility of medical and psychiatric diagnosis, see *O'Conner* v. *Donaldson,* 422 U.S. 563,584 (1975) (concurring opinion), we do not accept the notion that the shortcomings of specialists can always be avoided by shifting the decision from a trained specialist using the traditional tools of medical science to an untrained judge or administrative hearing officer after a judicial-type hearing. Even after a hearing, the nonspecialist decisionmaker must make a medical-psychiatric decision. Common human experience and scholarly opinions suggest that the supposed appropriateness of medical decisions for the commitment and treatment of mental and emotional illness may well be more illusory than real. See Albers, Pasewark & Meyer, Involuntary Hospitalization and Psychiatric Testimony; The Fallibility of the Doctrine of Immaculate Perception, 6 Cap. U.L. Rev. 11,15 (1976). . . .

Another problem with requiring a formalized, factfinding hearing lies in the danger it poses for significant intrusion into the parent-child relationship. Pitting the parents and child as adversaries often will be at odds with the presumption that parents act in the best interests of their child. It is one thing to require a neutral physician to make a careful review of the parents' decision in order to make sure it is proper from a medical standpoint; it is a wholly different matter to employ an adversary contest to ascertain whether the parents' motivation is consistent with the child's interests.

Moreover, it is appropriate to inquire into how such a hearing would contribute to the long range successful treatment of the patient. Surely, there is a risk that it would exacerbate whatever tensions already existed between the child and the parents. Since the parents can and usually do play a significant role in the treatment while the child is hospitalized and even more so after release, there is a serious risk that an adversary confrontation will adversely affect the ability of the parents to assist the child while in the hospital Moreover, it will make his subsequent return home more difficult. These unfortunate results are especially critical with an emotionally disturbed child; they seem likely to occur in the context of an adversary hearing in which the parents testify. A confrontation over such intimate family relationships would distress the normal adult parents and the impact on a disturbed child almost certainly would be significantly greater.

MR. JUSTICE BRENNAN, with whom MR. JUSTICE MARSHALL MR. JUSTICE STEVENS join, concurring in part and disenting in part.

• • •

II
Rights of Children Committed by Their Parents

A

Notwithstanding all this Georgia denies hearings to juveniles institutionalized at the behest of their parents. Georgia rationalizes this practice on the theory that parents act in their children's best interests and therefore may waive their children's due process rights. Children incarcerated because their parents wish them confined, Georgia contends, are really voluntary patients. I cannot accept this argument.

In our society, parental rights are limited by the legitimate rights and interests of their children. "Parents may be free to become martyrs themselves. But it does not follow they are free, in identical circumstances, to make martyrs of their children before they have reached the age of full and legal discretion when they can make that choice for themselves." *Prince* v. *Massachusetts,* 321 U.S. 158, 170 (1944). This principle is reflected in the variety of statutes and cases that authorize state intervention on behalf of neglected or abused children and that, *inter alia,* curtail parental authority to alienate their children's property, to withhold necessary medical treatment, and to deny children exposure to ideas and experiences they may later need as independent and autonomous adults.

First, the prospect of an adversarial hearing prior to admission might deter parents from seeking needed medical attention for their children. Second, the hearings themselves might delay treatment of children whose home life has become impossible and who require some form of immediate state care. Furthermore, because adversarial hearings at this juncture would necessarily involve direct challenges to parental authority, judgment or veracity, preadmission hearings may well result in pitting the child and his advocate against the parents. This, in turn, might traumatize both parent and child and make the child's eventual return to his family more difficult.

Because of these special considerations I believe that States may legitimately postpone formal commitment proceedings when parents seek in-patient psychiatric treatment for their children. Such children may be admitted, for a limited period, without prior hearing, so long as the admitting psychiatrist first interviews parent and child and concludes that short term in-patient treatment would be appropriate.

• • •

Georgia's present admission procedures are reasonably consistent with these principles. See maj. op., at 21. To the extent the District Court invalidated this aspect of the Georgia juvenile commitment scheme and mandated preconfinement hearings in all cases, I agree with the Court that the District Court was in error.

C

I do not believe, however, that the present Georgia juvenile commitment scheme is constitutional in its entirety. Although Georgia may postpone formal commitment hearings, when parents seek to commit their children, the State cannot dispense with such hearings altogether. Our cases make clear that, when protected interests are at stake, the "fundamental requirement of due process is the opportunity to be heard 'at a meaningful time and in a meaningful manner.'" *Matthews* v. *Eldridge,* 424 U.S. 319, 333 (1976), quoting in part from *Armstrong* v. *Manzo,* 380 U.S. 545, 552 (1965). Whenever prior hearings are impracticable, States must provide reasonably prompt postdeprivation hearings. Compare *North Georgia Finishing Inc.* v. *Di-Chem Inc.,* 419 U.S. 601 (1975), with *Mitchell* v. *W. T. Grant Co.,* 416 U.S. 600 (1974).

The informal postadmission procedures that Georgia now follows are simply not enough to qualify as hearings—let alone reasonably prompt hearings. The procedures lack all the traditional due process safeguards. Commitment decisions are made *ex parte*. Georgia's institutionalized juveniles are not informed of the reasons for their commitment; nor do they enjoy the right to be present at the commitment determination, nor the right to representation, the right to be heard, the right to be confronted with adverse witnesses, the right to cross-examine, or the right to offer evidence of the own. By any standard of due process, these procedures are deficient. See *Wolff* v. *McDonnell,* 418 U.S. 539 (1974), *Morrissey* v. *Brewer,* 408 U.S. 471 (1972), *McNeil* v. *Director,* 407 U.S. 245(1972), *Sprecht* v. *Patterson,* 386 U.S. 605,610 (1967). See also *Goldberg* v. *Kelly,* 397 U.S. 254, 269–271 (1970). I cannot understand why the court pretermits condemnation of these *ex parte* procedures which operate to deny Georgia's institutionalized juveniles even "some form of hearing," *Matthews* v. *Eldridge, supra,* at 333, before they are condemned to suffer the rigors of long term institutional confinement.

Judianne Densen-Gerber

What Pornographers
Are Doing to Children

Children between the ages of 3 and 14 are frequently featured in pornographic magazines, photographs, and movies. Sometimes the parents force the child to participate; in other cases the children claim to want to participate. What (if anything) is peculiarly *wrong with child pornography? Densen-Gerber obviously thinks it is wrong for parents to force children to pose for such pictures. But what exactly is wrong with this parental discretion? Is it the activity itself? Or is it because parents are forcing the children to participate? If it is the latter, why is it not also wrong to* force *children to clean their rooms, take their vitamins, or go to church? Would child pornography be so bad if the child really did want to participate? Why?*

On January 12, 1977, at the Crossroads, an adult bookstore in New York City, I purchased Lollitots, a magazine showing pornographic pictures of girls aged eight to 14 and Moppets, a magazine illustrated with pornographic photographs of children three to 12. I bought a deck of playing cards that pictured naked, spread-eagled children. I looked at a film showing children violently deflowered on their First Communion day at the feet of a crucified priest replacing Jesus on the Cross. I saw a film showing an alleged father engaged in bizarre sexual practices

From *Redbook*, August 1977. Reprinted by permission of Judianne Densen-Gerber.

36

with his four-year-old daughter. Of 64 films presented for viewing, 35 showed children; 16 of these involved incest.

In the months since January, I have personally purchased magazines carrying the titles Nudist Moppets, Chicken Delight, Lust for Children, Schoolgirls, Naughty Horny Imps, Chicken Love, and Child Discipline and seen films such as *Children Love* and *Lollipops #10*. I found them in New York, Philadelphia, Boston, Washington, New Orleans, Detroit, Flint, Chicago, San Francisco, San Jose and Los Angeles—and even in Sydney, Melbourne, and Canberra, Australia. And I have become angered beyond description.

I first became aware of the million-dollar sex-for-sale industry that is exploiting America's children through my work with Odyssey Institute's Concerns of Children Division.* Since then I have traveled all over the country amassing evidence, holding news conferences, determined to bring this disgrace to the attention of the public—and to put a stop to it.

According to the book *For Money or Love: Boy Prostitution in America*, by Robin Lloyd, an investigative reporter for NBC News in Los Angeles, there are at least 264 different boy and girl porn magazines being sold in adult bookstores nationwide. These magazines—slickly produced—sell for prices averaging more than $7 each. Most of the children exploited are runaways from extremely abusive and neglectful homes—most of the children, that is, who are eight years old or older. But younger children used in the production of pornography—some as young as three—must be provided by their parents or guardians, who themselves often are drug addicts, porn performers, prostitutes or, more frequently, parents having incestuous relationships with their children that they wish to memorialize in photographs or movies to exchange with others who belong to clubs or

---

*Odyssey Institute, headed by Dr. Densen-Gerber, is a nationwide organization committed to the delivery of health care to the socially disadvantaged. The Concerns of Children Division of the Institute has been working not only on the problems of child pornography, but also with the problems of abuse and neglect. For instance, the staff of the division assisted Congress in the research and writing of the Child Abuse and Neglect Act of 1973. Presently, they are lobbying for establishment of a cabinet level post for children. Eds.

groups advocating this type of activity. There is one group in southern California—it claims 2,500 members!—whose slogan is "Sex by eight or it's too late." Too late for what? To grow up loved and protected and unscarred?

Robin Lloyd's book documented the involvement of 300,000 boys, aged eight to 16, in activities revolving around sex for sale, including both pornography and prostitution. A common-sense "guesstimate" on my part leads me to believe that if there are 300,000 boys, there must be a like number of girls, but no one has bothered to count the females involved. (Lloyd postulated but cannot substantiate that only half the true number of these children is known. That would put the figure closer to 1.2 million nationwide—a figure that is not improbable to me, considering the nation's 1 million runaways. How many ways are there for a 12-year-old to support himself or herself?)

In an April Ms. magazine article titled "Incest: Sexual Abuse Begins at Home," the following startling fact was noted: "One girl out of every four in the United States will be sexually abused in some way before she reaches the age of 18." Researchers working with deviant women report that 50 to 70 per cent were sexually traumatized as children. This is truly an illustration of the sins of the parents' being visited upon the children.

We hide from the knowledge of incest; we have been even more ostrichlike in the area of the commercial sexual abuse of children. Only six states specifically prohibit the participation of minors in an obscene performance that could be harmful to them (Connecticut, North Carolina, North Dakota, South Carolina, Tennessee and Texas), although other states are considering such legislation. There is no Federal statute that specifically regulates or restricts the production, distribution or marketing of pornographic material involving children. Neither is there a Federal statute prohibiting the distribution of pornographic material to children.

Forty-seven states and the District of Columbia have laws in some way pertaining to the dissemination of obscene materials to minors. But state criminal statutes that deal with sex crimes often are not helpful, either because the physical activity does not meet the criteria of the statute—for example, rape, sodomy, sexual abuse—or because they are so broadly worded as to discourage courts from applying them in terms of significant penalties.

Many states have child-welfare provisions within their education laws that regulate the employment of children in commercial activities. Unfortunately either these same laws abdicate control when the child is working for a parent or the sanctions are so limited—a $10 fine or ten days in jail—as to pose no deterrent.

Given the paucity of legislation that relates specifically to child pornography, there can be little wonder at the relatively few attempts at law enforcement. The problems of case-finding and evidence are compounded by a confusion between sexploitation as a form of child abuse and adult-obscenity matters. These problems and the attitudes of many judges discourage and actually thwart the few criminal investigations attempted.

This year, for instance, when one of America's leading pornographers, Edward Mishkin, was arrested in New York, one third of the enormous quantity of material confiscated involved children. Mr. Mishkin pleaded guilty, and in spite of the fact that he had had many previous convictions, acting Justice Irving Lang, of the New York State Supreme Court, sentenced him to 27 consecutive weekends in jail—I assume so that his workweek destroying children would not be interrupted. We as citizens must ask why Judge Lang did not give Mishkin the seven-year maximum sentence. Mishkin went right back to work, and was rearrested on like charges within one week.

If you want to do your part in putting an end to this vicious abuse of children, I urge you to write to your Federal and state legislators, asking that they support the three-pronged approach suggested by Odyssey's Law and Medicine Institute. First, to make changes in your state education law to require licensing of all media involving children and to prohibit children from participating in any sexually explicit acts, any material produced in violation to be confiscated. Second, to strengthen the child-abuse and -neglect statutes to include commercial sexual exploitation of children and to make the finding of venereal disease in children under 12 an automatic presumption of child abuse and neglect. (In 1976 Connecticut passed such a law on venereal disease because there had been two cases of gonorrhea of the throat in children under 18 months of age and one in a child nine months old within that state.) And third, to create greater penalties under the obscenity laws if the offending material involves persons under 16.

There comes a point at which we no longer can defend atrocities by intellectualization or forensic debate. We must simply say: "I know the difference between right and wrong and I am not afraid to say no or to demand that limits be imposed."

Common sense and maternal instinct tell me that these abuses are not a question of freedom of speech and press. Children are not consenting adults; they are victims whose spirits are mutilated as their bodies are violated. This is a matter of child abuse and should be dealt with through child-abuse laws.

It is outrageous for someone to publish a primer instructing a sex molester on how to pick up a child in the park and subsequently assault her sexually ("Lust for Children"), or for someone else to issue a booklet advocating that a father have incestuous relations with his daughter and illustrating positions to be used if she, at nine, is too small for normal penetration ("Schoolgirls" and "Preteen Sexuality").

We are not going to produce mentally healthy and happy children by issuing an executive order that all children must be loved. But we can author legislation to protect them and give them a fighting chance in this world. To paraphrase the French writer Camus, speaking for all of us who in some way work with children or care about them:

"Perhaps we cannot prevent this America from being an America in which children are tortured . . . but we can reduce the number of tortured children. And if you don't help us . . . who else in this world can . . . . ?"

You and I can make a difference. Since my initial news

conference in January, 1977, in front of the Crossroads store, much of "kid porn" has disappeared from New York's adult bookstores—and the Crossroads itself has been closed. It was so simple, the answer was so clear: If we can still be outraged, if we can still care, we can begin to nurture a soil for all children to grow straight and strong.

As psychoanalyst Erik Erikson wrote: "Someday, maybe there will exist a well-informed, well-considered and yet fervent public conviction that the most deadly of all possible sins is the mutilation of a child's spirit; for such mutilation undercuts the life principle of trust, without which every human act, may it feel ever so good, and seem ever so right, is prone to perversion by destructive forms of consciousness."

Court Returns Foster Son to Biological Mother

The Idaho Supreme Court took custody of six year old Danny Dennis from his foster parents and returned him to his biological mother who had abandoned him at birth. What could be the rationale for this decision? Why are biological parents thought to have some special claim over their offspring? If you think the child should have had an important say in this custody decision, should the child's wishes carry absolute weight? Would the child's age make any difference? Should a child also have an important say during custody hearings following divorce?

BOISE, Idaho (AP)—Six-year-old Danny Dennis, raised by foster parents since he was four days old, cried when he was taken from them by sheriff's deputies and sent to California to live with the natural mother he has never known.

The Idaho Supreme Court overturned on Wednesday a decision which said the boy could stay with the foster parents and ordered him returned to his mother, Marilyn Mitchell, a San Diego secretary.

The court refused to stay its order for 24 hours while it is appealed to the U.S. Supreme Court.

Blue-eyed, blond-haired Danny, whose legal name is Christopher Mitchell, was in church in Eagle, Idaho, on Thursday with his foster parents, DeLoy and Lois Dennis, when deputies came without warning to pick him up.

From the *Johnson City Press Chronicle* (Johnson City, Tenn.) March 3, 1978. Reprinted by permission of the Associated Press.

"He just hugged me and held on to me," said Mrs. Dennis. "He didn't want to leave. He said how scared he was. He cried."

Mrs. Dennis said she didn't understand how the court ruled against them. "We expected these men to protect our rights. I just don't understand how they could do it without considering his welfare."

Legal Aid attorney Deborah Bail, who represented Miss Mitchell, said the decision "puts Idaho on record that this isn't a state where you deliberately ignore the decrees of another state in custody matters."

The struggle over custody of Danny began with his birth on Nov. 30, 1971, in LaMesa, Calif. According to the Idaho decision, Miss Mitchell signed a release form allowing Mrs. Dennis, then married to a man named Pincock, to take the infant home from the hospital four days after birth.

Kenneth Wooden

Case History of Charles Manson

Wooden suggests that Manson was more or less driven to commit the gruesome Tate-LaBianca murders by an uncaring and ineffective foster care system and by brutal juvenile detention workers. How do you think Manson should have been treated as a child? How should foster care systems operate? Can the juvenile justice system actually create criminals?

Charles Manson was thirty-five years old when he stood trial for the Sharon Tate-LaBianca murders. The macabre multimurders and the trial that convicted Manson commanded national media attention. So absorbing was the story that even Richard Nixon, President of the United States, found time in August of 1970 to say, "Here is a man who was guilty, directly or indirectly, of eight murders. Yet here is a man who, as far as the coverage is concerned, appeared to be a glamorous figure."

Today, Manson sits in a maximum security cell at San Quentin Prison in northern California. What was called one of the most baffling and horrifying murder cases of this century is now well-known history. What is not well known is the early childhood of Charles Manson and the effect of some twenty-two years spent in more than a dozen penal institutions.

Manson was born to sixteen-year-old Kathleen Maddox on November 12, 1934, in Cincinnati. His mother was allegedly violated by a Colonel Scott, so Charlie's birth certificate read: "No Name Maddox." Two years later Kathleen Maddox filed a bastard suit in Boyd County, Kentucky, and the father agreed to a judgment of twenty-five dollars and a five-dollar-a-month support for the child. She later married a William Manson, and gave his name to the illegitimate boy—Charles Milles Manson.

During the first few years of his life, Charlie was bounced between the care of his grandmother and maternal aunt because his mother, leaving the baby with neighbors "for an hour," would disappear for days and weeks at a time. In 1939, Kathleen and her brother were arrested for armed robbery when they knocked a service station attendant unconscious with a Coke bottle. She was sentenced to five years in the West Virginia State Penitentiary. Manson also went to West Virginia, to live with an aunt and uncle, who, he later told prison authorities, had a "difficult marriage until they found religion . . . and became very extreme." During this time, he started school.

Charlie was eight years old when his mother was released from prison. The youngster then began to live with a long line of "uncles," who, like his mother, drank heavily. Home was an assortment of run-down hotel rooms, where many times Charlie was forced to stay alone all day. He ran away, but returned.

Manson was next placed with foster parents for about a year—perhaps the best situation of his young life. But it was short-lived. His mother moved to Indianapolis with a salesman and sent for her son. A later report would state: "Manson received little attention from his mother and from the many men who were reputed to have lived with her."

In 1947 his mother tried to place him in another foster home, but there was none available. So Charlie became a ward of the county, who sent the unwanted boy to his first of many institutions, the Gibault Home for Boys in Terre Haute, Indiana. His record there revealed: "Poor institutional adjustment . . . his attitude toward schooling was at best only fair . . . during the short lapses when Charles was pleasant and feeling happy, he presented a likeable boy . . . a tendency towards moodiness and a persecution complex." (Mrs. Angles McMoney, a volunteer at his second institution in Plainfield who tried to help Manson, told me: "He was very quiet, very shy, didn't want anything to do with anyone else." Teachers said, "He professed no trust in anyone.")

After ten months at Gibault, Manson ran away to his mother, who again rejected him. (This "return-rejection" pattern was to persist right up to the time of the Tate-LaBianca murders.)

Manson now drifted toward a life of crime. From the take of burglarizing a grocery store, he was able to rent a room. Later, however, he was caught stealing a bike and sent to the Juvenile Center in Indianapolis. He escaped but was apprehended and sent to Father Flanagan's Boys Town. Four days into that institution, he and another boy stole an old Plymouth and made it to a ditch in Johnsonville, Iowa. Along the way, they committed two armed robberies—a gambling casino and a grocery store. They hitched the rest of the way to the other boy's uncle—a World War II disabled veteran, who tutored them in "slipping through skylights." Their first take was $1,500; the second time they were arrested. Manson was still only thirteen.

He was incarcerated at the Indiana Boys School at Plainfield. He stayed three years and attempted to run away eighteen times. On his nineteenth try, with two other youths, Charles Manson finally made good his escape from the thousand-acre youth jail with its own cemetery of over 135 graves. Stealing cars and burglarizing gas stations for transportation and support, they headed for California but were stopped near Beaver, Utah, at a roadblock set up for another robbery suspect. Crossing state lines with a stolen car is a federal offense (Dyer Act). Sixteen-year-old Manson was now under federal jurisdiction and was sent to the National Training School for Boys in Washington, D.C., to which he was sentenced to stay until he reached twenty-one.

In the late fall of 1974 I visited the Gibault Home in Terre Haute. The Catholic brothers there declined to discuss Manson and were embarrassed that he had ever been under their care. They told me it would take approval by the board of trustees for me to review his record. I was, however, given the opportunity to tour the facilities and see some of the buildings and grounds where Manson, the neglected child of thirteen, had been forced to live. I was struck by the old dormitories where the boys slept. Eight beds lined the walls and in the middle of one end of the room was a toilet within a windowed structure resembling a telephone booth. I also learned that discipline was meted out via the rod. I don't know how severe the beatings were. No one was talking.

When the Manson murder story broke, the Indiana Boys School at Plainfield refused anyone in the media permission to see his file in its entirety. So again, very little is known about Manson's treatment during a critical time of his young life. An enterprising New Yorker offered superintendent Al Bennett a good price if he would review and reveal the records, but Bennett declined. However, when I visited the Indiana school, Bennett did tell me that when Manson or any inmates ran, they were beaten, then thrown into solitary. He showed me the leather straps that were used. They were 26 inches long, 3 inches wide and ½ inch thick. The handles were stained from sweat, the ends worn thin by those who administered the beatings. The youngsters who were to be disciplined were placed on wooden racks at an appointed time (4 P.M.) "with their ass up in the air." The big debate was "should they beat the boys with their trousers on or off." When the leather strap had no effect, the guards would "take them out in the cornfield and beat the piss out of them."

According to the superintendent, records hidden from press and public reveal that on several occasions Manson was beaten so severely that he received treatment at a local hospital. Many years too late, in January of 1974, the United States Court of Appeals for the Seventh Circuit ruled on the Indiana Boys School:

In beating the juveniles, a "fraternity paddle" between ½" to 2" thick, 12" long, with a narrow handle was used. There is testimony that juveniles weighing 160 lbs. were struck five blows on the clothed buttocks, often by a staff member weighing 285 lbs. . . . It is . . . constitutionally cruel and unusual punishment.

It was also at Plainfield that Charles Manson was first homosexually attacked and raped. Thereafter he too engaged in homosexuality.

From Manson's records at the National Training School for Boys, Washington, D.C., a profile emerged: Though he had had four years of schooling, he was illiterate, with an IQ of 109. His first caseworker found him a "sixteen year old boy who has had an unfavorable family life, if it can be called a family life at all" and "aggressively antisocial." Three months later: "It appears that this boy is a very emotionally upset youth who is definitely in need of some psychiatric orientation."

Still, during the early years in the training school, a psychiatrist noted that though Charles Manson had a number of strikes against him, he hadn't quite given up on the world: "Because of a marked degree of rejection, instability, and psychic trauma—because his sense of inferiority in relationship to his mother was so pronounced, he constantly felt it necessary to suppress any thoughts about her. However, because of his diminutive stature, his illegitimacy, and the lack of parental love, he is constantly striving for status with the other boys . . . has developed certain facile techniques for dealing with people, those for the most part consist of a good sense of humor and an ability to ingratiate himself. . . . This could add up to a fairly slick institutionalized youth, but one is left with the feeling that behind all this lies an extremely sensitive boy who has not yet given up in terms of securing some kind of love and affection from the world."

In a special progress report during Charlie's stay at the National Training School, the following entry was made in his file:

He got along fairly satisfactory at the school although it was felt that he might be a custody risk unless something could be done to work out his feelings of depression and moodiness. He had a fairly good attitude and was cooperative when not in a depressed mood.

Shortly thereafter, officials at the National Training School decided that the Natural Bridge Honor Camp, a minimum security institution, would be the best possible place for the youth. Three weeks later he turned seventeen and was visited by his aunt, Mrs. W. L. Thomas of McMechen, West Virginia, who promised him a home and employment if he was released to her supervision. Manson was due for a parole hearing three months later, and with his aunt's offer his chances for release were very good. However, one month before the hearing, he pressed a razor blade against a fellow inmate's throat and sodomized him.

For that offense Manson was transferred to the federal reformatory at Petersburg, Virginia, and classified as dangerous. He became more and more involved in homosexual acts and increasingly entered into institutional mayhem. He served time in solitary confinement for "stealing food from the kitchen, shirking his assigned duties in the kitchen, fighting with another inmate, etc." During this time he had no visits from anyone and received only a few letters from his aunt and mother.

Finally officials felt that for the protection of Manson as well as others, it would be best to transfer him to a more secure prison, the federal reformatory at Chillicothe, Ohio. He arrived on September 23, 1952, and by now it was written: "in spite of his age, he is criminally sophisticated." And later: he ". . . has no foresight for the future, is thoroughly institutionalized and doesn't appear to be the type that will take advantage of the opportunities afforded him." The report concluded: "He has been a neglected child all his life."

Manson's conduct improved at Chillcothe, however, and he was granted parole on May 8, 1954. He was nineteen. He went to live with his aunt in McMechen, where he married seventeen-year-old Rosalie Jean Willis in early 1955. He worked at a number of odd jobs, from busboy to parking-lot attendant. During this time he saw his mother briefly.

He began to hustle cars, two of which he took across state lines, and was arrested again for violation of the Dyer Act. He pleaded guilty in a federal court and requested medical assistance by telling a judge: "I was released from the Federal

Penitentiary in Chillicothe, Ohio, in 1954 and having been confined for nine years, I was badly in need of psychiatric treatment. I was mentally confused and stole a car as a means of mental release from the confused state of mind that I was in.''

The judge had Dr. Edwin McNeil examine Manson on October 26, 1955, in the Los Angeles county jail. The psychiatrist commented on both Manson's early family life and his years of incarceration: ''It is evident that he has an unstable personality and that his environmental influences throughout most of his life have not been good. . . . This boy is a poor risk for probation; on the other hand, he has spent nine years in institutions with apparently little benefit except to take him out of circulation.''

Manson told the psychiatrist he had spent so much time in institutions that he never really learned much of what real life on the outside was all about. Commenting on his wife, Charlie said: ''She is the best wife a guy could want. I didn't realize how good she was until I got in here. I beat her at times. She writes to me all the time. She is going to have a baby.'' He opined that since he was about to become a father, it was important for him to be with his wife on the outside. ''She is the only one I have ever cared about in my life.'' The judge placed Manson on probation for five years.

But Manson still had another charge to face—auto theft in Florida. A hearing was set, but he skipped town. A warrant was issued; he was arrested and sentenced to three years at Terminal Island, San Pedro, California. The new father held his baby son in the courtroom just before he left for prison.

At Terminal Island, a caseworker observed: ''We have here a young man who comes from a very unfavorable background, has no worthwhile family ties and has been subjected to institutional treatment since early childhood. He is an almost classic textbook case of the correctional institution inmate. . . . His is a very difficult case and it is impossible to predict his future adjustment with any degree of accuracy.''

In April of 1957, ''the only one I have ever cared about in my life'' ceased to visit Manson. His mother brought the news that his wife was living with another man. Charlie attempted to escape from the minimal custody unit to which he had been transferred. A parole committee commented: "This episode, however, is in keeping with the pattern he has exhibited from early childhood of attempting to evade his responsibilities by running away" and refused parole. Rosalie then filed for divorce, which was granted in 1958. She was given custody of their child. Manson has never seen either of them again.

Now, because his institutional conduct and behavior became intolerable to prison officials—he would not dress properly and "contraband[ed] food"—the man was placed in "punitive segregation on a restricted diet for indefinite periods of time." His medical and psychiatric record revealed that he had now become totally dependent on institutional life and had anxiety over leaving the security of confinement. Bill Casey, an official at Terminal Island, told me during an interview that he felt Manson was a "real introvert, a loner and a quiet type—like a cat . . . strictly an institutionalized person who didn't want to leave prison." Casey said he was a little surprised at the violent behavior of Charlie Manson, but "when they grow up in institutions, they have a tendency toward violence. It gives them an identity and makes them somewhat of a hero, a leader, something they never were."

When released from prison, Manson quickly returned to the routine of stealing cars. He then started to pimp and he was arrested for trying to cash a stolen government check for $37.50. After a series of such episodes, Manson, at twenty-six, was back in jail, this time the United States penitentiary on McNeil Island, Washington. Staff evaluation summarized a neglected childhood and years of incarceration:

The product of an emotionally disruptive formative period, Manson has never really reconciled the overt rejecting aspects of his maternal relationship and has functioned primarily in a dependent manner, hiding his loneliness, resentment, and hostility behind a facade of superficial ingratiation. In many respects, he has a childish need for acceptance without knowing how to go about securing such acceptance in an adult manner. He has commented that institutions have become his way of life and that he receives security in institutions which is not available to him in the outside world.

During his last five years of imprisonment before the Tate–LaBianca murders, total institutionalization was effected. A second marriage, just prior to incarceration, to Leona Musser (1959) failed and terminated in divorce. It was now that Manson struck up a friendship with the last survivor of Ma Barker's gang, Alvin Karpis, who taught him to play the guitar, opening a whole new world to Charlie. He also developed a keen interest in scientology and, according to the annual progress report of the penitentiary, that interest "has led him to make a semi-professional evaluation of his personality which strangely enough, is quite consistent with the evaluations made by previous social studies." Another year, the report read: "Even these attempts and his cries for help represent a desire for attention, with only superficial meaning. . . . In view of his deep-seated personality problems . . . continuation of institutional treatment is recommended."

Finally, in June of 1966, Charles Manson was transferred back to Terminal Island Prison in California for release. His last report read: "Manson is about to complete his ten-year term. He has a pattern of criminal behavior and confinement that dates to his teen years. This pattern is one of instability whether in free society or a structured institution community. Little can be expected in the way of change in his attitude, behavior or mode of conduct. . . . He has come to worship his guitar and music . . . has no plans for release as he says he has nowhere to go."

On the morning of his release from prison, Charles Manson begged his jailers to allow him to remain: "Prison has become my home"; he doubted he could "adjust to the world outside." His request was denied. On March 21, 1967, Manson hit the free world and drifted into the Haight-Ashbury section of San Francisco. There the Manson family, which was to terrorize and take the lives of forty-odd people, was born.

Manson did not choose his own pathway to oblivion and

crime. It was charted for him, first by parental abandonment, and then, in a far greater sense, by the massive failure of the correctional system, particularly those in charge of juvenile offenders. Manson was the product of too many impersonal institutions, too many endless days in solitary confinement, too many sexual assaults by older boys and far too many beatings by guardians and institutional personnel. The U.S. Court of Appeals, which ruled the use of wooden paddles cruel and unusual punishment, also documented the destructiveness of beating: ". . . the practice does not serve as useful punishment or as treatment, and it actually breeds counter-hostility, resulting in a greater aggression by a child."

A review of all Manson's prison records reveal some interesting facts: Of twenty-two years in prison, seventeen were spent in federal facilities for crimes that, under state jurisdiction, would carry sentences totaling less than five years. There was never once a serious treatment program for young Manson. At the federal reformatory at Petersburg, Virginia, his rehabilitation program consisted of helping in the kitchen; he bitterly opposed being enrolled in elementary school, so he never showed up after the first class. Also he was always physically "fit for regular duty," and reports consistently recommended that he "continue on the same program." But what was the program?

Although Manson had held a razor blade against the throat of an inmate and sodomized him, no psychiatric help was "indicated." Treatment for Charles was "Close Custody" and "continue on same program."

Manson and the countless thousands of children locked away from society during the late forties and fifties became part of the bitter harvest of crime this country reaped in the late sixties and early seventies. What of future children? According to the FBI's annual report, more than 80,000 children under ten were arrested in 1972. Charges were placed against 585,000 children between eleven and fourteen years of age. Without proper treatment, without proper care and education, how many future Charles Mansons will emerge from these statistics? How many, in a new harvest of failure, will echo the words Charles Manson spoke just before being convicted of murder?

. . . I haven't decided yet what I am or who I am. I was given a name and a number and I was put in a cell and I have lived in a cell with a name and a number. . . . I never went to school, so I never growed up in the respect to learn, to read and write too good. So I stayed in that jail and I have stayed stupid, and I have stayed a child while I have watched your world grow up. . . . I have ate out of your garbage cans to stay out of jail. I have wore your secondhand clothes. I have done my best to get along in your world and now you want to kill me. . . . Ha! I'm already dead, have been dead all my life. I've lived in your tomb that you built. I did seven years for a $37.50 check. I did 12 years because I didn't have any parents. . . . When you were out riding your bicycle, I was sitting in your cell looking out the window and looking at pictures in magazines and wishing I could go to high school and go to the proms, wishing I could go to the things you could do, but oh so glad, oh so glad, brothers and sisters, that I am what I am.

Ingraham v. Wright

45 USLW 4364
(April 19, 1977)

The U.S. Supreme Court ruled in Ingraham v. Wright *that corporal punishment in the schools was not unconstitutional. Notice the court's rationale. In particular, note that the decision is largely based on the social consequences of outlawing corporal punishment in the schools. Is that an appropriate rationale for this decision? If not, what alternative is there? Also, what could explain the difference between the U.S. court's decision and the action, described in the next selection, of the Swedish parliment outlawing all corporal punishment?*

MR. JUSTICE POWELL delivered the opinion of the Court.

This case presents questions concerning the use of corporal punishment in public schools: first, whether the paddling of students as a means of maintaining school discipline constitutes cruel and unusual punishment in violation of the Eighth Amendment; and second, to the extent that paddling is constitutionally permissible, whether the Due Process Clause of the Fourteenth Amendment requires prior notice and an opportunity to be heard. . . . .

Petitioners', evidence may be summarized briefly. In the 1970–1971 school year many of the 237 schools in Dade County used corporal punishment as a means of maintaining discipline pursuant to Florida legislation and a local school board regulation. The statute then in effect authorized limited corporal punishment by negative inference, proscribing punishment which was "degrading or unduly severe" or which was inflicted without prior consultation with the principal or the teacher in charge of the school. . . . In an apparent reference to Drew, the District Court found that "[t]he instances of punishment which could be characterized as severe, accepting the students' testimony as credible, took place in one junior high school." The evidence, consisting mainly of the testimony of 16 students, suggests that the regime at Drew was exceptionally harsh. The testimony of Ingraham and Andrews, in support of their individual claims for damages, is illustrative. Because he was slow to respond to his teacher's instructions, Ingraham was subjected to more than 20 licks with a paddle while being held over a table in the principal's office. The paddling was so severe that he suffered a hematoma requiring medical attention and keeping him out of school for 11 days. Andrews was paddled several times for minor infractions. On two occasions he was struck on his arms, once depriving him of the full use of his arm for a week.

• • •

II

In addressing the scope of the Eighth Amendment's prohibition on cruel and unusual punishment, this Court has found it useful to refer to "[t]raditional common law concepts." *Powell v. Texas,* 392 U.S. 514, 535 (1968) (plurality opinion), and to the "attitude[s] which our society has traditionally taken." *Id.,* at 531. So too, in defining the requirements of procedural due process under the Fifth and Fourteenth Amendments, the Court has been attuned to what "has always been the law of the land." *United States v. Barnett,* 376 U. S. 681, 692 (1964), and to "traditional ideas of fair procedure." *Green v. McElroy,* 360 U. S. 474, 508 (1959). We therefore begin by examining the way in which our traditions and our laws have responded to the use of corporal punishment in public schools.

The use of corporal punishment in this country as a means of disciplining schoolchildren dates back to the colonial period. It has survived the transformation of primary and secondary education from the colonials' reliance on optional private arrangements to our present system of compulsory education and dependence on public schools. Despite the general abandonment of corporal punishment as a means of punishing criminal offenders, the practice continues to play a role in the public education of schoolchildren in most parts of the country. Professional and public opinion is sharply divided on the practice, and has been for more than a century. Yet we can discern no trend toward its elimination. . . .

Against this background of historical and contemporary approval of reasonable corporal punishment, we turn to the constitutional questions before us.

III

The Eighth Amendment provides, "Excessive bail shall not be required, nor excessive fines imposed, nor cruel and unusual punishments inflicted." Bail, fines and punishment traditionally have been associated with the criminal process, and by subjecting the three to parallel limitations the text of the Amendment suggests an intention to limit the power of those entrusted with the criminal law function of government. An examination of the history of the Amendment and the decisions of this Court construing the proscription against cruel and unusual punishment confirms that it was designed to protect those convicted of crimes. We adhere to this long-standing limitation and hold that the Eighth Amendment does not apply to the paddling of children as a means of maintaining discipline in public schools. . . .

B

In light of this history, it is not surprising to find that every decision of this Court considering whether a punishment is "cruel and unusual" within the meaning of the Eighth and Fourteenth Amendments has dealt with a criminal punishment. See *Estelle* v. *Gamble*,—U. S.—(1976) (incarceration without medical care); *Gregg* v. *Georgia*, 428 U. S. 153 (1976) (execution for murder); *Furman* v. *Georgia, supra* (execution for murder); *Powell* v. *Texas,* 392 U. S. 514 (1968) ($20 fine for public drunkenness); *Robinson* v. *California,* 370 U. S. 660 (1962) (incarceration as a criminal for addiction to narcotics); *Trop* v. *Dulles,* 356 U. S. 86 (1958) (plurality opinion) (expatriation for desertion); *Louisiana ex rel. Francis* v. *Resweber,* 329 U. S. 459 (1947) (execution by electrocution after a failed first attempt); *Weems* v. *United States, supra* (15 years' imprisonment and other penalties for falsifying an official document); *Howard* v. *Fleming,* 191 U.S. 126 (1903) (10 years' imprisonment for conspiracy to defraud); *In re Kemmler, supra* (execution by electrocution; *Wilkerson* v. *Utah,* 99 U. S. 130 (1879) (execution by firing squad); *Pervear* v. *Commonwealth,* 5 Wall. 475 (1867) (fine and imprisonment at hard labor for bootlegging).

These decisions recognize that the Cruel and Unusual Punishments Clause circumscribes the criminal process in three ways: first, it limits the kinds of punishment that can be imposed on those convicted of crimes, *e. g., Estelle* v. *Gamble, supra; Trop* v. *Dulles, supra;* second, it proscribes punishment grossly disproportionate to the severity of the crime. *e. g., Weems* v. *United States, supra,* and third, it imposes substantive limits on what can be made criminal and punished as such, *e. g., Robinson* v. *California, supra.* We have recognized the last limitation as one to be applied sparingly. "The primary purpose of [the Cruel and Unusual Punishments Clause] has always been considered, and properly so, to be directed at the method or kind of punishment imposed for the violation of criminal statutes. . . ." *Powell* v. *Texas,* 392 U. S., at 531–532 (plurality opinion). . . .

In the few cases where the Court has had occasion to confront claims that impositions outside the criminal process constituted cruel and unusual punishment, it has had no difficulty finding the Eighth Amendment inapplicable. Thus, in *Fong Yue Ting* v. *United States,* 149 U. S. 698 (1893), the Court held the Eighth Amendment inapplicable to the deportation of aliens on the ground that "deportation is not a punishment for crime." *Id.,* at 730; see *Mahler* v. *Eby,* 264 U. S. 32 (1924); *Bugajewitz* v.

Adams, 228 U. S. 585 (1913). And in *Uphaus* v. *Wyman,* 360 U. S. 72 (1959), the Court sustained a judgment of civil contempt, resulting in incarceration pending compliance with a subpoena, against a claim that the judgment imposed cruel and unusual punishment. It was emphasized that the case involved "essentially a civil remedy designed for the benefit of other parties . . . exercised for centuries to secure compliance with judicial decrees." *Id.,* at 81, quoting *Green* v. *United States,* 356 U. S. 165, 197 (1958) (dissenting opinion).

C

Petitioners acknowledge that the original design of the Cruel and Unusual Punishments Clause was to limit criminal punishments, but urge nonetheless that the prohibition should be extended to ban the paddling of school children. Observing that the Framers of the Eighth Amendment could not have envisioned our present system of public and compulsory education, with its opportunities for noncriminal punishments, petitioners contend that extension of the prohibition against cruel punishments is necessary lest we afford greater protection to criminals than to schoolchildren. It would be anomalous, they say, if schoolchildren could be beaten without constitutional redress, while hardened criminals suffering the same beatings at the hands of their jailors might have a valid claim under the Eighth Amendment. See *Jackson* v. *Bishop,* 404 F. 2d 571 (CA8 1968); cf. *Estelle* v. *Gamble, supra.* Whatever force this logic may have in other settings, we find it an inadequate basis for wrenching the Eighth Amendment from its historical context and extending it to traditional disciplinary practices in the public schools.

The prisoner and the schoolchild stand in wholly different circumstances, separated by the harsh facts of criminal conviction and incarceration. The prisoner's conviction entitles the State to classify him as a "criminal," and his incarceration deprives him of the freedom "to be with family and friends and to form the other enduring attachments of normal life."

Morrissey v. *Brewer;* 408 U. S. 471, 482 (1972); see *Meachum* v. *Fano,* 427 U. S. 215, 224–225 (1976). Prison brutality, as the Court of Appeals observed in this case, is "part of the total punishment to which the individual is subjected for his crime and, as such, is a proper subject for Eighth Amendment scrutiny." 525 F. 2d, at 915. Even so, the protection afforded by the Eighth Amendment is limited. After incarceration, only the "unnecessary and wanton infliction of pain," *Estelle* v. *Gamble,*—U.S., at—, quoting *Gregg* v. *Georgia, supra,* at 173, constitutes cruel and unusual punishment forbidden by the Eighth Amendment.

The schoolchild has little need for the protection of the Eighth Amendment. Though attendance may not always be voluntary, the public school remains an open institution. Except perhaps when very young, the child is not physically restrained from leaving school during school hours; and at the end of the school day, the child is invariably free to return home. Even while at school, the child brings with him the support of family and friends and is rarely apart from teachers and other pupils who may witness and protest any instances of mistreatment.

The openness of the public school and its supervision by the community afford significant safeguards against the kinds of abuses from which the Eighth Amendment protects the prisoner. In virtually every community where corporal punishment is permitted in the schools, these safeguards are reinforced by the legal constraints of the common law. Public school teachers and administrators are privileged at common law to inflict only such corporal punishment as is reasonably necessary for the proper education and discipline of the child; any punishment going beyond the privilege may result in both civil and criminal liability. See Part II, *supra.* As long as the schools are open to public scrutiny, there is no reason to believe that the common law constraints will not effectively remedy and deter excesses such as those alleged in this case.

We conclude that when public school teachers or administrators impose disciplinary corporal punishment, the Eighth Amendment is inapplicable. The pertinent constitutional question is whether the imposition is consonant with the requirements of due process.

IV

The Fourteenth Amendment prohibits any State deprivation of life, liberty or property without due process of law. Application of this prohibition requires the familiar two-stage analysis: we must first ask whether the asserted individual interests are encompassed within the Fourteenth Amendment's protection of "life, liberty or property"; if protected interests are implicated, we then must decide what procedures constitute "due process of law." *Morrissey* v. *Brewer*, 408 U. S., at 481; *Board of Regents* v. *Roth*, 408 U. S. 564, 569–572 (1972). See Friendly, "Some Kind of Hearing," 123 U. Pa. L. Rev. 1267 (1975). Following that analysis here, we find that corporal punishment in public school implicates a constitutionally protected liberty interest, but we hold that the traditional common law remedies are fully adequate to afford due process. . . .

B

"[T]he question remains what process is due." *Morrissey* v. *Brewer*, 408 U. S., at 481. Were it not for the common law privilege permitting teachers to inflict reasonable corporal punishment on children in their care, and the availability of the traditional remedies for abuse, the case for requiring advance procedural safeguards would be strong indeed. But here we deal with a punishment—paddling—within that tradition, and the question is whether the common law remedies are adequate to afford due process. . . . Whether in this case the common law remedies for excessive corporal punishment constitute due process of law must turn on an analysis of the competing interests at stake, viewed against the background of "history, reason, [and] the past course of decisions." The analysis requires consideration of three distinct factors: "first, the private interest that will be affected . . . ; second, the risk of an erroneous deprivation of such interest . . . and the probable value, if any, of additional or substitute procedural safeguards; and, finally, the [state] interest, including the function involved and the fiscal and administrative burdens that the additional or substitute procedural requirement would entail." *Mathews* v.

62 THE POPULAR DEBATE

Eldridge, 424 U. S. 319, 335 (1976). Cf. *Arnett* v. *Kennedy,* 416 U. S. 134, 167–168 (1974) (POWELL, J., concurring).

Florida has continued to recognize, and indeed has strengthened by statute, the common law right of a child not to be subjected to excessive corporal punishment in school. Under Florida law the teacher and principal of the school decide in the first instance whether corporal punishment is reasonably necessary under the circumstances in order to discipline a child who has misbehaved. But they must exercise prudence and restraint. For Florida has preserved the traditional judicial proceedings for determining whether the punishment was justified. If the punishment inflicted is later found to have been excessive—not reasonably believed at the time to be necessary for the child's discipline or training—the school authorities inflicting it may be held liable in damages to the child and, if malice is shown, they may be subject to criminal penalties. . . .

3

But even if the need for advance procedural safeguards were clear, the question would remain whether the incremental benefit could justify the cost. Acceptance of petitioners' claims would work a transformation in the law governing corporal punishment in Florida and most other States. Given the impracticability of formulating a rule of procedural due process that varies with the severity of the particular imposition, the prior hearing petitioners seek would have to precede *any* paddling, however moderate or trivial.

Such a universal constitutional requirement would significantly burden the use of corporal punishment as a disciplinary measure. Hearings—even informal hearings—require time, personnel, and a diversion of attention from normal school pursuits. School authorities may well choose to abandon corporal punishment rather than incur the burdens of complying with the procedural requirements. Teachers, properly concerned with maintaining authority in the classroom, may well prefer to rely on other disciplinary measures—which they may view as less effective—rather than confront the possible disruption that prior notice and a hearing may entail. Paradoxically, such an alteration of disciplinary policy is most likely to occur in the ordinary case where the contemplated punishment is well within the common law privilege.

Elimination or curtailment of corporal punishment would be welcomed by many as a societal advance. But when such a policy choice may result from this Court's determination of an asserted right to due process, rather than from the normal processes of community debate and legislative action, the societal costs cannot be dismissed as insubstantial. We are reviewing here a legislative judgment, rooted in history and reaffirmed in the laws of many States, that corporal punishment serves important educational interests. This judgment must be viewed in light of the disciplinary problems commonplace in the schools. As noted in *Goss* v. *Lopez,* 419 U. S., at 580, "[e]vents calling for discipline are frequent occurrences and sometimes require immediate, effective action."[1]

"At some point the benefit of an additional safeguard to the individual affected . . . and to society in terms of increased assurance that the action is just, may be outweighed by the cost." *Mathews* v. *Eldridge,* 424 U. S., at 348. We think that point has been reached in this case. In view of the low incidence of abuse, the openness of our schools, and the common law safeguards that already exist, the risk of error that may result in violation of a schoolchild's substantive rights can only be regarded as minimal. Imposing additional administrative safeguards as a constitutional requirement might reduce that risk marginally, but would also entail a significant intrusion into an area of primary educational responsibility. We conclude that the Due Process Clause does not require notice and a hearing prior to the imposition of corporal punishment in the public

---

[1] If a prior hearing, with the inevitable attendant publicity within the school, resulted in rejection of the teacher's recommendation, the consequent impairment of the teacher's ability to maintain discipline in the classroom would not be insubstantial.

schools, as that practice is authorized and limited by the common law.

MR. JUSTICE WHITE, with whom MR. JUSTICE BRENNAN, MR. JUSTICE MARSHALL, and MR. JUSTICE STEVENS join, dissenting.

• • •

A

The Eighth Amendment places a flat prohibition against the infliction of "cruel and unusual punishments." This reflects a societal judgment that there are some punishments that are so barbaric and inhumane that we will not permit them to be imposed on anyone, no matter how opprobrious the offense. See *Robinson* v. *California,* 370 U. S. 660, 676 (1962) (Douglas, J., concurring). If there are some punishments that are so barbaric that they may not be imposed for the commission of crimes, designated by our social system as the most thoroughly reprehensible acts an individual can commit, then *a fortiori,* similar punishments may not be imposed on persons for less culpable acts, such as breaches of school discipline. Thus, if it is constitutionally impermissible to cut off someone's ear for the commission of murder, it must be unconstitutional to cut off a child's ear for being late to class. Although there were no ears cut off in this case, the record reveals beatings so severe that if they were inflicted on a hardened criminal for the commission of a serious crime, they might not pass constitutional muster.

Nevertheless, the majority holds that the Eighth Amendment "was designed to protect [only] those convicted of crimes," *ante,* at 12, relying on a vague and inconclusive recitation of the history of the Amendment. Yet the constitutional prohibition is against cruel and unusual *punishments;* nowhere is that prohibition limited or modified by the language of the Constitution. Certainly, the fact that the Framers did not choose to insert the word "criminal" into the language of the Eighth Amendment is strong evidence that the Amendment was designed to prohibit all inhumane or barbaric punishments, no matter what the nature of the offense for which the punishment is imposed.

No one can deny that spanking of school children is "punishment" under any reasonable reading of the word, for the similarities between spanking in public schools and other forms of punishment are too obvious to ignore. Like other forms of punishment, spanking of school children involves an institutionalized response to the violation of some official rule or regulation proscribing certain conduct and is imposed for the purpose of rehabilitating the offender, deterring the offender and others like him from committing the violation in the future, and inflicting some measure of social retribution for the harm that has been done. . . .

In fact, as the Court recognizes, the Eighth Amendment has never been confined to criminal punishments. Nevertheless, the majority adheres to its view that any protections afforded by the Eighth Amendment must have something to do with criminals, and it would therefore confine any exceptions to its general rule that only criminal punishments are covered by the Eighth Amendment to abuses inflicted on prisoners. Thus, if a prisoner is beaten mercilessly for a breach of discipline, he is entitled to the protection of the Eighth Amendment, while a school child who commits the same breach of discipline and is similarly beaten is simply not covered.

The purported explanation of this anomaly is the assertion that school children have no need for the Eighth Amendment. We are told that schools are open institutions, subject to constant public scrutiny; that school children have adequate remedies under state law; and that prisoners suffer the social stigma of being labeled as criminals. How any of these policy considerations got into the Constitution is difficult to discern, for the Court has never considered any of these factors in determining the scope of the Eighth Amendment.

The essence of the majority's argument is that school children do not need Eighth Amendment protection because corporal punishment is less subject to abuse in the public schools than it is in the prison system. However, it cannot be reasonably suggested that just because cruel and unusual punishments may occur less frequently under public scrutiny, they will not occur at all. . . .

Nor is it an adequate answer that school children may have other state and constitutional remedies available to them. Even assuming that the remedies available to public school students are adequate under Florida law, the availability of state remedies has never been determinative of the coverage or of the protections afforded by the Eighth Amendment. The reason is obvious. The fact that a person may have a state-law cause of action against a public official who tortures him with a thumb screw for the commission of an antisocial act has nothing to do with the fact that such official conduct is cruel and unusual punishment prohibited by the Eighth Amendment. Indeed, the majority's view was implicitly rejected this Term in *Estelle* v. *Gamble*, when the Court held that failure to provide for the medical needs of prisoners could constitute cruel and unusual punishment even though a medical malpractice remedy in tort was available to prisoners under state law.

D

By holding that the Eighth Amendment protects only criminals, the majority adopts the view that one is entitled to the protections afforded by the Eighth Amendment only if he is punished for acts that are sufficiently opprobrious for society to make them "criminal." This is a curious holding in view of the fact that the more culpable the offender the more likely it is that the punishment will not be disproportionate to the offense, and consequently, the less likely it is that the punishment will be cruel and unusual. Conversely, a public school student who is spanked for a mere breach of discipline may sometimes have a strong argument that the punishment does not fit the offense, depending upon the severity of the beating, and therefore that it is cruel and unusual. Yet the majority would afford the student no protection no matter how inhumane and barbaric the punishment inflicted on him might be.

The issue presented in this phase of the case is limited to whether corporal punishment in public schools can *ever* be prohibited by the Eighth Amendment. I am therefore not suggesting that spanking in the public schools is in every instance prohibited by the Eighth Amendment. My own view is that it is not. I only take issue with the extreme view of the majority that corporal punishment in public schools, no matter how barbaric, inhumane, or severe, is never limited by the Eighth Amendment. Where corporal punishment becomes so severe as to be unacceptable in a civilized society, I can see no reason that it should become any more acceptable just because it is inflicted on children in the public schools. . . .

The reason that the Constitution requires a State to provide "due process of law" when it punishes an individual for misconduct is to protect the individual from erroneous or mistaken punishment that the State would not have inflicted had it found the facts in a more reliable way. See, *e. g., Mathews* v. *Eldridge,* 424 U. S. 319, 335, 344 (1976). In *Goss* v. *Lopez,* 419 U. S. 565 (1975), the Court applied this principle to the school disciplinary process, holding that a student must be given an informal opportunity to be heard before he is finally suspended from public school.

> *"Disciplinarians, although proceeding in utmost good faith, frequently act on the reports and advice of others;* and the controlling facts and the nature of the conduct under challenge are often disputed. *The risk of error is not at all trivial,* and it should be guarded against if that may be done without prohibitive cost or interference with the educational process." *Id.,* at 580. (Emphasis added.)

To guard against this risk of punishing an innocent child, the Due Process Clause requires, not an "elaborate hearing" before a neutral party, but simply "an informal give-and-take between student and disciplinarian" which gives the student "an opportunity to explain his version of the facts." *Id.,* at 580, 582, 584.

The Court now holds that these "rudimentary precautions against unfair or mistaken findings of misconduct," *id.,* at 581, are not required if the student is punished with "appreciable physical pain" rather than with a suspension, even though both punishments deprive the student of a constitutionally protected interest. Although the respondent school authorities provide absolutely *no* process to the student before the punishment is finally inflicted, the majority concludes that the student is nonetheless given due process because he can later sue the teacher and recover damages if the punishment was "excessive." Even if the student could sue for good faith error in the infliction of punishment, the lawsuit occurs after the punishment has been finally imposed. The infliction of physical pain is final and irreparable; it cannot be undone in a subsequent proceeding. There is every reason to require, as the Court did in *Goss,* a few minutes of "informal give-and-take between student and disciplinarian" as a "meaningful hedge" against the erroneous infliction of irreparable injury. 419 U. S., at 583–584.

There is, in short, no basis in logic or authority for the majority's suggestion that an action to recover damages for excessive corporal punishment "afford[s] substantially greater protection to the child than the informal conference mandated by *Goss.*" The majority purports to follow the settled principle that what process is due depends on " 'the risk of an erroneous deprivation of [the protected] interest . . . and the probable value, if any, of additional or substitute procedural safeguards' "; it recognizes, as did *Goss,* the risk of error in the school disciplinary process and concedes that "the child has a strong interest in procedural safeguards that minimize the risk of wrongful punishment . . . ," *ante,* at 24; but it somehow concludes that this risk is adequately reduced by a damage remedy that never has been recognized by a Florida court, that leaves unprotected the innocent student punished by mistake, and that allows the State to punish first and hear the student's version of events later. I cannot agree.

The majority emphasizes, as did the dissenters in *Goss,* that even the "rudimentary precautions" required by that decision would impose some burden on the school disciplinary process. But those costs are no greater if the student is paddled rather than suspended; the risk of error in the punishment is no smaller; and the fear of "a significant intrusion" into the disciplinary process, *ante*, at 31 (compare *Goss, supra,* at 585) (POWELL, J., dissenting), is just as exaggerated. The disciplinarian need only take a few minutes to give the student "notice of the charges against him and, if he denies them, an explanation of the evidence the authorities have and an opportunity to present his side of the story." *Id.,* at 581. In this context the Constitution requires, "if anything, less than a fair-minded principal would impose upon himself" in order to avoid injustice.

I would reverse the judgment below.

Swedes Outlaw Spanking

*This newspaper article describes the public reaction to the
new Swedish law outlawing all corporal punishment in the
schools. Clearly one of the functions of the law is to
protect children from abuse. Is this an effective way to
achieve this worthy goal? Is it an acceptable way? Notice
the Maranta sect's criticism of the law. Spokesmen for the
sect argue that the statute violates their religious liberty.
But how far should a parent's religious liberty go? Can
you reasonably differentiate between the Maranta's claim
and the parent's refusal to grant a transfusion (in* Wallace
v. Labrenz)?

STOCKHOLM (AP)—A new law that forbids parents from
beating, spanking, cuffing or otherwise harming their children
takes effect in Sweden in July, but some parents are not happy
about it.

One father questioned said he thought spanking was good for
children, and a spokesman for the small Maranata religious sect
said frankly: "We will go underground if we have to but we will
continue to exercise our natural rights."

Sweden will become the first nation with such a law, adopting
it in the International Year of the Child. The law is a new step in
a long process aimed at protecting children's rights here. A
children's ombudsman and an emergency phone watch for
youngsters already exist.

When the minority Liberal government introduced the bill to
ban parents from spanking last March, Justice Minister Sven

From *The Express* (Easton, Pa.), May 21, 1979. Reprinted by permission of
the Associated Press.

Romanus said it means "our society has taken an increasingly negative view of beating or spanking as a means of bringing up children."

There has been no organized opposition to the law but reactions from jurists, lawmakers, and parents have been mixed. Said one annoyed father of three:

"Spanking and spanking . . . there's a difference between a deliberate spanking and what I would call an outburst of temper. I never spanked my kids in cold blood, only on the spur of the moment. I am sure it does not hurt them but help them."

Most critical of the law were spokesmen for the Maranata sect, a group of about 300 persons who split from the Pentecostal Church in the 1960s. It sees physical chastisement by parents as a natural means of correction and an "ethical, moral and religious right."

The sect operates its own "pilgrim" schools in protest against the public school system, and Hans Brynte, principal of one Maranata school, said:

"If the authorities try to stop us we will go underground and fight on. They are suddenly outlawing an old cultural tradition and parents are declared idiots incapable of rearing their children. People in other countries will laugh at this and a whole generation will be criminalized because some sociologists shall have their way."

When the new law was debated in Parliament, Conservative Tore Nilsson protested it. Quoting the Bible, ancient Icelandic life rules of the book Havamal and a centuries-old Swedish law document, he said, "The law against spanking conflicts with our cultural tradition, with parents rights and personal integrity and with Western humanism."

Justice Minister Romanus took a different view. "This development reflects the now-dominant view that the child is an independent individual who can demand full respect for his person, integrity and own value," he said.

The new law prohibits "any act which, for the purpose of punishing, causes the child physical injury or pain, even if the disturbance is mild and passing." It is meant to include psychological punishment, but legal experts have criticized the wording on this as too vague.

Many child psychiatrists, physchologists, sociologists and doctors have welcomed the new law as necessary to protect children.

Grade school children aged 8–10 polled at a recreational center were definitely against being spanked—not surprisingly—though they found it natural to occasionally beat a brother or sister themselves.

Peter, 10, noted, "My sister is always riling me. Then I hit her but that's OK because we are evenly matched. If my dad would hit me, or mom, it would not be fair but I would hit back too . . .

"Hitting is no good," he continued. "But some parents think they cannot bring up kids without spanking them. There the only thing is to run away for awhile so they become anxious and regret it."

Legal medical officer Sven-Olof Lidholm took a stern view of parents who beat their children. Criticizing authorities for laxness in caring for maltreated youngsters, he said he receives more than 600 reports of child beatings annually, about 10 of them fatal. And he believes there are perhaps some 5,000 other children who are beaten regularly without it being reported.

William Kessen

The Chinese Paradox

Kessen recounts his impressions of child rearing and educational practices in the Peoples' Republic of China. He wonders why children behave so differently there than in most Western cultures. Consequently, he poses some very important questions concerning just how our unexamined beliefs and assumptions affect our treatment of children and our moulding and conditioning of them to become what we want them to be. How exactly does ideology mould our character? How does ideology in the United States, Australia, or England affect the way we rear our children?

Near the end of our three-week stay in the People's Republic of China, a member of the American Kindergarten Delegation—thirteen psychologists, educators, and sociologists—asked our chief Chinese host and guide, "You spend so much time, energy, and money on agricultural research; why do you spend almost nothing on research with children?" Mr. Hsieh's answer was deliberate: "Plants are different; it is important for us to believe that all children are the same."

Hsieh's answer, on its surface, seemed at best ingenuous, at worst deceitful. We had visited two dozen schools, we had seen hundreds of Chinese children from the first year of life to the twentieth, and we had met with scores of teachers. We knew that all Chinese children are not the same, and we knew that

---

Reprinted with permission from the February 1978 issue of the *Yale Alumni Magazine;* copyright © Yale Alumni Publications, Inc.

Hsieh knew it too. What did he mean? In the four years since our trip, I have often returned—detective with only circumstantial evidence—to Hsieh's paradox. Looking at the present confusion and disorder in American attitudes about our children, I have formed some guesses about ". . . all children are the same" that may be relevant to my children as well as Hsieh's.

Before I put forward my guesses, let me persuade you that the behavior of Chinese children is worth understanding. Our first school visit was to The-East-is-Red Kindergarten in Canton (a standard part of the standard tour for foreigners). Four-and five-year-old children sat in a semicircle around their teacher, feet flat on the floor and hands grasping the chair rungs behind them. Nobody jumped up, nobody shoved his neighbor, nobody spoke out of turn. When the teacher asked a question, the response of the children was orderly, lively, and correct. "Showcase," we said. But the observation was repeated over and over and at earlier and earlier ages until the delegation stood mutely and without explanation when we watched fourteen-month-old children sit in a semicircle around their teacher. Nobody jumped or shoved; nobody spoke out of turn.

But there were other marvels. We saw no "learning disabled" children in China and no "hyperactives." We saw little or no squirming or thumb-sucking or tics or inattention. We watched urban high school classes of fifty children and one teacher work quietly and with concentration. We also saw almost no eye-glasses on Chinese children. The answer to that specific wonder was a series of eye exercises which every Chinese child performs for twenty minutes each day of his school life. Do many Chinese children walk about seeing poorly, or is the regimen of exercise effective in the prevention of myopia or—surely the most provocative and inscrutable possibility—is the absence of eyeglasses in China another example of the way in which, in human societies, ideology becomes fact?

Perhaps a single story will bring together the reasons why Americans are wide-eyed and perplexed by what they see in China. We went to the Star Kindergarten of Peking where, among the children of Chinese bureaucrats, there were also the children of foreign diplomats. The teacher brought out an engaging mechanical ping-pong game that the children had never before seen. The Chinese children gathered around it; they watched closely the movements of the toy at a respectful distance, apparently delighted by the novelty of the gadget but patient and at ease. Then, one of the care-takers who had been holding a foreign child in her arms (Chinese children in the school are not held in arms or given candy or fed by bottle or permitted to mess their food—privileges uniformly available to the Swedish, Pakistani, and English children there) put the child down. Without hesitation, he broke through the circle of watching Chinese children to lunge at the toy. What a singular image of the contrast between the Chinese way and ours!

Unless the Chinese systematically hide their mentally retarded children, their hyperactive, their neurotic—unless we were, for all our years of watching children in many cultures, suddenly blind—then there was a phenomenon to be explained, even understood. And so, on to my guesses, supported at least in part by the testimony of better observers of China than I.

As in many other traditional societies, China is characterized by a remarkable *stability of expectations*. Children are born, grow, learn, many in the same places where their parents were born and grew. The stability is most obvious in rural villages (particularly in the villages where all males have the same surname and the generational lines can be traced for centuries), but much the same stability can be found in the cities. There are no private automobiles in China; the mobility that we Americans have come to see as normal is unthinkable in China, and the immobility of residence is more than matched by the immobility of attitude.

Children, like the rest of us, are defined by the people they meet. The social definition of children in late twentieth-century America is a curious conglomeration: a five-year-old Connecticut child is one kind of person for his parents, another for his kindergarten teacher, yet another for his eurhythmics teacher, his swimming teacher, his friends, the parents of his friends, the folks in the supermarket, and his mute, uncomprehending grandparents. The contemporary American child is a crazy quilt of expectations and, it follows as it should, a crazy quilt of definitions. Not surprisingly, the child here and now *sees himself* as a polymorph, a man for any season, a magic slate on whom anybody can write a recipe.

Not so in China. A thousand years and more of commitment to order, restraint, and respect for the established (to say nothing of the Chinese freedom from late-nineteenth-century sociology and psychology) have produced, in adults and children alike, *a shared sense of what a child is*. Every adult in the village or in the commune or in the neighborhood (true urban villages) appears to have precisely the same vision of the appropriate conduct of children. Of course children will sit quietly in their chairs; of course they will learn to use chopsticks by three; of course they will wait in front of the toy until the teacher authorizes their touching it. The phrase "of course" is, in the Chinese image of the child, brought back to its full intention. You need only to think of the experience of a contemporary American child to recognize what a great distance separates the two cultures. We live in a zoo of variety, with relatives, physicians, psychologists, novelists, journalists, and television all providing different—sometimes even contradictory—messages about the nature of children. My hunch, which cannot be worked out here, is that the only consistent residual instruction to American children in all the variety is "Get promoted."

Easily as noteworthy as the consistency of expectations about children among Chinese adults—teachers and educational administrators included—is the pale expression of an analytic attitude toward the study of children. One of the themes wrapped up in ". . . all children are the same" is a lack of interest in probing the varieties of development. Let me make the point in another contrast. Even the best American teachers of my observation, as well as well-put-together parents, possess a sense of *instrumentality* about their exchanges with children. *If* I behave in such and such a way, *then* the child will do so; *if* the child behaves in such and such a way, then *I* should do so.

Human interactions, particularly those between teacher and pupil, are interactions of contingency, a stringing together (often quite unsystematically) of desired behavior on one side and the disposal of esteem or disgrace (Locke's words) on the other. The image of development by contingency, deeply embedded in our culture, seems inapplicable to the attitudes of Chinese adults charged with caring for children. To be sure, they use rewards and punishments—so strictly and often so puritanically that the culture might have been designed by B. F. Skinner and St. Paul. But the Chinese *attitude* toward the development of children contains the expectation that the developmental approach to desired behavior is inevitable, regular, and without need of instrumental manipulation. The shock for American observers is to see how smoothly and without symptom Chinese children meet the expectations of adults and become socially adept, calm, and dutiful school children who amaze the Western visitor.

It is not surprising, if my speculations are on target, that Chinese teachers, by and large, did not easily comprehend our culture-bound questions about pedagogical methods. They usually answered our questions with a repetition akin to "That's just the way children are," or with a careful citation from the works of Mao Tsetung. And herein lies other striking evidence of the integrality (and consequent unconsciousness) of Chinese attitudes toward child development. In the first place, the pedagogical techniques and the more subtle exchanges of adults and children are not Maoist in structure; they can be seen in Hong Kong or Taipei and, not so long ago, could be seen in New York and San Francisco. Once more, the argument is too long to make here, but Chinese teachers seem to have little awareness of how much in the behavior of children that they assign to Communist ideology is rather the continuation of a centuries-old tradition. Can it be that, unlike those of the Soviet Union and Western Europe, the traditions of child-rearing in China are in neat congruence with the aims of Communist state-building? After all, restraint, respect for authority, intricate bureaucracies, and calm pleasantness are not inventions of the Communist leadership; they are old China in a new five-button jacket.

The failure of Chinese pedagogues and bureaucrats to recognize the intimate relation between traditional child-rearing and the new Communist citizen is best expressed in the policy of sending educated urban youths into the countryside to live in peasant communes and villages, theoretically for the rest of their lives. Imagine, if you will, a sixteen-year-old who has grown up in the neighborhood where his parents grew up, who has participated in the excitement of Shanghai or Canton, who sees himself as belonging to a new generation of educated Chinese trained in revolutionary fervor—imagine this sophisticate sent off to a village in Singkiang or Mongolia, where the people who live just down the river are, in tangled ways, outsiders. The disruption of sending off is a disruption in the lives of millions of adolescents (the policy, by the way, has resulted in the largest forced migration in the history of the world); it is also a grotesque disruption of the traditions of child-rearing in China. We do not yet know the consequences of Mao's radical policy of separating young people from their origins and putting them in settings almost certain to isolate and to reject them; we do not even know if Hua Kuofeng will continue the exile of sending off. What is notable, and what should reflect back on our own awareness of ideology, is that the Chinese leaders chose to enter on an educational policy that contradicts the lifelong experience of Chinese children. How often do we do likewise? A glimpse of Chinese children nowadays is not valuable primarily because it tells us how to rear our children—the procedures of the Chinese are deeply locked into cultural values and are neither detachable nor exportable. Rather, a visit to China forces us to ask painful questions about American child-rearing and education: what is *our* fact, what is *our* ideology, and—the question at the heart of the matter— what burden do we lay on our children to live out the tension between the two? How much does our exquisite variety cost?

United Nations Declaration of the Rights of the Child

Some people have hailed the U.N. Declaration of the Rights of Children as a bold, inventive document advocating children's rights. But notice, in the preamble as well as in several of the principles, children are viewed as being incompetent and in need of strong paternalistic protection. Is it legitimate to assume that all children need to be treated paternalistically? Why? Also, what is the precise nature of the rights claimed here? Are they rights which the General Assembly wants each nation to legally recognize? If not, what force do such right claims have?

A five-point Declaration of the Rights of the Child was stated in 1923 by the International Union for Child Welfare, with 1948 revisions in a seven-point document. The League of Nations adopted the IUCW declaration in 1924. The following Declaration of the Rights of the Child was adopted by the United Nations General Assembly in 1959.

Declaration of the Rights of the Child Preamble

Whereas the peoples of the United Nations have, in the Charter, reaffirmed their faith in fundamental human rights and in the dignity and worth of the human person and have determined to promote social progress and better standards of life in larger freedom,

---

United Nations General Assembly Resolution 1386 (XIV), November 20, 1959. Published in the *Official Records of the General Assembly, Fourteenth Session, Supplement No. 16*, 1960, p. 19.

Whereas the United Nations has, in the Universal Declaration of Human Rights, proclaimed that everyone is entitled to all the rights and freedoms set forth therein, without distinction of any kind, such as race, color, sex, language, religion, political or other opinion, national or social origin, property, birth, or other status,

Whereas the child, by reason of his physical and mental immaturity, needs special safeguards and care, including appropriate legal protection, before as well as after birth,

Whereas the need for such special safeguards has been stated in the Geneva Declaration of the Rights of the Child of 1924, and recognized in the Universal Declaration of Human Rights and in the statutes of specialized agencies and international organizations concerned with the welfare of children,

Whereas mankind owes to the child the best it has to give,

Now therefore,

The General Assembly

Proclaims this Declaration of the Rights of the Child to the end that he may have a happy childhood and enjoy for his own good and for the good of society the rights and freedoms herein set forth, and calls upon parents, upon men and women as individuals, and upon voluntary organizations, local authorities, and national governments to recognize these rights and strive for their observance by legislative and other measures progressively taken in accordance with the following principles:

Principle 1

The child shall enjoy all the rights set forth in this declaration. All children, without any exception whatsoever, shall be entitled to these rights, without distinction or discrimination on account of race, color, sex, language, religion, political or other opinion, national or social origin, property, birth, or other status, whether of himself or of his family.

Principle 2

The child shall enjoy special protection, and shall be given opportunities and facilities, by law and by other means, to enable him to develop physically, mentally, morally, spiritually, and socially in a healthy and normal manner and in conditions of freedom and dignity. In the enactment of laws for this purpose the best interests of the child shall be the paramount consideration.

Principle 3

The child shall be entitled from his birth to a name and a nationality.

Principle 4

The child shall enjoy the benefits of social security. He shall be entitled to grow and develop in health; to this end special care and protection shall be provided both to him and to his mother, including adequate prenatal and postnatal care. The child shall have the right to adequate nutrition, housing, recreation, and medical services.

Principle 5

The child who is physically, mentally, or socially handicapped shall be given the special treatment, education, and care required by his particular condition.

Principle 6

The child, for the full and harmonious development of his personality, needs love and understanding. He shall, wherever possible, grow up in the care and under the responsibility of his parents, and in any case in an atmosphere of affection and of moral and material security; a child of tender years shall not, save in exceptional circumstances, be separated from his mother. Society and the public authorities shall have the duty to extend particular care to children without a family and to those without adequate means of support. Payment of state and other assistance toward the maintenance of children of large families is desirable.

Principle 7

The child is entitled to receive education, which shall be free and compulsory, at least in the elementary stages. He shall be given an education which will promote his general culture, and enable him on a basis of equal opportunity to develop his abilities, his individual judgment, and his sense of moral and social responsibility, and to become a useful member of society.

The best interests of the child shall be the guiding principle of those responsible for his education and guidance; that responsibility lies in the first place with his parents.

The child shall have full opportunity for play and recreation, which should be directed to the same purposes as education; society and the public authorities shall endeavor to promote the enjoyment of this right.

Principle 8

The child shall in all circumstances be among the first to receive protection and relief.

Principle 9

The child shall be protected against all forms of neglect, cruelty, and exploitation. He shall not be the subject of traffic, in any form.

The child shall not be admitted to employment before an appropriate minimum age; he shall in no case be caused or permitted to engage in any occupation or employment which would prejudice his health or education, or interfere with his physical, mental, or moral development.

Principle 10

The child shall be protected from practices which may foster racial, religious, and any other form of discrimination. He shall be brought up in a spirit of understanding, tolerance, friendship among peoples, peace and universal brotherhood, and in full consciousness that his energy and talents should be devoted to the service of his fellow men.

John Holt

Liberate Children

*John Holt claims that our present treatment of children is
abhorrent and ought to be abolished. We should then
make available to children all the rights, privileges,
duties, and responsibilities of adults. Would most
children—even most teenagers—be capable of undertaking these responsibilities? Notice that Holt claims that
these rights and duties should be made available to
children. That suggests that children would have an
option to accept or reject them. If you agree that they
should have the option, should a child be able to pick and
choose? For example, could he take the right to vote but
refuse to take legal responsibility for his actions? Why
should a child, but not an adult, be given such options?*

For a long time it never occurred to me to question [the
institution of childhood]. . . . Only in recent years did I begin to
wonder whether there might be other or better ways for young
people to live. By now I have come to feel that the fact of being a
"child," of being wholly subservient and dependent, of being
seen by older people as a mixture of expensive nuisance, slave,
and superpet, does most young people more harm than good.

I propose instead that the rights, privileges, duties, responsibilities of adult citizens be made *available* to any young

---

person, of whatever age, who wants to make use of them. These would include, among others:

1. The right to equal treatment at the hands of the law—*i.e.*, the right, in any situation, to be treated no worse than an adult would be.

2. The right to vote, and take full part in political affairs.

3. The right to be legally responsible for one's life and acts.

4. The right to work, for money.

5. The right to privacy.

6. The right to financial independence and responsibility—*i.e.*, the right to own, buy, and sell property, to borrow money, establish credit, sign contracts, etc.

7. The right to direct and manage one's own education.

8. The right to travel, to live away from home, to choose or make one's own home.

9. The right to receive from the state whatever minimum income it may guarantee to adult citizens.

10. The right to make and enter into, on a basis of mutual consent, quasi-familial relationships outside one's immediate family—*i.e.*, the right to seek and choose guardians other than one's own parents and to be legally dependent on them.

11. The right to do, in general, what any adult may legally do.

I have not tried to list these in any order of importance. What some young people might find most important others would find less so. I do not say, either, that these rights and duties should be tied into one package, that if a young person wants to assume any of them he must assume them all. He should be able to pick and choose. On the other hand, some of these rights are in the nature of things tied to others. Thus, the right to travel and to choose one's own home could hardly have much meaning to any young person who did not also have the right to legal and financial responsibility, to work, and to receive an income.

Some of these rights, much more than others, are linked to and depend on other kinds of change, in law, custom, or attitudes. Thus, we are likely to give young people of a given age—say, fourteen— the right to drive a car some time before we give them the right to vote, and we are likely to allow them to vote for some time before we give them the right to marry or to manage their own sex lives. And we are not likely to give young people the right to work at all in a society which, like the U.S. in 1973, tolerates massive unemployment and poverty. A country would have to make a political decision, like Sweden or Denmark, to do away with severe poverty and to maintain a high level of employment before adults would even consider allowing young people to compete for jobs. By the same token, no society is likely to give to young people the right to equal treatment before the law if it denies this right to adult women or to members of racial or other minority groups.

Part II
Transition Essay

After reading the selections from the popular debate you should now be familiar with the range and complexity of problems concerning state and parental treatment of children. You may well feel angry or bewildered. No doubt questions are buzzing in your head. But familiarity with the problems or sympathy with the victims is not enough. We also need to critically think about these problems and try to find some reasonable solutions. That is why we will now shift the tenor of the discussion from these journalistic, judicial, and literary selections to the philosophical reflections on the treatment of children.

What Philosophers Can Contribute

I imagine many people wonder what philosophers can add—other than more confusion—to this already burgeoning discussion about children. Why, in a book like this, should there be any philosophical contribution whatsoever? Why not just include more detailed selections from the authors and sources already cited?

There are four good reasons for including the philosophical essays. *First,* if we reflect on our initial reactions to the popular essays we find that our intuitions about the appropriate treatment of children are often confused. Consider the case of J.J. (p. 24). Upon reading the story, one immediately feels sympathy for J.J. and admiration for his parents and sister. But after further reflection, one begins to wonder if the interests of the donor sister are being unjustly sacrificed. Our intuitions about this kind of case are unsettled. More rigorous, systematic thought is necessary if we are to find a way to resolve our confusions, and systematic thinking is one of the principal tasks of the philosopher.

Actually, it is really not all that surprising that our intuitions about children are so confused. Historically, most energy has been spent thinking about moral dilemmas involving adults—capital punishment, war, euthanasia, sexual behavior, etc. We all have fairly fixed views about moral matters affecting adults: one shouldn't kill, steal from, or limit the liberty of an adult, except under unusual circumstances. However, most children differ from adults in several important respects. Generally, children are less experienced, less reasonable, and less mature than adults. And so, at first glance, anyway, there are some relevant differences between (most) adults and (most) children, differences that appear to justify differences in treatment. Where the real difficulty comes, of course, is in deciding exactly how different the treatment can justifiably be. In other words, adults are seen as full moral agents—creatures with moral rights and responsibilities. Children differ from adults in seemingly relevant ways; so how should children be viewed morally? Are they also full moral agents? Our struggles to answer this pressing question usually involve attempts to extend the more settled principles concerning proper treatment of adults to the more problematic cases concerning children. Since we have no established ways to extend these principles, we find, not surprisingly, that our initial thoughts are often confused.

Lawrence Houlgate, in his essay, "The Child as a Person: Recent Supreme Court Decisions," argues that this confusion is not just a confusion over initial intuitions. Rather it deeply pervades and disturbs the thought even of the highest judicial court in the United States. The Supreme Court often makes judgments about the fate of children by claiming that children are persons (in the full legal sense). But, Houlgate claims, the court is reluctant to consistently apply this doctrine; and so is in desperate need of a full normative theory of juvenile rights.

If Houlgate is right, as he certainly seems to be, his analysis shows how confused most people's thinking about children is and therefore, how important it is that philosophers attempt to resolve these confusions with careful, systematic thinking.

The *second* function of the philosophical essays is to identify the features or considerations common to the various issues. It is easy to get bogged down in or distracted by particular details. A more general examination, however, will reveal that the same question or belief often crops up in seemingly distinct issues, though in somewhat different guises. By focusing on these more general considerations, as the philosopher does, one is more likely to find satisfactory solutions to these problems concerning children.

It is important to realize that how one thinks about one of these issues often reflects how one does, or should, think about other issues concerning children. For example, someone who finds the Idaho Supreme Court's decision (p. 42) to return six year old Danny Dennis to his biological mother repulsive, probably thinks the child's stated wishes should be given strong, if not absolute, consideration in this case. The operative presumption seems to be that the child knows what he wants, and ought to be able to do what he wants. Yet if one does hold that a six year old is mature enough to make such an important decision about his future, then there are some rather direct implications for how one ought to think about other issues, say deprogramming or "voluntary" child pornography. For example, one would have to explain why a child's wishes in a custody case should be so weighty if a child's desire to be the subject of pornographic movies is considered totally illicit.

On the other hand, if one thinks the court's decision to return Danny Dennis to his biological mother was entirely appropriate, it is probably because he thinks biological parents have some special right or authority over birthed children. This conviction would probably affect what one thought the appropriate state response to child abuse should be. For example, someone with this belief would be more likely to want every effort made to reunite the abused child with her biological parents than would someone who did not see the biological bond as being morally significant.

The point of these examples is not to claim that someone who reacts to a case one way must necessarily react to another case in the same way. The point is that in many cases what is really at issue are not the details of the specific case, but rather the more general views or beliefs. That is, the disagreement about the appropriate dispensation of Danny Dennis is probably more a product of one's convictions about the biological bond or a six year old's ability to know what is in his best interests, than it is a squabble about specific details of the situation (like the fact that he was in church when he was taken away).

Consequently, progress is more often made by focusing on these more general considerations than on the unique minutiae. That is one of the advantages of the philosophical approach. The popular essays acquaint one with the nitty gritty of the cases, and thereby emotionally involve one with the issue. The philosophical essays primarily focus on these more general considerations, thereby illuminating the problem.

The *third* function of the philosophical essays is to uncover important unstated assumptions about children and the proper ways to treat them. This function is often closely related to the second, since many of these unstated assumptions are, in fact, the common features of the issues which philosophical exploratory surgery is designed to find. In the story about Danny Dennis we saw that some of the premier issues were general considerations about the moral importance of the biological bond and the rational abilities of children. Yet the judges in this case did not explicitly mention the moral or legal status of the biological bond. However, they must have assumed that the biological mother had special claim to her offspring. Otherwise their decision would have differed.

Or consider the normal reaction to child pornography. Most people think it obvious that children should not participate in pornography even if they claim they want to. But why? The answer seems to lie in a generally held assumption that children are incapable of making rational, informed choices about such important matters as public sexual display, and therefore ought to be treated paternalistically. This assumption will strongly influence opinions not only about child pornography but also about other controversial issues. Hence it is crucial to identify these assumptions if one is going to think rationally about the moral status of children. An important function of the philosophical essays is to identify these assumptions.

Suppose, now, that we have essays which successfully fulfill the first three functions of the philosophical essays—they help us to see our confused intuitions, discover the general features of these diverse issues, and identify the main unstated assumptions. Each function is a preliminary though necessary step toward the *fourth* and probably the paramount philosophical task, namely, critical evaluation. Without critical evaluation we have only a description of the status quo; we now understand how children are viewed and treated. But mere understanding is insufficient. If we want to solve these problems we must critically evaluate the intuitions and assumptions as well as the arguments about the preferred ways of treating children.

When philosophers evaluate *assumptions*, they frequently appeal to broader ethical considerations. Palmeri, for example, thinks it is beneficial to see our present treatment of children as analogous to our previous mistreatment of blacks and women. Feinberg attempts to elucidate questions about preparing a child for life as an adult by appealing to the moral notions of autonomy and self-determination.

When philosophers evaluate *policies* for treating children, they often scrutinize the arguments defending these policies. For example, Schrag criticizes the popular arguments defending children's rights by pointing out what he sees as unacceptable consequences of granting children rights. Young, on the other hand, rejects the arguments defending paternalism, at least in part, by citing empirical studies which show that adolescents have abilities to assess their own interests. Both of these evaluative strategies are necessary if we are going to construct a defensible view about how we should relate to and deal with children.

Some Concepts Philosophers Use

In the philosophical essays certain notions are repeatedly used, for example, 'rights,' 'obligations,' 'correlativity,' 'paternalism,' and 'interests.' This section should familiarize the reader with the common philosophical use of these concepts. Since in large part this book is about children's rights, it is appropriate to begin by examining the notion of 'a right.'

Talk about rights can be very confusing. How often have we heard: "you have no right to ask me to do that," "I have a right to keep that," "they are trying to take away my rights"? But what is a right?

Generally speaking, a right is a valid claim of someone to something against someone else. However, "to have a right" does not mean the same as "to do what is Right." To "do what is Right" is to do an action which is judged by a standard to be appropriate or correct, whereas "To have a right" is to have a valid claim to something. For example, I may have a right to keep my money when the United Way representative asks me for a contribution, even though it may be Right for me to give a contribution. It is important to see that these two uses of the word 'right' are distinct since it often happens that rights come into conflict. For example, if the parents of a child divorce, both may claim a right to the custody of their child. But the rights of both parents cannot be honored (or respected or protected) at the same time. They can not both be Right. The rights conflict. To settle this dispute we must adjudicate between the conflicting claims of rights and make a decision as to which right is most important (or which one is overriding, or which one takes precedent). Then we honor the appropriate claim of right. But this is still a bit confusing. What does honoring a right mean? How do we adjudicate conflicts of rights? And anyway, what good are rights?

When we speak of honoring or respecting a right we are dealing with a very serious business, for to fail to respect a right seems to be wrong; it is something that should not be done. Why is this? Since a right is a claim against someone there is a special relationship between the person who has the right (the right holder) and other people against whom the right is held (those who have a duty or obligation to abide by, honor, or respect the right.) One aspect of this relationship can be described by the metaphor of a leash, in which the right holder has another (the one with the obligation) as on a leash. A different aspect of this relationship can be described by another metaphor: the right-holder sits inside a fenced-in back yard and others have a duty not to climb the fence. So if you have a right, at least one other person has a duty toward you. If I borrow $5.00 from you and promise to pay you back, then you have a right to be repaid and I have an obligation to repay you. I am on your leash. If you have a right not to be killed, then all others have a duty not to kill you—we are outside of your fence. This connection between rights and duties is called correlativity. Rights and duties are correlative. Although there may be some duties that do not have correlative rights (for instance, the duty to be kind, or to give to charity), whenever there is a right there is also a correlative duty. Negative rights (liberties) protect individuals from unwarranted interference from others. Others have a duty to stay outside the fence. Positive rights (entitlements) grant individuals power over others to provide goods or services. Another is on my leash, and that person must give me what I am entitled to. Correlativity is important to understand since people sometimes make wild claims of rights. For instance they may claim that they have a right to the biggest house in town, or to living space of three acres, or to a happy, productive and fruitful life. The correlativity thesis requires us to carefully examine each claim of right to see if, realistically, it can have a correlated duty. Is it the duty of others to make me happy? Are they on my leash? Is it the duty of others to leave me alone entirely so that I may have living space—how extensive is my fenced-in back yard? Merely to claim a right to this or that is not enough to establish the right. It may be just idle wishing or dreaming about what it would be nice to have.

But how, then, do people "get" rights? One way people are granted rights is by rules conferring rights and duties. For example, in a football game, the offensive team is allowed four attempts to make a first down—it has a "right" to have four downs. The other team has a "duty" to respect this (unless it can cause a turnover!). Furthermore the referee enforces the rules. When a dispute arises, he also adjudicates between conflicting claims; he decides whose claim is overriding. This example provides a model for most rights talk. There are rules conferring rights (with correlative duties). In law this is clear. Legal rights are conferred and correlative duties are ascribed by rules (laws). When violations of rights occur, legal institutions enforce the laws. When a dispute breaks out—as in the child custody case—legal institutions adjudicate the conflict and make the decision. So some rights and duties are conferred by legal institutions. These are called legal rights.

But often rights talk is used to refer to other kinds of rights such as moral rights, human rights, and natural rights. Unlike legal rights, moral rights need not be conferred by actual laws. For example, people once had a legal right to own another person as a slave. But even while this invidious practice was legal, still some people maintained that all human beings had a moral right to be free from slavery and that all others, including slave owners, had a duty to refrain from owning slaves. Much of the current debate over children's rights similarly contrasts legal rights with moral rights. Even though children may not have many legal rights, some people claim that they have moral rights which others are duty-bound to respect—they too have a moral fence and a moral leash.

But if there are such moral rights, where do they come from? If they are not derived from written laws, how are they derived? This is a source of great controversy. Some claim that Natural

Law (a moral law above the law of governments) confers natural rights upon people. Others maintain that the rules which ought to pertain in a moral society confer them. Others believe that human rights are not derived from any rules, they are simply known by the intuition of morally sensitive persons. Still others maintain that rational persons would agree to respect certain rights, therefore moral rights are derived from hypothetical agreements. But however moral rights are grounded, it is important to see that they differ from legal rights. They may serve as "presumptive" rights; that is, as what ought to be embodied in law. Or they may be seen as higher critiques of law, having a stronger claim to our allegiance than law. But they differ from legal rights since legal rights are protected by the state. Enforcement of duties to respect rights is very important for those advocating the rights of children. In fact, many of these advocates argue that moral rights should be protected by law; that is, become legal rights. This leads to controversy for if the moral rights of children are enforced by laws then the state as protector of children's rights could force parents to respect those rights. Some opponents of children's rights object to such rights on the grounds that this intervention would introduce a hostile and adversary element into the natural, trusting, loving, and nurturing relationship between children and their parents. So it is important to remember that moral rights may or may not be protected by laws; but when they are, they also become legal rights which the state will protect, by force if necessary.

Is the purpose of all this talk about rights, then, simply to encourage a change in the laws? If so, why bother with rights talk at all?—why not just talk about law? The answer comes, at least in part, by focusing on one very important aspect of rights talk. Remember the fence metaphor? When an entity has rights it has a sphere of autonomy of its own. It is granted an independent status. An individual with rights must be given respect. It is assumed that an individual with rights is owed a certain type of treatment. The rightholder does not have to prove that he/she should be allowed to do something or have something—it is his/her due. The "burden of proof" is on others to show that there is a very compelling reason why the right should be overridden. The rightholder need not justify the exercise of right. But why is this so important? An example will illustrate. If children have a right to an education then it is owed them as their due; others have a duty to provide it. But what if they did not have such a right? What would happen? Undoubtedly some parents would not want their children to become educated—they believe it will poison their minds with idolatrous ideas. Other parents might want the money which their children could earn working in the fields or the factory or may not want to "waste" money on education. Under these circumstances, children could only plead, beg, or petition their parents to allow them to receive an education. They could only hope for parental kindness, benevolence, generosity, or aquiescence. But if they have a right to an education they can demand it as their due. Having rights gives them power over others.

This element of autonomy and being "worthy of respect," this power over others, persists even for moral rights. For example, it is not illegal to discipline children with physical force (as it is for private citizens to "discipline" other adults with assault and battery). But if children have moral rights to their physical well-being, then this right ought to be respected by parents even when "disciplining" their children, regardless of what the law permits. Having rights is important because entities with rights should be treated differently than entities without them.

Some thinkers believe moral rights language does not correctly apply to children even though normal adults do have such rights. On this view children do not have full moral standing or complete moral status. They are not yet the kind of entity which can have rights (because they are not rational, autonomous, responsible, competent, etc.). Normally, the parents should decide what is best for the child and act accordingly. Children do not have moral standing apart from their parents. They are dependent, developing entities which stand in a special relationship with their parents. Their parents may have certain duties with regard to them, but they have no rights against their parents. The relationship between child and parent is not, on this model, an adversary one enforced by laws and coercion. It is a natural kinship relationship in which parents know and do what is best for their children. The interests of children are carefully protected and developed by adults. There is no need for the hostile language of rights to even enter into the picture.

This is in stark contrast to the framework of rights talk. True, rights talk is a language of respect. But it is also a language of conflict wherein individuals are adversaries who pursue their own interests within the limits placed on them by others. Each individual is seen as an autonomous responsible agent capable of abiding by the rules. Each takes on the burden of respecting the rights of others and reaps the benefit of having their own rights respected. Each makes autonomous decisions and is held accountable for his actions.

But children, some claim, are not yet ready for this world of responsibility, autonomy, rights, and duties. They must be given a special form of treatment which the framework of rights simply cannot capture. This special treatment is generally called paternalism. Instead of focusing on rights of children, these thinkers maintain, we should focus upon the interests of children. Instead of seeing parental duties as correlative of children's rights, we should stress parental or adult responsibility to develop children's interests and long-term good. Actions benefitting children are not done because they are owed to them as if to a rightholder, and they cannot be demanded as due.

Generally when rights talk is used we are not looking ahead to goals, purposes, or aims which we wish to accomplish. Rights talk is not "teleological" (goal oriented). But this other frame of reference, paternalism, is highly teleological and in many ways is even more complicated than rights talk. We can understand the framework best by looking at the case of normal adults. It is generally assumed that adults act upon goals and aims which they believe to be best for them. Sometimes, though, they seem to act foolishly. They let short-term interests (desires, wants, wishes) distract them from their long-term well-being. For instance, they may drink or smoke too much and thereby ruin their health. They have an interest in good health, but sometimes they choose to act against their own best interest (what is good for them in the long run). Generally we assume adults are rational and autonomous and thus we let them choose their own goals and act accordingly. As long as they do not harm anyone else, we let them decide and act upon what is in their own best interest—what is for their "own good".

But what about children? Many believe that children should not be granted the autonomy to decide what is in their own best interest nor be left alone to pursue their chosen goals. The welfare or well-being or best interest of children must be identified and promoted by adults. Why is this? Presumably because children are not mature enough to know what things are good for them in the long run. If given the choice of immediate gratification or long-term fulfillment, they choose immediate gratification. If left to choose between playing or going to school, they might never get an education. And even if they do know what is in their long-term best interests, they may not be mature enough to act upon it. They may let immediate pleasures control their better judgment, and so not have the will power to act in their best interests. Even though they know they should not eat only cake and candy, if left totally without "guidance", chances are they would not eat a balanced meal.

So adults must not only decide what is best for the child—what is in the child's interest—they must also, when necessary, force the child to act in accordance with his/her best interest. This is what paternalism is all about—being a loving "pater" who knows and does what is best for the child whether the child agrees or not. Here the language of rights is somewhat inappropriate, since the conflicts which arise between what the child wants and what is really best for the child are not *real* conflicts—they are only apparent. If the child knew what the parent knows, there would be no conflict. If the child had the will which the parent does, there would be no conflict.

However, the assumptions underlying paternalism are questionable. Some argue that even children should be entitled to choose their own goals, decide what is in their interest, and be given the liberty (with accompanying rights) to pursue those goals without interference, even from their parents. But generally, the concession is made that some sort of paternalism is necessary, at least for very young children. But even if we agree that some paternalism is necessary, who should decide what is in the best interest of the child? The parents of the child? If so, is there not a danger that parents will make mistakes? We admitted earlier that adults sometimes act foolishly with regard to their own interests. Are they not sometimes as foolish when it comes to their children? Some parents do have some very peculiar ideas about what is "good" for a child. Perhaps they believe that severe beatings will make the child a hard working adult; that complete isolation from other children will make a mature adult; that a protein-less diet will make a pure and happy adult; that incestuous sexual experiences will make a good adult lover; that cultivating a caustic, cruel, and selfish character will make a "dog-eat-dog" successful adult; that a childhood devoid of affection or tenderness will spare the adult of emotional involvement and consequent heartache. Parents do have some very strange beliefs about what is in the best interest of their children. And these beliefs affect child rearing practices. Should the state step in to protect the child's interests against the parents? Should the state take on the responsibility of identifying and promoting the best interests of children even if this conflicts with parental judgment?

If one adopts the paternalistic standpoint, who should decide what really is in the best interest of children? The traditional presumption has been that parents naturally love their children and so will want to do what is best for them. Parents are in a better position to know what is in the best interests of their children than is a (impersonal? oversized? cumbersome?) bureaucracy of a state enforcement agency. But whether state paternalism or parental paternalism, the paternalistic framework differs in some important respects from the framework of rights. Still, some thinkers attempt to combine them by asserting that children have a right to receive certain kinds of paternalistic treatment. For example, children are sometimes said to have rights to be given a compulsory education, or rights to have their long term best interests promoted by others, or rights to the conditions which will maximize their possibility of obtaining well-being.

When you read the following philosophical essays, it is imperative that you critically examine the use of the concepts from these two frameworks. Be sure you understand exactly what is being claimed. When someone talks about paternalism, determine what it is that is claimed to be in the child's best interest, who is making the judgement, and who is enforcing it. When someone talks about rights, determine what right is being claimed, whether it is seen as a moral or legal right, and who has the correlative duty. Careful attention to the way these concepts are used will make it easier for you to understand the arguments put forth in the philosophical essays.

Part III
The Philosophical Debate

Ann Palmeri

Childhood's End: Toward the Liberation of Children

After considering several analogies between our past mistreatment of minorities and women and our present treatment of children, Palmeri argues that our current beliefs about and treatment of children are flawed. Particularly notice her discussion of institutional paternalistic practices. Do you think Feinberg would agree with Palmeri's analysis of paternalism? How, if at all, would adoption of Palmeri's views alter the parent-child relationship?

"None worried except a few philosophers."

Arthur C. Clarke

The "Children's Rights Movement" has clearly drawn its inspiration from the civil rights and women's liberation movements. Not too long ago minorities and women were not considered people, all kinds of scientific explanations were offered about why this was so. The advocates of present liberation movements deny first, that most so-called racial and sexual differences are real, and second, that any actual differences have bearing on the rights to be ascribed. Since the analogy has been drawn between minorities, women, and children, what light can it shed on our treatment of children, in other words, how apt is this analogy?

This article has not been published previously.

Yet, this is not a paper on children's rights. Instead, I wish to talk about the concept of "childhood,"[1] what kind of "person" a child is. We cannot answer the question about what rights should be ascribed to children unless we can answer the more general question about what kinds of beings can be accorded what kinds of rights. Furthermore, many of the arguments for our paternalistic behavior towards children have depended upon the assumption that the differences between children and adults warranted our acting paternistically on their behalf. The analogy drawn above, if it is at all apt, brings into question whether such paternalistic behavior towards other persons can in fact be justified, especially by appeal to the fact they are "children."[2]

This paper is divided into three parts: the first is a general discussion of paternalism with respect to the analogy drawn between minorities, women, and children; the second is a discussion of some of the arguments justifying our paternalistic behavior towards children, ((1) that children are not rational and (2) that children do not have enough experience); the third, through the use of specific examples, discusses what children's liberation might mean.

I

In recent years, paternalistic behavior has been a focus of heated discussion. Although enough intuitively acceptable examples can be given, paternalistic acts require explicit moral justification. The reason we need moral justification, Gert and Culver point out, is because such acts necessarily involve the violation of various moral rules. Their definition of paternalistic behavior is worth our consideration.

"A is acting paternalistically toward S if and only if A's behavior (correctly) indicates that A *believes that:*

(1) his action is for S's good
(2) he is qualified to act on S's behalf
(3) his action involves violating a moral rule (or doing that which will require him to do so) with regard to S

(4) he is justified in acting on S's behalf independently of S's past, present, or immediately forthcoming (free, informed) consent

(5) S believes (perhaps) falsely that he (S) generally knows what is for his own good."[3]

Before discussing the other features of paternalistic behavior, our immediate concern is with feature (5). For A to be acting paternalistically toward S, it is assumed that S is capable of thinking about what is for his or her own good. This condition is made, Gert and Culver state, to exclude those acts on behalf of infants or animals (and any other beings without such "self-consciousness") from the category of paternalism. Clearly, we cannot be acting paternalistically towards those who cannot even think about what is in their own behalf. I have no quarrel with this claim. To say I act paternalistically towards my plants when I prune them because I often will claim it is "for their own good" certainly extends paternalism too far.

But the important and interesting part of this condition is not just whether S is in fact capable of thinking on his own behalf. For Gert and Culver claim "We can be paternalistic only toward those *whom we regard* as believing themselves to be capable of acting on their own behalf."[4] It is the character of A's belief about S's belief that is central to characterizing any behavior as paternalistic. Social criticism of recent years has pointed out the *patterns* of paternalistic thinking. If such a pattern became institutionalized, it was not considered paternalistic because it needed no *special* moral justification. Often those who seem to us to be acting paternalistically do not believe they are acting paternalistically at all precisely because they do not believe S to be capable of thinking, at least initially, about what is in his own best interest. A traditional text will illustrate this point.

John Locke explaining "paternal power" says:

The power, then, that parents have over their children arises from that duty which is incumbent on them—to take care of their offspring during their imperfect state of childhood. To inform the mind and govern the actions of their yet ignorant nonage till reason shall take its place and ease them of that trouble is what the children want and the parents are bound to . . .[5]

The important case Gert and Culver have left out is whether we can be acting paternalistically when we do not believe ourselves to be acting paternalistically. If we convince ourselves that we are not acting paternalistically then we also escape needing to justify our violation of moral rules. John Locke's account of "paternal power" is not offered as a moral justification of paternalistic practices (in Gert's and Culver's sense), rather, it is an account that denies that children have the ability to know what is good for them except in the minimal sense that they "know" their parents should act for them.

In addition to distinguishing between those beings toward whom we can be paternalistic and those to whom we cannot be, we must further distinguish acceptable institutional paternalism from paternalism which needs a case by case justification. For it may be that a certain class of beings, say infants, about which we have plausible generalizations, can justifiably be subjected to standard institutional forms of paternalism. However, with other classes where these generalizations cannot be made, for example, older children, we would have to justify paternalistic treatment of them on a case by case basis.

Many paternalistic practices occur with A's denial that they are paternalistic, while many others occur with A's systematic justification of how S believes falsely that he or she knows what is for his or her own good. These latter practices are recognized as paternalistic and in need of justification. The plausibility of A's belief is often a historical and moral matter; what might have seemed an acceptable or plausible social or biological theory one hundred years ago has often been superseded on scientific and moral grounds. Any full account of paternalistic behavior must adjust its account of plausibility to suit both present and past beliefs. We could say that in recent years we have *discovered* paternalistic practices—in the past we did not recognize them as such.

In the case of minorities and women, we have been uncovering the elaborate justifications for practices we must label as paternalistic. One such example of a scientific theory offered as a guide to medical practice is given in the following account, offered in 1869 by Dr. Dirix, of the causes of disorders in women from sore throats to curvature of the spine:

Thus, women are treated for diseases of the stomach, liver, kidneys, heart, lung, etc.; yet, in most instances, these diseases will be found, on due investigation to be, in reality, no diseases at all, but merely the sympathetic reactions or the symptoms of one disease, namely, a disease of the womb.[6]

A consequence of the "frailty of woman" theme of the nineteenth century was the medical treatment of confinement and inactivity for the upper class woman. An account of the differing beliefs of the woman and the doctor on what is for her own good can be found in Charlotte Perkins Gilman's *The Yellow Wallpaper*.

Are there any comparable theories about children that lead to paternalistic practices towards them? One real characteristic of children is that they are small—that is, smaller than adults. This physical difference seems, John Holt argues, to give us license to bully children or to think of them as cute. "Much of what we respond to in children is not strength or virtue, real or imagined, but weakness, a quality which gives us power over them or helps us to feel superior."[7] But specific similarities in the analogy are not sufficiently illuminating for understanding a whole range of paternalistic practices. Our problem in recognizing paternalistic practices in general is to figure out what constitutes a moral justification for such a practice and whether any such justifications can be correlated with plausible beliefs about children.

Just as there are disanalogies between the histories of minorities and women, so there are important differences between those histories and that of children. That blacks and women have so often been thought to be "childlike" and, on the basis of that claim, been paternalistically treated shows how much deeper the claims for paternalistic practices with respect to children are entrenched. Most importantly, the category of "children" is just too broad to make any sense in examining how we ought to treat children. Yet historical justifications for the paternalistic treatment have certainly used some arguments indiscriminately applied to "children," from toddlers of three to young adolescents of fourteen who are biologically capable of being parents. Only by looking at these arguments can we ever make sense of whether *any* paternalistic practices towards children are in fact justified.

II

The Argument from Mental Maturity
Version A: Children are not rational

The most serious argument for the paternalistic treatment of children has come from whose who think that children are not mentally mature enough to make their own decisions. Children, it is said in this argument, do not know what is right or wrong, or how to reason correctly. They are not, in short, morally responsible human beings because they are not rational. Therefore, we are justified in "teaching" them how to behave by issuing commands like "Don't hit Mary over the head, it's not nice" until such time when they can truly understand why they should not do those things.

We can identify two premises to support the conclusion that children are not morally responsible: 1) A person is morally responsible if and only if he or she is rational or (perhaps to beg the question) is capable of being rational and 2) the factual claim that *children* are not rational.

The identification of being rational with being moral has obvious modern roots in the Kantian tradition of ethics. Basing his view on Piaget and others, John Rawls, for instance, has specified three successive stages of moral development: 1) the morality of authority, 2) the morality of association, and 3) the morality of principles. The stage of the morality of principles is the only stage in which, according to Rawls, a person has a true "sense of justice," the only stage in which he or she is acting on rational principles. Until children reach the final stage in which they rationally determine on what principles they ought to act, it follows that children cannot be held morally responsible.[8]

We must carefully notice that implicit in the description of the child's behavior as developing towards this goal is an evaluation of the "normal human adult" as a state that *"ought to be reached."*[9] Such states of mental maturity are "ethical ideals of human development."[10] But it is very difficult to tell what meaning this ethical ideal is supposed to have, it seems to be only a vague and intuitive notion.[11] We lack an adequate psychological account of the process of development and, therefore, we also lack satisfactory criteria for recognizing the "end product" of this development. How we are to determine when children possess such a capacity is very unclear. Accordingly, we have only the vaguest idea of what counts as a "moral being."

One important question to be answered here is whether age is a reliable index in gauging rationality and moral responsibility.[12] A plausible case might be made for acknowledging a difference between infants and fourteen-year-olds in their being able to exercise their rationality. On Piaget's (and others') theory, one of the first requirements is to be able to differentiate between oneself and others. The infant is in the process of making this distinction while a "normal" fourteen-year-old already operates with such a distinction. Consequently, our expectations of an infant as opposed to a fourteen-year-old are quite different. When an infant pulls your glasses off and breaks them by throwing them to the ground, we plausibly assume the infant had no real idea of what he or she was doing. We would be hard put to morally excuse a fourteen-year-old who performed the same action. So in a gross way age can be an index (although not always a fully sufficient one) of how we can expect people to behave and how responsible we can expect them to be.

But we must be careful here. Since we seem so unclear about the "end product," we must be equally skeptical of the present social and psychological theories which claim to give an accurate chart of the development. Many social critics of our treatment of children have claimed that children are far more capable than we think and our paternalistic practices pervert these capabilities. For instance, in response to being treated as cute, John Holt argues,

A cute child soon learns to do everything he or she does, at least around adults, to get an effect. Such children become self-conscious, artful, calculating, manipulative . . . They become specialists in human relationships which they can see more and more as a kind of contest to see who can get the most out of others.[13]

These traits, he suggests, resemble the psychological picture of a subservient class: lack of self worth, emotional instability, and manipulative relations with others.

Our dilemma is that children are "developing persons." Feeding an infant a well-balanced diet may not be considered a paternalistic practice, but feeding a child of eight a well-balanced diet when that child has other ideas certainly is. Whether this practice is justifiable then becomes another question. We have often used the argument that children are not rational in a way that obscures our paternalistic practices. If we believe an eight-year-old cannot possess a rational life plan, for instance, then we can ignore his or her protests by citing this general claim of incapacity. We often forget, because of the institutionalized nature of our justification, that such an incapacity must be demonstrable to count as an adequate moral justification.

Right now, it seems impossible to demonstrate that children lack such a capacity. By assuming they do lack the capacity to reason we restrict their behavior and give them little opportunity to demonstrate or further develop such a capacity. Further, we often wish and indeed *act* as if children are accountable for their actions. In short, we are inconsistent and irresponsible when we do hold children accountable—we simply adopt whatever notion we seem to find convenient.

Often, when we judge children incapable of making decisions for themselves, we seem, on more careful reflection, to be saying that they will not make the "right" decisions; or, that if the right decisions have been made, that they will have been made for the wrong reasons. What we must be careful about is that in our efforts to guarantee a child's final moral end we do not blind ourselves into thinking that differences between a child's thinking and our own necessarily marks her or his thinking as defective. Our knowing that a young person goes through this process of development should not make us believe a child *must be* in some morally inferior or defective stage. In other words, our judgment about a child's moral incapacity may not always be right and may indicate that we are often unclear about just what a rational decision might be.

As a consequence, making socially restrictive judgments about what children can and cannot do must be done with the utmost care. If Piaget is right that such a process is inevitable,[14] it can be argued that this does not imply that we must exercise adult restraint and authority in all areas in those early years. Rather, its inevitability may equally cogently lead us to question very seriously our institutionalized paternalistic practices.

So what if an eight-year-old wants to eat only Twinkies? We have it on good evidence that prolonged eating of this sort of junk food rots your teeth and may cause ill health. Wanting such an end, rotten teeth and ill health, we think, would be irrational. But just because an eight-year-old wants to eat Twinkies, we cannot assume that he or she wants this end, any more than we would assume an adult would. (We would assume the adult either does not know the relationship between eating Twinkies and rotten health or has decided the joy of gorging on Twinkies now is worth risking rotten teeth or ill health later.) We cannot make such an assumption of knowledge and valuation in the eight-year-old child—not because he or she is incapable, but perhaps because such learning may not have been available or the child was not ready until now for such information. Until such time we may be quite right as parents to try and inculcate eating habits which do not result in ill health. But after a child understands such a relationship are we then justified in acting paternalistically? What justification could we have?

What is clear is that interfering with a child's liberty should be as serious a matter as interfering with an adult's liberty. Our special duties as parents and teachers is to pass on important knowledge about living in the world, evaluating different life plans and imparting a sense of self worth through our love and care. The trouble with the notion of "interfering with another's liberty" is that it assumes that letting someone alone is the most liberty enhancing. If we let anyone follow a path of self-destruction at whatever age, is that enhancing his or her liberty? We can recognize such self-destructive behavior in a child or an adult and, it seems to me, we are obligated to help each other, first, to stop such behavior and then to help each other reevaluate our lives. Our belief that we are a better judge of what is best for a child or an adult, however, cannot be assumed from the authority that age or position gives us, but only from an acceptable moral justification presumably demonstrable to others. To return to our example, the end of a healthy growing child must be weighed over the deprivation of self-determination and the immediate pleasure of eating what one wants. If the parent opts for depriving the child of Twinkies, the responsibility of the parent to educate is all that more compelling—to explain why the opportunity for eating Twinkies is being diminished.

One last comment on this argument. Because what we consider to be rational behavior or a rational life plan may be very limited, it is in tension with the principle of accepting the different behavior of other people. One thing, though, is clear—children *do not fail* to make decisions and plans on matters that they know about.[15] What we really think of them is not that they cannot make decisions but rather that they are *incapable* of making *good* ones. We do not protect young people by making their decisions for them, rather, we keep them from gaining the most from their experience—we may keep them from "being rational," and, we do not let them take the responsibility in areas where they are quite capable of making decisions.

Version B: Children are inexperienced

A further rationalization of our paternalistic treatment of children runs somewhat as follows: I respect children's abilities as persons in their own right; the main problem, though, is that they do not know anything. So the real gap between adults and children is a function of the fact that children are inexperienced. Their "formative years" are, accordingly, to be set aside (unlike the era of child labor) to provide them with enough experience to become full-fledged moral beings capable of making important decisions.

But clearly we do not, and we do not for good reasons, accept this general claim when it comes to other categories of people. Should we accept it in this case? What needs to be demonstrated is that the lacks a particular child or children of a certain age have are relevant to the specific set of decisions being discussed. We do not think ignorance of the issues although an undesireable state of affairs, is sufficient to exclude people from voting. Our moral obligation to all citizens is to give them the opportunity to read, free access to all information and educational opportunities.[16]

The fact is we treat experiential or cognitive deficiencies in various ways. Our difficulties with children, however, are not, in general, different from our moral problems in any situation involving the complex interrelationships of those with more knowledge who are teaching those with less. We, of course, wish to protect *anyone* who steps in front of a car, whatever may be his or her state of knowledge of the dangers of doing so, but we appear to have more difficulty in extending this general benevolence in matters that require a certain level of experience for practice. With regard to driving a car, and also to practicing medicine, we feel that the practice of state licensing protects people from harm, and we feel no compunction about keeping people off the road or from practicing medicine when they do not have the proper experience. Yet, for certain kinds of experience, we cannot make such a fine judgment as to the level of experience required, for the kind of experience required is of a different sort. If we examine the patient-doctor case more closely we will see why.

Often, a patient who uses a doctor's services is told very little about the diagnosis or prescribed treatment. Even when the patient asks, the doctor often gives simple-minded answers and treats the patient as if he or she were incapable of "really" understanding. While a patient may fail to have the knowledge that comes both from study and from years of practice, by no means should the patient be considered incapable of understanding or, more importantly, of participating in decisions affecting his or her own health. This participation may require careful guidance and explanation by the doctor as to the consequences of different decisions, nevertheless, the choice must be the patient's.

The fact that we do sometimes hold children responsible for their actions and call upon them to justify their actions shows our willingness to recognize children's growing capacities and knowledge. At those times, we do not allow young people to give their being children as an excuse; if they do, they turn our own classification against us.[17] What is acceptable as an excuse is not a recounting of one's age but some accounting of not being in a position to know, or that circumstances were beyond one's control, and so on.

The times when we wish to hold children responsible for their actions gives us an indication of our "common sense" views of how much experience children need to have to engage in certain practices. For the moment, let us say that there is no legal restriction on the age a person can drive; we only require that drivers pass a driving test. As cars are now constructed, it is clear only older children would have the physical capability to drive a car. Should we allow anyone with the requisite physical capability to drive a car? One of the arguments against allowing younger teenagers to drive cars is that they will not be responsible drivers—not only do many of them lack a sense of courtesy, but they often engage in destructive behavior like driving while drunk. The statistics for older teenagers, the argument goes, bear out their recklessness. Our legal restrictions are supported by such statistical generalizations. If we were to take away this legal argument we might be more inclined, as we do in the case of adult recklessness, to make a judgment on the basis of each individual case. There is no easy test, prior to long term driving, of driver responsibility and there is no good evidence for saying that teenage recklessness is *inevitable*; in fact, most teenagers are not reckless at all and maybe younger ones would be less so.

What then would be the justification for restricting a particular young person from driving? Our justification should be no different than in an adult case of the same kind. We restrict only those who are emotionally immature in such a way as to endanger a life. Although age may indicate certain kinds of immaturity, for example, in sexual or political matters, we cannot automatically assume that justifies paternalism. Although we might make broader generalizations on the basis of a person's age, acts of paternalism with respect to children involve the same *kinds* of moral justifications as in the adult cases. The reason we get confused is because we have special responsibilities towards children to help them develop and to act in their behalf when they are not ready to do so. Yet this in no way excuses us from supplying the same sort of justifications for paternalism that we must have in other sorts of cases. Doctors, teachers, and clergypersons all have special responsibilities and their paternalistic practices are no less suspect.

The experience argument is a powerful one and *can* be used in all sorts of cases to justify specific paternalistic behavior. But the violation of a moral rule like deception or the denial of an opportunity must be outweighed by the promotion of other values. Assuming our every action as parents has the best interest of our children at heart is simply not enough, if minimizing paternalism is our end.

III

I would like to turn now away from considerations of paternalism to a more positive view of a child as a "developing person" and to what the "liberation" of children might mean. Let us return to our original analogy for the moment. Presently, our society seems embroiled in debates over how to compensate for past injust treatment of minorities and women. On the one hand, we wish to compensate for the unequal treatment by affirmative actions, on the other, we also wish to recognize differences when they call for different sorts of resources and institutional arrangements, for example, giving birth. For children, both forms of liberation are relevant.

Often our repressive way of treating children is not a direct consequence of our recognition that children are materially different beings than ourselves, that is, physically and mentally developing, but appears, rather, to be put forward on the basis of some explicit moral assumptions about what such developmental characteristics should lead to in constructing our social institutions. Those who argue that adults have total authority to tell children what to do on the grounds that children need protecting are confusing the need for special treatment in certain respects with the assumption that those respects provide grounds for restriction of children's personal autonomy.

In the first sense of liberation, we wish to ferret out all the ways our social theorizing has stereotyped children—epithets like "cute," "innocent," "the little beasts,"—which influence adult behavior and deny that children are "persons." Other characteristics attributed to children such as smallness (relative to adults), lack of experience are certainly recognizable in what it means to be a child. Two points must be made here. First, just as giving birth to a child should not necessarily entail exclusion from other activities like holding a job, just being small should not exclude a person from being mobile. Second, our social institutions must be responsive to the fact that children develop, they have different needs and lacks at different times. It would be a mistake to argue, then, that all social institutions constructed on the basis of special needs are oppressive. Education, for instance, is not inherently oppressive, although present day schools, it can be argued, are not at all, or are only intermittently, responsive to the various needs of the children in them. When "educators" believe the main task of the schools is to control the behavior of the children, to transmit values by mere assertion of authority, physical or mental, then it would be easy to argue that children would be better off without those schools, and instead that we should establish learning centers which would involve people of all ages. We might then expand the notion of a "developing person" to all ages and discard the notion of "child" as being too imprecise to be of any use.

The danger here is that the special responsibility of parents to educate may become diffuse and depersonalized in social institutions. Our problem here is not in "liberating children" but what we often take the notion of "liberty" to mean. "Liberty," in the classical liberal sense, has meant the absence of external impediments. Yet, the other sense, deriving from that tradition, is the sense of being a person, meaning being responsible, having reasons, acting with intentions and purposes. We want a society that enhances the liberty of a person to develop (creatively) in the fullest sense possible. What has been missed, or confused, in "liberation" talk is that giving people complete liberty, in the sense of letting them do whatever they want, may undermine liberty in the second sense. We interfere with children by not letting them defecate where they please, eat what they want, or view what they desire, often on the basis that it will somehow inhibit their becoming a person in the fullest creative sense of using all the gifts and capabilities they have and of being involved in a close intimate way with other people. Teaching people how to read can enhance liberty but the manner in which we do it may not. If the situation is made so uncomfortable that a person does not want to read, then perhaps it would be more "liberating" to give up trying under those conditions and find some other way.

It may be that real liberation requires closer ties with people than we now have, more interference with the first sense of liberty rather than less. For instance, many feminists would argue that beauty contests, pornographic (rather than erotic) films exploit women, make them into objects and would think it proper to interfere in the liberty of people to engage in these events. Although legal interventions are not desirable, nor very effective, we do wish to find a way to keep people from promoting such values.

Pluralism should not include making objects of other people or making yourself into an object. Perhaps, at this time, we can only cogently argue for interference in the liberty of those with whom we have ties and have a basis for rational discourse and a more than casual concern for their welfare. The danger is always that I will coerce someone solely for my own benefit in the guise that it is for theirs.

Despite the dangers of coercion, I think it is possible to enhance the liberty of children if we allow them to participate more in the decisions about their own education. Clearly, the level and kind of participation would change over the course of the years. The conflict of values we often find between children and adults may involve visions of the future. An adult, unlike a child, recognizes the importance of reading or practicing the piano not just for the present but for the future success as an independent person with hopes of an enjoyable life. This future vision may not seem so important to the child. Our main responsibility is to get the child to recognize the importance of preparing for the future, to incline them to give more importance to other values. How much is sacrificed of the present desire for the future can be a matter of discussion and negotiation. Unless the adult and the child are willing to engage in the process of offering reasons, coercion of the child or manipulation of the adult is more likely to occur. In turn, adults might alter their values in response to the strength of children's needs. New modes of production, education, and family life may evolve with the creative vision of children involved.

Often, we hear children remark on our bigotry, question our unjustifiable rules, uncover our most dogmatic beliefs. Our exchange of ideas with the young could be much more fruitful and exciting if we took young people seriously and did not pass their ideas off as childish rubbish. Not only can we learn from children, but we may hope to become freer in imagining, more careful in justifying our beliefs, in short, more "childlike." Like the society we hope to attain with the full liberation of women, we hope that the liberation of children will produce a world where people have the best characteristics of both adults and children.

Our differences should not let us fail to recognize our

common humanity, for until we can recognize it, children may continue to be controlled in the name of education, and abused in the name of love.[18]

NOTES

1. Philippe Ariès, *Centuries of Childhood: A Social History of Family Life* (New York: Vintage Books, 1962).

   Only beginning in the seventeenth century was the period of childhood distinguished from all others as a period of dependence. Thus Ariès writes,

   > One could leave childhood only by leaving the state of dependence, or at least lower degrees of dependence. That is why the words associated with childhood would endure to indicate in a familiar style, in the spoken language, men of humble rank whose submission to others remained absolute: lackeys, for instance, journeymen and soldiers. (p. 26)

   Especially important is Ariès finding that the vocabulary of childhood was characteristically used for anyone in a state of subservience. This reverberates to our own day.

   In contrast, Lloyd de Mause, ed. in *The History of Childhood* (New York: Harper Torchbooks, 1975), cites this modern period as saving these small beings from the physical exploitation by adults, and, therefore, as a positive soc:..' development. It is possible to resolve these historical interpretations, but even if one were to adopt one position to the exclusion of the other, it is not relevant to the case being made here. Whether we once treated this "age of life" as a period of dependency or not, or whether we see our historical development as progressively humane treatment is not the telling point here about whether we can and *ought* to move into a different era of social relations.

2. Three social critics who have examined this treatment and have made some suggestions for remedy are: Shulamith Firestone, *The Dialectic of Sex* (New York: Bantam Books, 1971); Richard Farson, *Birthrights* (New York: Macmillan, 1974); John Holt, *Escape From Childhood* (New York: E.P. Dutton, 1974).

3. Bernard Gert and Charles M. Culver, "Paternalistic Behavior" in *Philosophy and Public Affairs,* Vol. 6, No. 1, Fall, 1976, pp. 49-50.

4. Gert and Culver, p. 53. Italics mine.

5. John Locke, *The Second Treatise on Government* (Indianapolis: Bobbs-Merrill, 1952), p. 33 (Section VI).

6. Quoted in Barbara Ehrenreich and Deirdre English, *Complaints and Disorders: The Sexual Politics of Sickness* (Old Westbury: The Feminist Press, 1973), p. 30.

7. Holt, p. 82.

8. See, for example, R. S. Peters, *Ethics and Education* (London: G. Allen & Unwin, Ltd., 1966);
John Rawls, *A Theory of Justice* (Cambridge: Harvard University Press, 1971):

> "this initial situation is fair between individuals as moral persons, that is, as rational beings with their own ends and capable, I shall assume, of a sense of justice." (12)

> ". . . provided the minimum for moral personality is satisfied, a person is owed all the guarantees of justice." (507)

> ". . . It follows that a full grasp of moral conceptions must await maturity; the child's understanding is always primitive . . ."

> "the child lacks the concept of justification altogether, this being acquired much later. Therefore, he cannot with reason doubt the propriety of parental injunctions." (463);

R. P. Wolff, *In Defense of Anarchism* (New York: Harper Torchbooks, 1970)

> "It is quite appropriate that moral philosophers should group together children and madmen as being not fully responsible for their actions, for madmen are thought to lack freedom of choice, so children do not yet possess the power of reason in a developed form." (12)

9. D. W. Hamlyn has pointed this out in T. Mischel ed. *Cognitive Development and Epistemology* (New York: Academic Press, 1971) pp. 3–25.

10. This further moral point is made by Stephen Toulmin in "The Concept of Stages in Psychological Development" in Mischel, pp. 25–71.

11. A point made by Toulmin who further states,

> ". . . our choice of 'stages' in psychology will be at least as value loaded' as the same choice in developmental physiology; it commits us to some general view about the capacities which it is desirable for adolescents to develop—and so to an *ethical* opinion about the 'true' nature of Man." p. 53.

12. What is perplexing is that Rawls acknowledges our mistakes with

regard to other human beings. The capacity for a moral personality is a sufficient condition for being entitled to equal justice. "While individuals presumably have varying capacities for a sense of justice, this fact is not reason for depriving those with a lesser capacity of the full protection of justice." (505).

13. Holt, p. 91.
14. Jean Piaget, *The Moral Judgment of the Child* (New York: The Free Press, 1965).
15. Robert Coles in "Political Children" in *New York Review of Books,* February 20, March 6, and March 20, 1975 gives credence to the claim that children are quite capable of making political assessments.
16. Just what we have to provide to make opportunities substantively equal is not an easy question. See Onora O'Neill "How Do Know When Opportunities Are Equal?" in Jane English ed. *Sex Equality* (Englewood Cliffs: Prentice Hall, 1977), pp. 14–153.
17. This point came out of a discussion with Iris Young.
18. This paper is dedicated to Richard S. Rudner. I would also like to thank SWIP, Iris Young, Mary Ellen MacGuigan, Joyce Trebilcot, members of the Philosophy Department at Washington University, Ben Daise, Susanne McNally, Marilyn Kallet, Hugh LaFollette, and William Aiken for helpful criticism.

Joel Feinberg

The Child's Right to an Open Future

In the first two sections of this essay Feinberg discusses "the child's right to an open future," and tries to show how recognition of this right might alter the ways that parents rear their children. Then, in the remainder of the paper, he considers two attempts to justify this right.

Notice Feinberg's discussion of the claim that the child's self-fulfillment depends on interests the parents decide to create. If Feinberg's views on this matter are correct, how if at all, would Bishop's discussion of the right of determination be affected?

Would Palmeri agree with Feinberg's claim that paternalism toward children is inevitable?

Given Feinberg's argument for the right to self-determination, is there any principled way to justify extensive paternalistic treatment of children but not adults?

1

How do children's rights raise special philosophical problems? Not all rights of children, of course, do have a distinctive character. Many whole classes of rights are common to adults and children; many are exclusive possessions of adults; perhaps none at all are necessarily peculiar to children. In the common

---

This article has not been published previously.

category are rights not to be mistreated directly, for example the right not to be punched in the nose or to be stolen from. When a stranger slaps a child and forcibly takes away his candy in order to eat it himself, he has interfered wrongfully with the child's bodily and property interests and violated his or her rights just as surely as if the aggressor had punched an adult and forcibly helped himself to her purse. Rights that are common to adults and children in this way we can call "*A-C*-rights"

Among the rights thought to belong only to adults ("*A*-rights") are the legal rights to vote, to imbibe, to stay out all night, and so on. An interesting subspecies of these are those autonomy-rights (protected liberties of choice) that could hardly apply to small children, the free exercise of one's religion, for example, which presupposes that one has religious convictions or preferences in the first place. When parents choose to take their child to religious observances and to enroll him in a Sunday School, they are exercising *their* religious rights, not (or not yet) those of the child.

The rights which I shall call "*C*-rights", while not strictly peculiar to children, are generally characteristic of them, and possessed by adults only in unusual or abnormal circumstances. Two subclasses can be distinguished, and I mention the first only to dismiss it as not part of the subject matter of this essay, namely those rights that derive from the child's dependence upon others for the basic instrumental goods of life—food, shelter, protection. Dependency-rights are common to all children, but not exclusive to them, of course, since some of them belong also to handicapped adults who are incapable of supporting themselves and must therefore be "treated as children" for the whole of their lives.

Another class of *C*-rights, those I shall call "rights-in-trust," look like adult autonomy rights of class *A*, except that the child cannot very well exercise his free choice until later when he is more fully formed and capable. When sophisticated autonomy rights are attributed to children who are clearly not yet capable of exercising them, their names refer to rights that are to be *saved* for the child until he is an adult, but which can be violated "in advance," so to speak, before the child is even in a position to exercise them. The violating conduct guarantees *now* that when the child is an autonomous adult, certain key options will already be closed to him. His right while he is still a child is to have these future options kept open until he is a fully formed self-determining adult capable of deciding among them. These "anticipatory autonomy rights" in class *C* are the children's rights in which I am most interested, since they raise the most interesting philosophical questions. They are, in effect, autonomy rights in the shape they must assume when held "prematurely" by children.

Put very generally, rights-in-trust can be summed up as the single "right to an open future," but of course that vague formula simply describes the form of the particular rights in question and not their specific content. It is plausible to ascribe to children a right to an open future only in some, not all respects, and the simple formula leaves those respects unspecified. The advantage of the general formula, however, is that it removes temptation to refer to certain rights of children by names that also apply to rights of adults that are quite different animals[1]. The adults's right to exercise his religious beliefs, for example, is a class *A* right, but the right of the same name when applied to a small child is a right-in-trust, squarely in class *C*. One can avoid confusing the two by referring to the latter simply as part of the child's right to an open future (in respect to religious affiliation). In that general category it sits side by side with the right to walk freely down the public sidewalk as held by an infant of two months, still incapable of self-locomotion. One would violate that right in trust *now,* before it can even be exercised, by cutting off the child's legs. Some rights with general names are rather more difficult to classify, especially when attributed to older, only partly grown, children. Some of these appear to have one foot in class *A* and the other in the rights-in-trust subclass of the *C* category. For example, the right of free speech, interpreted as the freedom to express political opinions, when ascribed to a ten year old is perhaps mainly an actual *A*-right, but it is still partly a *C*-right-in-trust, at least in respect to those opinions which the child might one day come to form but which are presently beyond his ken.

People often speak of a child's "welfare" or his "interests." The interests protected by children's A-C-rights are those interests the child actually has *now*. Their advancement is, in a manner of speaking, a constituent of the child's good *qua* child right now. On the other hand the interests he might come to have as he grows up are the one's protected by his rights-in-trust of class C. While he is still a child these "future interests" include those that he will in fact come to have in the future and also those he will never acquire, depending on the directions of his growth.

It is a truism among philosophers that interests are not the same things as present desires with which they can, and often do, clash. Thus if the violation of a child's autonomy right-in-trust can not always be established by checking the child's *present* interests, *a fortiori* it cannot be established by determining the child's present *desires* or *preferences*[2]. It is the adult he is to become who must exercise the choice, more exactly, the adult he will become if his basic options are kept open and his growth kept "natural" or unforced. In any case, that adult does not exist yet, and perhaps he never will. But the child is *potentially* that adult, and it is that adult who is the person whose autonomy must be protected now (in advance.)

When a mature adult has a conflict between getting what he wants now and having his options left open in the future, we are bound by our respect for his autonomy not to force his present choice in order to protect his future "liberty." His present autonomy takes precedence even over his probable future good, and he may use it as he will, even at the expense of the future self he will one day become. Children are different. Respect for the child's future autonomy, as an adult, often requires preventing his free choice now. Thus the future self does not have as much moral weight in our treatment of adults as it does with children. Perhaps it should weigh as much with adults pondering their *own* decisions as it does with adults governing their own children. In the self-regarding case, the future self exerts its weight in the form of a claim to prudence, but prudence cannot rightly be imposed from the outside on an autonomous adult.

2

Moral perplexity about children's C-rights-in-trust is most likely to arise when those rights appear to conflict with certain A-rights of their parents, and the courts must adjudicate the conflict. Typically the conflict is between the child's protected personal interests in growth and development (rather than his immediate health or welfare) and the parents' right to control their child's upbringing, or to determine their own general style of life, or to practice their own religion free of outside interference. Very often the interests of the general community as represented by the state are involved too, for example the concern that children not be a source of infection to others, that they grow up well enough informed to be responsible voting citizens, or that they not become criminal or hopeless dependents on state welfare support. Thus custody hearings, neglect proceedings against parents, and criminal trials for violating compulsory school attendance laws and child labor statutes often become three-cornered contests among the rights of children, parents, and the state as representative of the collective interests of the community.[3] Sometimes, however, the community's interests are only marginally involved in the case, and the stark conflict between parent and child comes most clearly to the fore. Among the more difficult cases of this kind are those that pose a conflict between the religious rights of parents and their children's rights to an open future.

Children are not legally capable of defending their own future interests against present infringement by their parents, so that task must be performed for them, usually by the state in its role of *parens patriae*. American courts have long held that the state has a "sovereign power of guardianship" over minors and other legally incompetent persons which confers upon it the right, or perhaps even the duty, to look after the interests of those who are incapable of protecting themselves. Mentally disordered adults, for example, who are so deranged as to be unable to seek treatment for themselves, are entitled, under the doctrine of *parens patriae,* to psychiatric care under the auspices of the state. Many "mentally ill" persons, however, are not cognitively deranged, and some of these do not wish to be confined and treated in mental hospitals. The government has no right to impose treatment on these persons, for the doctrine of *parens patriae* extends only to those unfortunates who are rendered literally incapable of deciding whether to seek medical treatment themselves; and even in these cases, the doctrine as liberally interpreted grants power to the state only to "decide for a man as we assume he would decide for himself if he were of sound mind."[4] When the courts must decide for *children,* however, as they presume the children themselves would (or will) when they are adults, their problems are vastly more difficult. As a general rule, the courts will not be so presumptuous as to speak now in the name of the future adult; but, on the other hand, there are sometimes ways of interferring with parents so as to postpone the making of serious and final commitments until the child grows to maturity and is legally capable of making them himself.

In 1944 in the case of *Prince v. Massachusetts*[5] the U.S. Supreme Court upheld a Massachusetts statute that had been applied to prevent Jehovah's Witnesses' children from distributing religious pamphlets on the public streets in what their parents claimed was the free exercise of their religion. The decision in this case has been severely criticized (and I think rightly) as a misapplication of the *parens patriae* doctrine,[6] but the court's statement of that doctrine is unusually clear and trenchant. The state is concerned, said the court, not only with the immediate health and welfare of children but also with—

... the healthy, well-rounded growth of young people into full maturity as citizens with all that implies [in a democracy] . . . Parents may be free to become martyrs themselves. But it does not follow that they are free in identical circumstances to make martyrs of their children before they have reached the age of full and legal discretion when they can make that decision for themselves.[7]

It was no doubt an overstatement to describe the exposure of children to the apathy or scorn of the passersby in the streets as "martyrdom", but the court's well-stated but misapplied principle suggests other cases where religious liberty must retreat before the claims of children that they be permitted to reach maturity with as many open options, opportunities, and advantages as possible.

Twenty years later, in a quite different sort of case, the religious rights of parents were upheld in a Long Island court at the expense of their three small children. The twenty-four year old mother, injured in an automobile collision, was allowed to die when her husband refused on religious grounds to allow doctors to give her a blood transfusion. The husband, like his wife a member of Jehovah's Witnesses, remained adamant despite the pleadings of doctors. Finally the hospital administrator appealed to State Supreme Court Judge William Sullivan, who refused to order the transfusion.

It is too easy to criticize a judge who was forced to make a life or death decision in a legally difficult case on only a moment's notice, and I have no intention of doing so. On balance his decision might well have been justified even though the case for reading the balancing scales in the children's favor in this instance was strong indeed. The three children whose interests in present welfare and future development were directly involved could not, of course, make the momentous decision for themselves, and both natural parents were determined to decide against the children's interests. Only the state in its capacity as protector of those who cannot help themselves (*parens patriae*) had the legal power to overrule the parents' decision. The religious beliefs of the parents were sincere and important; their contravention, according to the tenets of the parents' sect, would be serious sin, perhaps something akin to both cannibalism and adultery.[8] On the other balance pan was the diminished prospect of three children for a "healthy, well-rounded growth into full maturity", and their immediate and continuous need of maternal care and affection. The parents' "sin" would certainly be mitigated by the fact that it was "committed" involuntarily under governmental duress; whereas the children's deprivation, while perhaps being something short of "martyrdom," would be a permanent and possibly irreplaceable loss. On the other hand, some fathers might be able to replace their deceased wives quite effectively, either on their own or through prompt remarriage, so it is not perfectly clear that the case for applying the *parens patriae* doctrine in this instance ought to have been decisive.

Another close case, I think, but one where the interests of children do seem prior to the religious interests of their parents, was that in which the Kansas courts refused to permit an exemption for Amish communities from the requirement that all children be sent to state-accredited schools.[9] The Amish are descended from eighteenth century immigrants of strong Protestant conviction who settled in this country in order to organize self-sufficient farming communities along religious principles, free of interference from unsympathetic outsiders. There is perhaps no purer example of religious faith expressed in a whole way of life, of social organization infused and saturated with religious principle. The aim of Amish education is to prepare the young for a life of industry and piety by transmitting to them the unchanged farming and household methods of their ancestors and a thorough distrust of modern techniques and styles that can only make life more complicated, soften character, and corrupt with "worldliness". Accordingly, the Amish have always tried their best to insulate their communities from external influences, including the influence of state-operated schools. Their own schools teach only enough reading to make a lifetime of Bible study possible, only enough arithmetic to permit the keeping of budget books and records of simple commercial transactions. Four or five years of this, plus exercises in sociality, devotional instruction, inculcation of traditional virtues, and on-the-job training in simple crafts of field, shop, or kitchen are all that is required, in a formal way, to prepare children for the traditional Amish way of life to which their parents are bound by the most solemn commitments.

More than this, however, was required by law of any accredited private school in the state of Kansas. Education is compulsory until the age of sixteen, and must meet minimal curricular standards including courses in history, civics, literature, art, science, and mathematics more advanced than elementary arithmetic. Why not permit a limited exemption from these requirements out of respect for the constitutional right of the Amish to the free exercise of their religion and to the self-contained way of life that is inseparable from that exercise? The case for the exemption was a strong one. The Amish "sincerity" is beyond any question. The simple "unworldly" life that is part of their religion is *prima facie* inconsistent with modern education; and the virtues of simplicity and withdrawal are "important", that is, more than merely incidental or peripheral to the Amish religion. Moreover, the small size of the Amish sect would minimize the effect of an exemption on the general educational level in Kansas. Indeed, insofar as there is a *public* interest involved in this problem (in addition to the clash of private interests) it seems to weigh more heavily on the Amish side of the scale, for as Mill pointed out in *On Liberty*,[10] we all profit from the example of others' "experiments in living". They permit us to choose our own way of life more aware of the various alternatives that are open, thus facilitating our own reasoning about such choices and reducing the possibility of error in our selection. Living examples of radically different ways of life constantly before our eyes cannot help but benefit all of us, if only by suggesting different directions in case our majority ways lead to dead ends.

The case against the exemption for the Amish must rest entirely on the rights of Amish *children,* which the state as *parens patriae* is sworn to protect. An education that renders a child fit for only one way of life forecloses irrevocably his other options. He may become a pious Amish farmer, but it will be difficult to the point of practical impossibility for him to become an engineer, a physician, a research scientist, a lawyer, or a business executive. The chances are good that inherited propensities will be stymied in a large number of cases, and in nearly all cases, critical life-decisions will have been made irreversibly for a person well before he reaches the age of full discretion when he should be expected, in a free society, to make them himself. To be prepared for anything, including the worst, in this complex and uncertain world would seem to require as much knowledge as a child can absorb throughout his minority. These considerations have led many to speak of the American child's birth-right to as much education as may be available to him, a right no more "valid" than the religious rights of parents, but one which must be given reluctant priority in cases of unavoidable conflict.

Refusal to grant the exemption requested by the Amish only puts them in the same kind of position *vis-a vis* their children as all other parents. They are permitted and indeed expected to make every reasonable effort to transmit by example and precept their own values to their children. This is in fact a privileged position for parents, given their special relations of intimacy and affection with their children, even when compared to the rival influences of neighbors and schools; but still, in the interest of eventual full maturity, self-fulfillment, and natural many-sided development of the children themselves, parents must take their chances with outside influences.

The legal setback to the Amish at the hands of the Kansas Supreme Court was only temporary, however, and six years later in the case of *Wisconsin v. Yoder*[11] they won a resounding victory in the Supreme Court of the United States. The Amish litigants in that case had been convicted of violating Wisconsin's compulsory school attendance law (which requires attendance until the age of sixteen) by refusing to send their children to public or accredited private school after they had graduated from the eighth grade. The U.S. Supreme Court upheld the Wisconsin Supreme Court's ruling that application of the compulsory school-attendance law to the Amish violated their rights under the Free Exercise of Religion Clause of the First Amendment.[12] The Court acknowledged that the case required a balancing of legitimate interests but concluded that the interest of the parents in determining the religious upbringing of their children outweighed the claim of the state in its role as *parens patriae* "to extend the benefit of secondary education to children regardless of the wishes of their parents."

Mr. Chief Justice Burger delivered the opinion of the Court which showed a commendable sensitivity to the parental interests and the ways they are threatened by secular public education:

The concept of a life aloof from the world and its values is central to their faith . . . High school attendance with teachers who are not of the Amish faith, and may even be hostile to it, interposes a serious barrier to integration of the Amish child into the Amish religious community . . . Compulsory school attendance to the age of sixteen for Amish children carries with it a very real threat of undermining Amish community and religious practice as they exist today; they must either abandon belief and be assimilated into society at large, or be forced to migrate to some other and more tolerant region.[13]

Burger shows very little sensitivity, however, to the interests of the Amish child in choosing his own vocation in life. At one point he begs the question against anyone who suggests that some Amish children might freely and even wisely decide to enter the modern world if given the choice:

The value of all education must be assessed in terms of its capacity to prepare the child for life. It is one thing to say that compulsory education for a year or two beyond the eighth grade may be necessary when its goal is the preparation of the child for life in modern society as the majority live, but it is quite another if the goal of education be viewed as the preparation of the child for life in the separated agrarian community that is the keystone of the Amish faith.[14]

But how *is* "the goal of education" to be viewed? That is the question that must be left open if the Court is to issue a truly neutral decision, to *assume* that "the goal" is preparation for modern commercial-industrial life is to beg the question in favor of the state, but equally, to assume that "the goal" is preparation for a "life aloof from the world" is to beg the question in favor of the parents. An impartial decision would assume only that education should equip the child with the knowledge and skills that will help him choose whichever sort of life best fits his native endowment and matured disposition. It should send him out into the adult world with as many open opportunities as possible, thus maximizing his chances for self-fulfillment.

More than eighty percent of the way through his opinion, the Chief Justice finally addresses the main issue—

> The state's case . . . appears to rest on the potential that exemption of Amish parents from the requirements of the compulsory education law might allow some parents to act contrary to the best interests of their children by foreclosing their opportunity to make an intelligent choice between the Amish way of life and that of the outside world.[15]

That is indeed the argument that Burger must rebut, and his attempt to do so is quite extraordinary—

> The same argument could, of course, be made with respect to all church schools short of college. [Burger forgets that church schools must satisfy certain minimal curricular standards if they are to be accredited by the state. The state of Wisconsin has not prohibited the Amish from establishing parochial schools that meet the same standards that other church schools do.] Indeed it seems clear that if the State is empowered, as *parens patriae,* to "save" a child from himself or his Amish parents by requiring an additional two years of compulsory formal high school education, the State will in large measure influence if not determine, the religious future of the child. Even more markedly than in *Prince,* therefore, this case involves the fundamental interest of parents, as contrasted with that of the State, to guide the religious future and education of their children.[16]

Burger seems to employ here a version of the familiar argument that to prevent one party from determining an outcome is necessarily to determine a different outcome, or to exercise undue "influence" on the final outcome. So it has been argued in similar terms that to prevent one party's coercion of a second party's decision is itself to influence that decision coercively.[17] Often this sort of argument is directed at inactions as well as actions so that the would-be guarantor of impartiality is beaten from the start. Thus it is sometimes said that to abstain from

coercion is to permit an outcome that could have been pre-
vented and thus to exercise undue influence, or (in other
contexts) that not to punish is to "condone." The upshot of
these modes of reasoning is the conclusion that state neutrality
is not merely difficult but impossible in principle, that by doing
nothing, or permitting no other parties to do anything that will
close a child's options before he is grown, the state in many
cases itself closes some options.

There are two ways of replying to this argument of Burger's.
The first is to claim that there is some reasonable conception of
neutrality that is immune to his blanket dismissal, so that while
there are severe practical difficulties that stand in the way, they
are not insolvable in principle, and that in any event, even if
perfect neutrality is unachievable in an imperfect world, there is
hope that it can be approached or approximated to some degree.
Ideally, the neutral state (in this "reasonable conception")
would act to let *all* influences, or the largest and most random
possible assortment of influences, work equally on the child, to
open up all possibilities to him, without itself influencing him
toward one or another of these. In that way, it can be hoped that
the chief determining factor in the grown child's choice of a
vocation and life-style will be his own governing values, talents,
and propensities. The second reply to Burger is to ask, on the
supposition that neutrality *is* impossible, why the Court should
automatically favor the interests of the parents when they
conflict with those of their children.

Despite these animadversions on Mr. Chief Justice Burger's
reasoning, I do not wish to contend that the decision in *Yoder*
was mistaken. The difference between a mere eight years of
elementary education and a mere ten years of mostly elementary education seems so trivial in the technologically complex
modern world, that it is hard to maintain that a child who has
only the former is barred from many possible careers while the
child who has only the latter is not. It is plausible therefore to
argue that what is gained for the educable fourteen year old
Amish child by guaranteeing him another two years of school is
more than counterbalanced by the corrosive effect on the
religious bonds of the Amish community. From the philosophi-

cal standpoint, however, even the sixteen year old educable youth whose parents legally withdraw him from school has suffered an invasion of his rights-in-trust.

I am more sympathetic to the separate concurring opinion in the *Yoder* case, written by Mr. Justice White and endorsed by Justices Brennan and Stuart, than to the official majority opinion written by the Chief Justice, and I should like to underline its emphasis. These justices join the majority only because the difference between eight and ten years is minor in terms of the children's interests but possibly crucial for the very survival of the Amish sect. (Secular influences on the children had been minimal during the first eight years since they attended a "nearby rural schoolhouse," with an overwhelming proportion of students of the Amish faith, none of whom played rock records, watched television, or the like.) Nevertheless, even though the facts of this case are not favorable for the State's position, the case is still a close one, and had the facts been somewhat different, these justices would have upheld the C-rights represented by the state whatever the cost to the Amish sect. "This would be a very different case for me," Mr. Justice White wrote, "if respondents' claim were that their religion forbade their children from attending any school at any time and from complying in any way with the educational standards set by the State."[18] In that hypothetical case, as in various intermediate ones where we can imagine that the respondents withdrew their children after two or four years of schooling, no amount of harm to the parents' interest in the religious upbringing of their children could overturn the childrens' rights-in-trust to an open future.

White gives eloquent answer to Burger's claim that compulsory education of Amish youth in large modern high schools is in effect a kind of indoctrination in secular values. Education can be compulsory, he argues, only because, or only when, it is neutral:

. . . the State is not concerned with the maintenance of an educational system as an end in itself; it is rather attempting to nurture and develop the human potential of its children, whether Amish or non-Amish: to expand their knowledge, broaden their sensibilities, kindle their imagination, foster a spirit of free inquiry, and increase their human understanding and tolerance. It is possible that most Amish children will wish to continue living the rural life of their parents, in which case their training at home will adequately equip them for their future role. Others, however, may wish to become nuclear physicists, ballet dancers, computer programmers, or historians, and for these occupations, formal training will be necessary . . . A State has a legitimate interest not only in seeking to develop the latent talents of its children but also in seeking to prepare them for the life style that they may later choose, or at least to provide them with an option other than the life they have led in the past.[19]

The corrective emphasis of the White concurring opinion then is on the danger of using *Yoder* uncritically as a precedent for finding against Children's *C*-rights when they are clearly in conflict with the supervisory rights of their parents. A quite different case, involving a child custody decision, will illustrate the equal and opposite danger, of overruling parental rights for the suppositious future interests of a child interpreted in a flagrantly "non-neutral" manner. This horror story is an example of a court taking far too seriously its right under *parens patriae* by enforcing on a child its own special and partisan conception of the way of life that is truly best for it. I refer to the case of six year old Mark Painter of Ames, Iowa.[20] An automobile accident took the lives of his mother and sister. His father then left him temporarily with his prosperous maternal grandparents on a large Iowa farm, and went himself to a suburb of San Francisco to begin a new career. A year later, having remarried, he went back to Iowa to pick up his son and return with him to his new home. The grandparents refused to give up the boy, however, and the case went to court. A lower court decision returning the boy to the custody of his natural father was eventually overturned by a state Supreme Court decision favoring the grandparents. The U. S. Supreme Court refused to review that decision, and thus a father was legally deprived of the custody of his own son.

The opinion of the Iowa Supreme Court is a melancholy

document. Mr. Painter's new home, it concluded, would not satisfy the child's right to well-rounded growth into full maturity:

> Our conclusion as to the type of home Mr. Painter would offer is based upon his Bohemian approach to finances and life in general . . . He is either an agnostic or an atheist and has no concern for formal religious training . . . He has read a lot of Zen Buddhism . . . [his new wife] Mrs. Painter is Roman Catholic . . . He is a political liberal and got into difficulty in a job at the University of Washington for his support of the activities of the American Civil Liberties Union . . . We believe the Painter household would be unstable, unconventional, arty, Bohemian, and probably intellectually stimulating.[21]

The home of Mark's Protestant Sunday school-teaching grandparents, on the other hand, was spacious and commodious, and sure to provide him "with a stable, dependable, conventional, middle-class, Middle West background."[22]

If a parent, as such, has a legally recognized right to the custody of his own child (and surely this must be the case) then we should expect courts to infringe that right only with the greatest reluctance and only for the most compelling reasons. One such reason would be conflict with an even more important right of the child himself. Parents who beat, torture, or mutilate their children, or who willfully refuse to permit them to be educated, can expect the state as *parens patriae* to intervene and assign the children to the custody of court-appointed trustees. Given satisfaction of reasonable moral standards of care and education, however, no court has the right to impose its own conception of the good life on a child over its natural parents' objections. The state can't properly select the influences that are best for a child; it can only insist that all public influences be kept open, that all children through accredited schools become acquainted with a great variety of facts and diversified accounts and evaluations of the myriad human arrangements in the world and in history. This is what it means for parents to "take their chances" with external influences. But apart from that, every parent is free to provide any kind of religious upbringing he chooses, or none at all; to send his child to public or accredited private schools, sectarian or non-sectarian; to attempt to transmit his own ideals, moral and political, whatever they may be, to his child; in short, to create whatever environment of influence he can for his child, subject to the state's important but minimal standards of humanity, health, and education. For a child to be exposed mainly and directly to unconventional values is still, after all, a long way from "martyrdom".

As to the content of the values of any particular parents, there the liberal state is and must be *neutral*. Indeed, the state must be as neutral between atheism and theism in the private households of citizens as it is between protestantism and Catholicism. The wretched decision in the Painter case, therefore, can be construed in part as a violation of a citizen's right to the free "non-exercise" of religion, for reasons that include no weighable interest or right of his child. It sounds innocuous enough to say that a child's welfare has priority even over a parent's right of custody; but this is no more than an empty platitude when the child's welfare is not objectively and unarguably at issue.

3

The coherence of the above account of the child's right to an open future is threatened by a number of philosophical riddles. The existence of such a right, as we have seen, sets limits to the ways in which parents may raise their own children, and even imposes duties on the state, in its role as *parens patriae,* to enforce those limits. The full statement of the grounds for these protective duties will invoke the interrelated ideals of autonomy(or self-determination) and self-fulfillment, and these concepts are notoriously likely to generate philosophical confusion. Moreover, both friends and enemies of the child's right to an open future are likely to use the obscure and emotionally charged epithet "paternalism," the one side accusingly, the other apologetically, a practice that can only detract further from conceptual clarity.

The pejorative term "paternalism" is commonly applied to

acts of authorities or rule-makers which are thought to treat adults as if they were children, for example orders prohibiting some sort of predominately self-regarding behavior, when they are issued for the subject's "own good" quite apart from his own considered preferences in the matter, or actions that deliberately impose some pattern on the subject's life without his consent or even against his wishes, but once more, like bitter medicine, "for his own good." How is it possible then for parents to be "paternalistic" in a similarly derogatory sense, toward their own children? The term can be applied pejoratively in this way only because there is a series of stages in a child's growth between total helplessness and incapacity at the beginning and near self-sufficiency at the threshhold of adulthood. Blameable "paternalism" must consist in treating the child at a given stage as if he were at some earlier, less developed, stage. But "paternalism" in the upbringing of children, in some sense, is inevitable and therefore wholly proper, whether imposed by the state in the child's interest or by the parents themselves, and that is because there will be some respects at least in which even an older child cannot know his own interest, some respects in which he must be protected from his own immature and uninformed judgment. Moreoever, since children are not born with a precisely determined character structure, they must be socialized by measures of discipline if they are to become fit members of the adult community, and this must be done even if it is against the wishes of the pre-socialized children themselves. As Kenneth Henley puts its: "We cannot always await their consent to the sometimes painful steps of growing up."[23]

It is characteristic of parents, of course, not only to protect children from their own folly, but also to protect them from external dangers generally, including the dangers posed by other persons. This is a task in which the state joins as a cooperative partner defining crimes against children and enforcing criminal laws by its police powers and the threat of punishment. Since the state shares this safeguarding function with willing parents, its protective policies are "paternalistic" in an innocent, non-pejorative sense, namely that of "protective in a manner characteristic of parents." In the cases we have considered in this essay, however, the state exercises its tutelary powers for the sake of children *against their own parents*. These state policies are "paternalistic" in the general sense of "characteristically parental," but the question of their justification in all but extreme cases is genuinely controversial. Insofar as the word "paternalism" has acquired a fixed derogatory overtone it can be applied to these difficult cases only at the risk of equivocation between pejorative and neutral senses and consequent question-begging against the defender of state intervention.

Typically the state must shoulder a greater burden of justification for its interferences with parents for the sake of their children than that which is borne by parents in justification of *their* interferences with children for the children's own sake. That is because state action by its very nature tends to be cumbersome, and heavy-handed, and because it constitutes a threat to such well-established parental rights as the right to supervise the upbringing of one's own children and the right to the free exercise of one's own religion (which unavoidably influences the developing attitudes and convictions of the children). But although the burden on the state is characteristically heavier than that shouldered by parents for their own interventions, it is essentially of the same general kind, requiring the same sorts of reasons. In either case, the justification appeals (to speak roughly at first) to the eventual *autonomy* and to *the good* of the child.

The word "autonomy," which plays such an essential role in the discussion of children's rights, has at least two relevant senses. It can refer either to the *capacity* to govern oneself, which of course is a matter of degree, or (on the analogy to a political state) to the *sovereign authority* to govern oneself, which is absolute within one's own moral boundaries (one's "territory," "realm," "sphere," or "business"). Note that there are two parallel senses of the term "independent," the first of which refers to self-sufficiency, the *de facto* capacity to support oneself, direct one's own life, and be finally responsible for one's own decisions, and the second of which, applied mainly to political states, refers to *de jure* sovereignty and the right of self-determination. In a nutshell, one sense of "autonomy" (and also of "independence") refers to the capacity and the other to the right of self-determination. When the state justifies its interference with parental liberty by reference to the eventual autonomy of the protected child, it argues that the mature adult that the child will become, like all free citizens, has a *right of self-determination,* and that that right is violated in advance if certain crucial and irrevocable decisions determining the course of his life are made by anyone else before he has the *capacity of self-determination* himself.

The child's own good is not necessarily promoted by the policy of protecting his budding right of self-determination. There is no unanimity among philosophers, of course, about that in which a human being's own good consists, but a majority view that seems to me highly plausible would identify a person's good ultimately with his *self-fulfillment*—a notion that is not identical with that of autonomy or the right of self-determination. Self-fulfillment is variously interpreted, but it surely involves as necessary elements the development of one's chief aptitudes into genuine talents in a life that gives them scope, an unfolding of all basic tendencies and inclinations, both those that are common to the species and those that are peculiar to the individual, and an active realization of the universal human propensities to plan, design and make order.[24] Self-fulfillment, so construed, is not the same as achievement and not to be confused with pleasure or contentment, though achievement is often highly fulfilling, and fulfillment is usually highly gratifying.

One standard way of deriving the right of self-determination is to base it solidly on the good of self-fulfillment. A given normal adult is much more likely to know his own interests, talents, and natural dispositions (the stuff of which his good is composed) than is any other party, and much more capable therefore of directing his own affairs to the end of his own good than is a government official, or a parent at an earlier stage who might preempt his choices for him. The individual's advantages in this regard are so great that for all practical purposes we can hold that recognition and enforcement of the right of self-determination (autonomy) is a causally necessary condition for the achievement of self-fulfillment (the individual's own good). This is the view of John Stuart Mill who argued in *On Liberty* that the attempt even of a genuinely benevolent state to impose upon an adult an external conception of his own good is almost certain to be self-defeating, and that an adult's own good is "best provided for by allowing him to take his own means of pursuing it."[25] Promotion of human well-being and the prevention of harms are primary in Mill's system, so that even so basic a right as that of self-determination must be derived from its conducibility to them. In those rare cases where we can know that free exercise of a person's autonomy will be against his own interests, as for example when he freely negotiates his own slavery in exchange for some other good, there we are justified in interfering with his liberty in order to protect him from harm.

The second standard interpretation of the right of self-determination holds that it is entirely *underivative,* as morally basic as the good of self-fulfillment itself. There is no necessity, on this view, that free exercise of a person's autonomy will promote his own good, but even where self-determination is likely, on objective evidence, to lead to the person's own harm, others do not have a right to intervene coercively "for his own good." By and large, a person will be better able to achieve his own good by making his own decisions, but even where the opposite is true, others may not intervene, for autonomy is even more important a thing than personal well-being. The life that a person threatens by his own rashness is after all *his* life; it *belongs* to him and to no one else. For that reason alone, he must be the one to decide—for better or worse—what is to be done with it in that private realm where the interests of others are not directly involved.[26]

A compromising way of regarding the adult's right of autonomy is to think of it as neither derivative from nor more basic than its possessor's own good (self-fulfillment), but rather as coordinate with it. In the more plausible versions of this third view,[27] a person's own good, in the vast majority of cases will be most reliably furthered if he is allowed to make his own choices in self-regarding matters, but where that coincidence of values does not hold, one must simply do one's best to balance autonomy against personal well-being, and decide between them intuitively, since neither has automatic priority over the other. In any case, the two distinct ideals of sovereign autonomy (self-determination) and personal well-being (self-fulfillment) are both likely to enter, indeed to dominate, the discussion of the grounding of the child's right to an open future. That right (or class of rights) must be held in trust *either* out of respect for the sovereign independence of the emerging adult (and derivatively in large part for his own good) or for the sake of the life-long well-being of the person who is still a child (a well-being from which the need of self-government "by and large" can be derived), or from both. In such ways the good (self-fulfillment) and the right (self-determination) of the child enter the justificatory discussion. And both can breed paradox from the start, unless handled with care.

The paradoxes I have in mind both have the form, *prima facie,* of vicious circles. Consider first the self-determination circle. If we have any coherent conception of the fully self-determined adult, he is a person who has determined both his own life-circumstances and his own character. The former consists of his career-type (doctor, lawyer, merchant, chief), his life-style (swinger, hermit, jogger, scholar), and his religious affiliation and attitude (piety, hypocrisy, indifference, total absorption), among other things. The latter is that set of habitual traits that we create by our own actions and cultivated feelings in given types of circumstances, our characteristic habits of response to life's basic kinds of situations. Aristotle analyzed these as deeply rooted *dispositions* to act or feel in certain ways in certain kinds of circumstances, and since his time it has become a philosophical truism that we are, in large part, the products of our own making, since each time we act or feel in a given way in a given kind of circumstance, we strengthen the disposition to act or feel in that (brave or cowardly, kind or cruel, warm or cold) way in similar circumstances in the future. Now, whatever policy is adopted by a child's parents, and whatever laws are passed and enforced by the state, the child's options in respect to life circumstances and character will be substantially narrowed well before he is an adult. He will have to be socialized and educated, and these processes will inevitably influence the development of his own values, tastes, and standards, which will in turn determine in part how he acts, feels, and chooses. That in turn will reenforce his tendencies to act, feel, and choose in similar ways in the future, until his character is set. If the parents and the state try to evade the responsibility for character and career formation by an early policy of drift, that will have consequences on the child too, for which they shall have to answer. And in any case, simply by living their own lives as they choose, the parents will be forming an environment around the child that will tend to shape his budding loyalties and habits, and they will be providing in their own selves ready models for emulation.[28] This inevitable narrowing of options can yet be done without violation of the child's *C-right* of self-determination provided it is somehow in accordance with the child's actual or presumptive, explicit or tacit *consent*. But we can hardly ask the child's actual explicit consent to our formative decisions because at the point when these processes start—where the "twig begins to be bent"—he is not developed enough to give his consent. But neither has he values and preferences of his own for the parents to consult and treat as clues to what his disposition to give or withhold consent would be. At the early stage the parents cannot even ask in any helpful way what the child *will* be like, apart from the parental policies under consideration, when he *does* have relevant preferences, values, and the capacity to consent. That outcome will depend on the character the child will have then, which in part depends, in turn, on how his parents raise him now. They are now shaping the him who is to decide later and whose presumptive later decision cannot be divined. As Henley puts it: "Whether a certain sort of life would please a child often depends upon how he has been socialized, and so we cannot decide to socialize him for that life by asking whether that kind of life would please him."[29]

The paradox of self-determination can be put even more forcefully as an infinite regress. If the grown-up offspring is to determine his own life, and be at least in large part the product of his own "self-determination," he must already have a self fully formed and capable of doing the determining. But he cannot very well have determined *that* self on his own, because he would have to have been already a formed self to do that, and so on, *ad infinitum*. The vicious circle is avoided only by positing an infinite series of prior selves, each the product of an earlier self.[30]

The paradoxes of self-fulfillment present much the same sort of appearance as the paradoxes of self-determination and can be expressed in quite parallel language. These arise, however, not when we ask what a child will come to prefer, choose, or consent to later in the exercise of his matured autonomy, but rather, simply, what would be good for him, his presumptive choice notwithstanding. To answer this question we must seek to learn his governing propensities, his skills and aptitudes, his highest "potential". We must gauge how his nature is "wound up" and in what direction he is faced, in order to determine what would fulfill his most basic tendencies. We stumble into the vicious circle when we note that if a person's own good is to be understood as self-fulfillment, we cannot fully know the small child's long term future good until its "nature" is fully formed, but equally we cannot determine how best to shape its nature until we know what will be for its own good. We cannot just leave the child's entire future open for him to decide later according to his settled adult values, because he must begin to acquire those values now in childhood, and he will in fact acquire his governing dispositions now, whatever we do. And in closing his future options in some ways now by our educating, our socializing, our choice of influential environments, we cannot be guided entirely by what accords with the child's own future character, because that character will in large part be a product of the self we are molding now. In a nutshell: the parents help create some of the interests whose fulfillment will constitute the child's own good. They cannot aim at an independent conception of the child's own good in deciding how to do this, because to some extent, the child's own good (self-fulfillment) depends on which interests the parents decide to create. The circle is thus closed.

4

Closed, but not closed tight. The plausible-sounding propositions that seem to lock us into paradox in reality are only approximate generalizations, merely partial truths whose soft spots make viable escape-hatches. The "paradoxes" stem from a failure to appreciate how various judgments used in their formulation are only partly true, and how certain central distinctions are matters of degree. It is an overstatement, for example, that there is any early stage at which a child's character is *wholly* unformed and his talents and temperament *entirely* plastic, without latent bias or limit, and another that there can be *no* "self-determination" unless the self that does the determining is already *fully* formed. Moreover, it is a distortion to represent the distinction between child and adult in the rigid manner presupposed by the "paradoxes".

There is no sharp line between the two stages of human life; they are really only useful abstractions from a continuous process of development every phase of which differs only in degree from that preceding it. Many or most of a child's C-rights-in-trust have already become A-rights by the time he is ten or twelve. Any "mere child" beyond the stage of infancy is only a child in some respects, and already an adult in others. Such dividing lines as the eighteenth or twenty first birthday are simply approximations (plausible guesses) for the point where *all* the natural rights-in-trust have become actual A-rights. In the continuous development of the relative-adult out of the relative-child there is no point before which the child himself has no part in his own shaping, and after which he is the sole responsible maker of his own character and life plan. The extent of the child's role in his own shaping is again a process of constant and continuous growth already begun at birth, as indeed is the "size" of his self, that is the degree to which it is already formed and fixed.

Right from the beginning the newborn infant has a kind of rudimentary character consisting of temperamental proclivities and a genetically fixed potential for the acquisition of various talents and skills. The standard sort of loving upbringing and a human social environment in the earliest years will be like water added to dehydrated food, filling it out and actualizing its stored-in tendencies. Then the child's earliest models for imitation will make an ineluctable mark on him. He will learn one language rather than another, for instance, and learn it with a particular accent and inflection. His own adult linguistic style will be in the making virtually from the beginning. For the first year or two he will have no settled dispositions of action and feeling of the kind Aristotle called virtues and vices (excellences and defects of character), but as Aristotle said, he is born with the capacity to acquire such dispositions, and the process is underway very early as his basic habits of response are formed and reenforced.

At a time so early that the questions of how to socialize and educate the child have not even arisen yet, the twig will be bent in a certain definite direction. From then on, the parents in promoting the child's eventual autonomy and well-being will have to respect that initial bias from heredity and early environment. Thus from the beginning the child must—inevitably will—have some "input" in its own shaping, the extent of which will grow continuously even as the child's character itself does. I think that we can avoid, or at least weaken, the paradoxes if we remember that the child can contribute towards the making of his own self and circumstances in ever-increasing degree. Always the self that contributes to the making of the new self is itself the product both of outside influences and an earlier self that was not quite as fully formed. That earlier self, in turn, was the product both of outside influences and a still earlier self that was still less fully formed and fixed, and so on, all the way back to infancy. At every subsequent stage the immature child plays an ever-greater role in the creation of his own life, until at the arbitrarily fixed point of full maturity or adulthood, he is at last fully and properly in charge of himself, sovereign within his terrain, his more or less finished character the product of a complicated interaction of external influences and ever-increasing contributions from his own earlier self. At least that is how growth proceeds when parents and other authorities raise a child with maximal regard for the autonomy of the adult he will one day be. That is the most sense that we can make of the ideal of the "self-made person," but it is an intelligible idea, I think, with no paradox in it.

Similarly, the parents who raise their child in such a way as to promote his self-fulfillment most effectively will at every stage try to strengthen the basic tendencies of the child as manifested at that stage. They will give him opportunities to develop his strongest talents, for instance, after having enjoyed opportunities to discover by various experiments just what those talents are. And they will steer the child toward the type of career that requires the kind of temperament the child already has rather than a temperament that is alien to him by his very nature. There can be no self-fulfillment for a child prone to sedentary activity by his native body type and endowed with fine motor control over his sensitive fingers if he is inescapably led into a job calling for a large muscled, energetic person with high gross motor control but no patience for small painstaking tasks, or vice-versa. The child will even have very basic tendencies toward various kinds of attitudes from an early stage, at least insofar as they grow naturally out of his inherited temperamental propensities. He may be the naturally gregarious, outgoing sort, or the kind of person who will naturally come to treasure his privacy and to keep his own counsels; he may appreciate order and structure more or less than spontaneity and freedom; he may be inclined, *ceteris paribus,* to respect or to challenge authority. Such attitudes grow from basic dispositions of temperament and are the germ in turn of fundamental convictions and styles of life that the child will still be working out and trying to understand and justify when he is an adult. The discerning parent will see all of these things ever more clearly as the child grows older, and insofar as he steers the child at all, it will be in the child's own preferred directions. At the very least he will not try to turn him upstream and make him struggle against his own deepest currents. Then if the child's future is left open as much as possible for his own finished self to determine, the fortunate adult that emerges will already have achieved, without paradox, a certain amount of self-fulfillment, a consequence in large part of his own already autonomous choices in promotion of his own natural preferences.

NOTES

1. John Locke preferred the more uniform usage according to which all human rights are *A-C* rights. In his usage, from which I here depart, we are all *born* with certain rights which we possess throughout our lives, from infancy through senectitude. Some of these rights, however, children cannot exercise, though they continue to possess them until they acquire the requisite capability. "Thus we are born free as we are born rational; not that we have actually the exercise of either; age that brings one, brings with it the other too." (*Second Treatise of Government,* Section 61). It would be a mistake to elevate this terminological difference into a philosophical quarrel. Obviously Locke can say everything in his terminology that I can in mine and *vice versa*. He was concerned to emphasize the similarity in the moral status of children and adults, whereas this paper focuses on the differences. I have no objection if people talk about *A*-rights as if they are actually possessed by small infants (e.g. the right to vote as one pleases) provided it is clearly understood that they are "possessed" in the sense that they are held in trust for the autonomous adults the children will (probably) become one day, and they are subject to violation now in a way that is *sui generis*.
2. *Pace* William O. Douglas in his dissenting opinion in *Wisconsin v. Yoder,* 406 U. S. 205 (1972).

3. For an illuminating analysis of these three sided conflicts, see Stuart J. Baskin, "State Intrusion into Family Affairs: Justifications and Limitations," 26 *Stanford Law Review* 1383 (1974).

4. Note on "Civil Restraint, Mental Illness, and the Right to Treatment," 77 *Yale Law Journal* 87 (1967).

5. *Prince v. Massachusetts,* 321 U. S. 158 (1944).

6. See Justice Frank Murphy's dissenting opinion in *Prince,* and also Donald Giannella, "Religious Liberty, Nonestablishment, and Doctrinal Development" Part I, "The Religious Liberty Guarantee," *Harvard Law Review,* Vol. 81 (1967), p. 1395.

7. *Prince v. Massachusetts,* op. cit. at 168, 170.

8. " 'If I allow blood to be given into her and if she lived, she wouldn't be considered my wife,' the police said Mr. Jackson had told the doctors."—*New York Times,* November 13, 1968.

9. *State v. Garber,* 197 Kan. 567 (1966).

10. J. S. Mill, *On Liberty,* Chap. 3, paragraph 2, 3.

11. *Wisconsin v. Yoder, et al.* 406 U. S. 205 (1972).

12. As made applicable to the states by the Fourteenth Amendment.

13. *Wisconsin v. Yoder, op. cit.,* pp. 209, 216.

14. Ibid., p. 213.

15. Ibid., p. 230.

16. Loc. cit.

17. Consider also the commonly heard argument that state policies that keep religious observances and practices out of the public schools have the effect of "establishing" one religion in preference to all the others, namely the "religion of secular humanism." The conclusion then presented is not that the state should try nevertheless to be as neutral as it can, but rather that since neutrality is absolutely impossible whichever policy is adopted, the state might as well permit Christian observances.

18. Ibid., p. 236.

19. Ibid., pp. 237–38.

20. See the book about the case by his father: Hal Painter, *Mark, I Love You* (New York: Simon & Schuster, 1968). The citations in notes 19 and 20 below are from Justice William C. Stuart's decision in the Iowa Supreme Court, reprinted as an Appendix in the paperback edition of *Mark, I Love You* (New York: Ballantine Books, 1969).

21. Ibid., p. 226f.

22. Ibid., p. 225.

23. Kenneth Henley, "The Authority to Educate" in *Having Children: Philosophical and Legal Reflections on Parenthood,* ed. by Onora O'Neill and William Ruddick (New York: Oxford University Press, 1978), p. 255. Henley's excellent article is strongly recommended.

24. For a further analysis of self-fulfillment, see my "Absurd Self-fulfillment: An Essay on the Merciful Perversity of the Gods," in *Time and Cause, Essays Presented to Richard Taylor,* edited by Peter van Inwagen (Dortrecht, The Netherlands: Reidel, 1979).

25. John Stuart Mill, *On Liberty,* Chapter V, paragraph 11.

26. This second interpretation of autonomy rights is defended in my essay "Legal Paternalism," *Canadian Journal of Philosophy,* Vol. 1 (1971), pp. 105–24, and also in my "Freedom and Behavioral Control" in *The Encyclopedia of Bioethics,* edited by Warren T. Reich (New York: The Free Press, 1978).

27. See for example Jonathan Glover, *Causing Death and Saving Lives* (New York: Penguin Books, 1977), pp. 74–85.

28. Henley (see note 23 above) makes this point especially well in his discussion of the parents' religious rights: "In the early years of the child's socialization, he will be surrounded by the religious life of his parents; since the parents have a right to live such religious lives, and on the assumption that children will normally be raised by their parents, parental influence on the child's religious life is both legitimate and unavoidable. But at such an early stage it can hardly be said that coercion is involved; the child simply lives in the midst of a religious way of life and comes to share in it. But surely the assertion that the child is born with religious liberty must entail that parents are under at least moral constraints not to *force* their religious beliefs upon the child once he is capable of forming his own views . . ." Op. cit. pp. 260–61.

29. Henley, Ibid., p. 256.

30. Cf. John Wisdom's not altogether playful argument that moral responsibility presupposes that we have *always* existed, in his *Problems of Mind and Matter* (Cambridge: Cambridge University Press, 1934), pp. 110–134.

Sharon Bishop

Children, Autonomy and the Right to Self-Determination

Bishop claims that even if children are not fully autono-
mous persons, the recognition that children have, or at least
will have, a right to self-determination puts significant
constraints on how we can now treat them. In particular,
recognition of this right dictates that children should be
reared so that they will not be forced into rigid sexual
roles.

Compare Bishop's and Feinberg's discussions of the
right of self-determination. If one grants that children
should be reared in the style Bishop describes, should the
state force parents to rear their children in just that style?

According to a liberal commonplace, children do not have a right to choose for themselves because they lack the knowledge and rational capacities to exercise choice wisely. It is said, for example, that children cannot postpone gratification long enough to assess the risks of tooth-decay, diabetes or obesity to have the prerogative to eat candy whenever they wish. Older children lack imagination and are too much influenced by peer pressures and rebellious desires to make rational choices about the use of alcohol. Nor can children appreciate the risks of

This essay is an adaptation of "Self-Determination and Autonomy" by the same author, published under the name Sharon Bishop Hill, in Richard Wasserstrom, ed., *Today's Moral Problems* (New York: Macmillan, 1975, 1979). Permission to reprint granted by Richard Wasserstrom.

illness from failure to wear sweaters and keep clean. And certainly they are not in a position to make important choices about their own training and future vocation; they know too little about the world and their own interests. It would be a disservice to them to regard them as having the right to make choices which might jeopardize their later lives; thus they should not be said to have a right to self-determination at all. Parents and educators are entitled to restrict and channel children's activities in the interests of the children, and the children have no right to complain that their choices are restricted.

It is important to notice that there is a large leap from particular examples of choice like the use of alcohol to the more general claim that children lack altogether the right to self-determination. The resulting picture of parent/educator-child relations is that someone in the know has the authority to make choices for the child, and though they are to be guided by what is good for the child in the long run, they need not restrict their attitudes and activities directly because of the child's choices. Here, I do not press the gap between some rather convincing examples in which it seems permissible to restrict children's choices and the claim that children do not have a right to self-determination. I shall accept as a starting point that they do not, but that as adults they will have the right to forge their own life styles and to choose vocations. Given this fact, I argue that certain kinds of educational policies and parental attitudes interfere with the rights the child will have as an adult.

In what follows, I discuss a dispute between two parents over their daughter's education. The resulting discussion is largely about sex roles, but the principles involved could be applied to other aspects of child rearing as well. First, I describe the dispute; then I sketch a way of understanding the right to self-determination as it pertains to adults, particularly with regard to the traditional domestic role for women. Finally, I argue that even on the supposition that children do not have this right, the fact that they will as adults has an important bearing on how we may treat our children now.

I. THE DISPUTE

Over the years, John and Harriet have had long arguments about women's liberation. Both have come a long way. When Harriet first decided that she could not find self-fulfillment without a paying job, John felt threatened and protested that it would not be proper. But now he is reconciled and even insists that women get equal pay for equal work. He supports the Equal Rights Amendment and urges his company to give talented and well-trained women an equal chance at job opportunities. He has given up as muddled his old belief that women are naturally inferior to men in intelligence, objectivity, emotional stability and the like. He acknowledges that women have often been treated in degrading ways, and like many liberals, he has tried hard to purge his vocabulary of such words as "chick," "broad," and "piece." He even tries, not always successfully, to avoid references like "the girls in the office." Women, he says, have as much right to happiness as men, and so he is ready to oppose any social scheme which makes them, relative to men, systematically discontent or unhappy. But this is as far as he will go.

Harriet says that this is not far enough. And the dispute came to a head when she protested to the school principal and finally to the school board about their daughter's education. Harriet was distressed that girls were encouraged in numerous ways to accept the traditional feminine role. For example, the practice at most school dances was for girls to wait to be asked by boys. The school had well-developed and financed athletic programs for boys, but few for girls, and very little staff to help girls to develop their skills. The counselors were comparatively uninterested in advising girls about their futures. When they did, they assumed that, for the most part, appropriate careers for girls were as secretaries, decorators, teachers, nurses or medical assistants. Students' programs were then tailored for these vocations. These, in turn, were viewed as stop-gap or carry-over measures to enable girls to get through any periods in which they were not married or supported by someone. If they did marry, it was assumed that there would be children and a home to which the woman should devote herself.

Harriet gradually came to see that her objections to these practices arose as she faced her own feelings of resentment and betrayal at the kinds of opportunities and counseling she had early in life. Though she acknowledged the occasion of her objections, she also became convinced that her complaints were well founded. She was less clear how to support them, but her way of life seemed unnecessarily restrictive and she believed that she had interests and capacities which should have been developed but were not. She was irked, too, that she had never had a genuine opportunity to choose the way of life in which she and other women were so deeply involved. Whatever she might have chosen and whether or not she liked having a family and the feminine virtues, she felt that she had never really had any choice. She realized that part of the problem was that she herself had not regarded these as proper objects of her own choice. The failure she thought was the result of a complicated and overlapping set of teachings which had it that women were almost inevitably unfulfilled without having children, that normally they were better at raising children than men and men better suited for earning a living. Consequently, as the story went, the current division of labor is really most efficient, better for almost everyone and thus best. Both men and women were said to have duties associated with these roles. She now resents these teachings, justifiably she believes. She became especially anxious as she saw her daughter falling into the patterns of behavior and belief to which she now objects and so she complained to the school board.

John found Harriet less than convincing on these matters. It is important to oppose sex roles, he argued, if the roles function in a way which humiliates or degrades women or deprives them of political or economic rights. If these abuses could be avoided, he thinks the current standard division of labor and roles would not only be legitimate but quite a good way to arrange things. Someone, after all, needs to care for children and most women seem quite content. These arrangements seem natural to him. He suspects that women are naturally more sensitive and so make better parents for the very young; moreover, those he knows who have either not married or not had children seem to be weak and stunted characters or else hostile and aggressive. These observations suggest to him that most people, including women, are well off under something like the current division of labor and role. He acknowledges some, at least, of the difficulties about his belief that women are naturally suited for the domestic role. He does not, for example, rely on personality inventories of women versus men, because the traits they test for are bound to be influenced by the culture in which people grow up including, of course, some of the practices Harriet finds obnoxious. He does not appeal to the obvious physical differences between men and women, and he regards as irrelevant, at least in the modern world, appeals to differences in brute strength. Still he believes that some of the relevant differences are natural. He supports his suspicion by appeals to anthropological evidence about widely divergent groups in which women have almost invariably had the domestic role and quite often the traits which suit them for raising children and managing households. Were this not natural, he thinks it would not be so frequent. He has been known to remark that estrogen is associated with passive as opposed to aggressive personality traits, reminding Harriet that women maintain a higher level of this hormone than men. He suspects that the thwarted and hostile women he finds among the unmarried and childless result from frustration of the natural capacities of women for close emotional relations. There are, he admits, extraordinarily ambitious women who would be frustrated in following the traditional pattern; but a society which grants full political and economic rights to all adults can accommodate these exceptional people. Consequently, he resists the idea that there is something wrong with encouraging in young girls the feminine traits he so likes. He wants his daughter to be ladylike in figure and personality and hopes, for her sake, that she will never choose a career at the expense of having a family. He communicates this to her in innumerable, sometimes subtle, sometimes direct ways.

It is at this point that Harriet becomes most exasperated and even despairing. By all the conventional criteria, John seems liberal enough. He believes in equal pay for equal work and equal opportunities for those of equal achievement, motivation and talent. He acknowledges that women have been deprived of income, opportunities, power and their associated satisfactions by unfair social practices of various sorts. What he envisages is a world in which these injustices are eradicated but one in which women remain sensitive, understanding and charming, and in which most take up a domestic life while most men take up a paying vocation. Since he thinks it only efficient to prepare people for these likely different but quite natural futures, he thinks sound educational policy calls for certain subtle differences in the training of males and females. Harriet, on the other hand, believes that her resentment is justified, that she has been wronged in some way and would continue to be wronged if the world were magically transformed to match John's dreams. She becomes most desperate when she thinks of her daughter who is being similarly wronged.

The perplexed, like John, may say, "But where is the difficulty?" They understand complaints about violations of political and economic rights, like the right to vote, hold office and receive equal pay for equal work. They admit that a person would be wronged if gratuitously insulted or deliberately injured. But none of these seem to fit the case of Harriet or her daughter at least in the world John wants. There is no reason to believe they will be insulted, and it is difficult to pick out any political or economic right which we could confidently claim would be violated. Even if we think that Harriet and her daughter have been injured by the workings of the social system in this world, it is not clear that the harm was deliberate. No definite person designed the social system for the purpose of keeping women down, much less for the purpose of harming Harriet; it, like Topsy, just growed. If that is the case, whatever harm they may have suffered seems in important respects like a natural misfortune and not a deliberate wrong. If Harriet's objections to John's views can be defended, it must be on some other pattern of reasoning.

In the following, I shall try to isolate and explain some

principles which could be used to justify Harriet's feelings about her own life and her protests of school practices. Roughly, I shall argue that if adults are viewed as having a right of self-determination, then Harriet and other adult women do nothing inappropriate in eschewing a traditional role nor do they have duties directly associated with such a role. Moreover, if as adults, we are to have a right of self-determination which is meaningful, we ought not to be treated in ways which distort or prevent the development of the capacity for autonomous choice. I do not attempt to justify the claim that adults have a right of self-determination nor the claim that viewing adults as having such a right is better than any of a variety of other ways of regarding them, for example, as potential contributors to the general welfare or to some social or economic ideal. I hope that some of what I say will make respect for a right of self-determination attractive, but here I only set out to explain something about the right.

I try this line of argument, first, because I think it is a promising one to explain the depth and kind of feeling generated in women who begin thinking seriously about their lives and their daughters' prospects. In the end, it may help explain why such pervasive changes are required and why some of them must be changes in attitude. Secondly, it seems possible with this reasoning to avoid some philosophical and empirical difficulties involved in more familiar arguments. For example, a number of people argue for sweeping changes in the treatment of women on the grounds that the resulting system will be more efficient in turning out happy individuals or in using the available pool of natural abilities. One problem here, of course, is to determine what is to count as being happy and so what is to count as evidence that some new system will be more efficient producing it than the present one. Others suggest that there has been a deliberate male conspiracy to keep women in the kitchen and out of the most lucrative and satisfying jobs. There are innumerable problems about what could be meant by "deliberate conspiracy" in this case; there does not seem to have been a conspiratorial meeting attended by anyone much less by most men or by representative men. It does not even seem plausible that some rather large number of men have consciously intended to keep women out of the mainstream of social and economic life at least in recent history. Even if some clear sense can be given to the notion, successful completion of the argument would require complicated empirical inquiries. Although it is true that a deliberate conspiracy to do wrong makes things rather worse, what seems important here is rather the wrong that has been done. If questions about the deliberateness of the wrongs are important at all, they seem to belong rather with attempts to decide to whom the burdens of change may legitimately fall. Finally, the line of reasoning I propose directly undercuts two of the kinds of arguments John suggested against Harriet. In the end, he claimed that his views about women and educational policy could be supported by appeals to efficient ways of arranging for child rearing as well as the natural suitability of current sex roles and the division of labor. Once a right of self-determination is granted, however, it does not matter whether the complex facts John appeals to are true or not, that is, it does not matter whether current sex roles are efficient means of rearing children or whether women, on the average, are better at domestic affairs than men. There are other considerations having to do with self-determination and autonomy which make these alleged facts irrelevant and which do justice to Harriet's response. She does not need to await empirical evidence about what is suitable for women and what makes women and children happy in order to know that something is wrong.

II. THE RIGHT OF SELF-DETERMINATION

To say that persons or states have a right of self-determination is to say minimally that they and only they have the authority to determine certain sorts of things. This does not necessarily mean that they have the power or capacity to determine these things, but rather that they have the title to. Sovereign states, for example, are widely regarded as having rather extensive authority to choose for themselves; they are said to have a right to determine how and who shall govern them, to have rights to determine for themselves what their ideals shall be, how they will allocate funds, what forms of culture they will support and devote themselves to, and the like. Having title to make these choices means that they have a right to expect others not to interfere with the legitimate exercise of their authority and a right to protect themselves from interference. It means, too, that they have a right to expect to carry on the processes of their government without foreign interest groups bribing their officials, and without being flooded with propaganda designed to influence the outcome of elections and the like. All this seems rather uncontroversial. More controversially, a small dependent state might claim that its right of self-determination was violated by threats of loss of essential support just because it failed to adopt the policies its larger, more affluent neighbor wanted. Withdrawal of such support makes it impossible to exercise its right of self-determination, consequently, threatening such withdrawal may be counted as incompatible with respecting the small nation's right. This may seem especially plausible where the support is well established, and where the threat is given for failure, say, to give up some local ritual or some trading policy mildly contrary to the interests of the affluent. Mature adults are often said to have a similar right, for example, to determine for themselves what their vocations shall be, whether to use their money for steaks or tennis balls, their leisure time for concerts or back-packing, and so on. Again, what is meant is that only they have the authority to make such choices, that others ought to refrain from interfering with the legitimate exercise of the title, and that they have the right to protect themselves from interference. Individuals may, if they wish, delegate parts of that authority. They give up some of it when they take a job, put themselves under the tutelage of an instructor or decide to let a friend choose the day's activities. Even in these cases, however, it is only they who may decide not to exercise the right.

Like other rights, this one is limited. Sovereign states do not have a right to make war on their neighbors for profit. Individuals do not have the right to harm or restrain one another simply for the fun of it however much they may want to. The limitations on this right will be roughly what is prohibited by other moral principles. Although these limitations cannot be spelled out here, we could get agreement about a number of cases like injuring another for one's own pleasure. While this does not give us a satisfactory criterion for what morality forbids, it is enough to permit us to focus on the right of self-determination confident that it need not commit us to silly views about the rights of sadists.

Obviously the right is not in fact granted or guaranteed to everyone by the state or culture in which they live. Like the rights to life, liberty and security, it is a natural right, that is, it is thought of as belonging to everyone simply by virtue of their being human and so it is a right which everyone has equally. Society can and should protect us in exercising it in some ways, for example, in choosing a vocation. A state should not, however, enforce all the behavior and attitudes which might be appropriate in someone who believes in the right of self-determination. For example, I suspect that some committed to honoring the right of self-determination would regard themselves as bound not to influence those close to them by exploiting any emotional dependence they might have. If this is a reasonable attitude, it does not seem that it would be wise for a society to protect us from the influence of those on whom we are dependent emotionally. The right of self-determination does not, in general, determine a particular outcome as the just or only acceptable one. It rather outlines a range of considerations which should come into play whenever we are trying to adjust our behavior or attitudes to persons making permissible choices. I call it a right because it is thought of as a title and because the considerations it picks out as relevant mark off an area in which we do not allow conclusions about either the general good or an individual's good to be decisive. The point of the right of self-determination is to enable people to work out their own way of life in response to their own assessments of current conditions and their own interests, capacities and needs, rather than to secure the minimal conditions for living or to maximize a person's expectations for satisfaction. In respecting an individual's right of self-determination, one expresses a certain view about that person which is not a belief that one is acting for the good of that person (at least in some narrow sense of the person's good having to do with his or her welfare or happiness). The rough idea is that persons are, among other things, creatures who have title to select what they will do from among the permitted options. This establishes a presumption that other people should refrain from interfering with our selections whatever their content. They should refrain even if they do not like the particular choice or if they correctly believe that it is not in the chooser's or society's long-term interests.

Applying the right of self-determination to questions about the treatment of women, John and Harriet readily agree on a number of conclusions. First, bending the will of a woman by force is wrong. Conquering nations violate the right of self-determination and so does the man who keeps a woman or harem in servitude however nice he may make their lives. The man who prevents his wife from attending her therapy session or sky-diving lessons by force also violates this right. He does not allow her to do what she has a right to do. He violates the right whether he prevents her because he fears the changes in her personality, or is jealous of her handsome teacher, or because he correctly and sincerely believes the group is harming her or that sky-diving is dangerous. So long as we are talking about a mature woman who is choosing nothing prohibited by morality, it does not matter whether he acts in her own interests or not, he will still have violated her right to determine on her own what she will do.

The husband who achieves similar results by threatening to divorce his wife who has no other means of support may also violate her right to self-determination. This would be like a powerful state that threatens to cut off aid whenever a dependent state acts contrary to its wishes. Some may feel more certain that the threatening husband makes a mistake than that the powerful state violates the right of self-determination of the smaller state. Someone may note that it is quite accepted that relations among nations proceed by threat and counter threat. Things do not go all that well when carried on in this manner, but they go on. When husband, wife, parents or friends resort to such tactics, the relation of friendship or love is effectively off. Someone who is prepared to use such tactics displays special callousness toward the friendship. If they care about maintaining it at all, they will have made a grave blunder. They will also have indicated that they are indifferent to the feelings of the individual they threaten. They show a willingness to harm them, and this may be considered a moral fault for which there is no analogue in the threatening state. These observations can be accepted, I think, without weakening the original claim. We began by saying that states and persons have a right to make certain sorts of choices for themselves without interference by force or threat of force or withdrawal of essential support. This implies in both the case of states and individuals that there is a special wrong in threatening those who are making perfectly permissible policy, namely the violation of this right; that other wrongs and blunders may also be involved is beside the point.

Finally, if a group of men were to conspire together to discourage their wives from taking jobs or joining groups where women work through their problems together, they would violate the women's right of self-determination. These conclusions are not a problem for a liberal like John. He is not tempted to prevent his wife from going anywhere by force. Nor is he tempted to use the threat of loss of support in order to win a battle. He knows that would be to lose the war, and he wants her love and respect, not simply her presence and obedience. He knows, too, that his wife could find other means of support in this world. She is able, and this is not the nineteenth century where his support may well have been essential. Moreover, he has always been inclined to resist the temptation to adjust his relation to his wife in response to or in concert with others. So far the right of self-determination adds nothing startling to the list of legitimate complaints that women might have.

It does, however, add something to the reasons we may have for objecting to a variety of policies. For example, it means that some wrong is involved in the above cases apart from the objectionable techniques used to bring about the desired result. The wrong is not either simply that someone made a conscious attempt to interfere with someone's legitimate choice, but rather that someone's selections were blocked or interfered with. In addition, the right of self-determination takes us a good way toward directly undermining John's views about women. He seemed to think that it was perfectly all right to advise adult women to engage in and stick with traditional domestic life styles on the grounds that it was efficient and natural for women to have them. What appears to be the case now, is that, even if it is efficient and natural, enticing women to take this role for these reasons is likely to interfere with their right of self-determination. It is likely to do this because it encourages the false belief that these reasons are or should be decisive in determining an important lifetime commitment. Instead the right of self-determination establishes a presumption that within the range of permissible selections a person's uncoerced, unforced spontaneous responses to her own interests and circumstances are or should be decisive. It does not matter whether the interference is deliberate or non-deliberate or whether it is well-intended guidance. Once it is known that a practice, policy or teaching interferes, there is good reason to believe it should be revised. That is not to say that there is always sufficient reason, for this presumption like others can be rebutted. If the rebuttal is to work, however, it must give something like an equally important reason, for example, that revising the policy will cause perpetual or irremediable disaster, that it represents the only possible way for anyone to have a decent life, that some other natural right would be violated or that some particular person is not capable of exercising the right for some special reason. While this is not an adequate account of what will rebut the presumption established by the right of self-determination, it does suggest that John's arguments were simply beside the point if he was trying to justify policies which encourage a group of people to take up some lifetime role.

It is even difficult to see why the argument from efficiency should be effective in persuading a particular person like Harriet to exercise her right of self-determination by choosing a traditional domestic role. It seemed to be an argument that society in general will run more efficiently under the current role division, and it is not obvious that it is wise to make important lifetime commitments on the grounds that society in general is likely to run more efficiently. If the argument is rather that Harriet's life would work more smoothly and efficiently if she has a domestic role, then the right of self-determination says that it is up to her whether to take these facts (supposing them to be determinate) as decisive. If she does not want to struggle or if she does not fancy some other definite way of life, she may prefer the so-called efficient way. At the same time, it should be noted that it is a little difficult to determine what is meant by saying that her life would be more efficient, for surely that will depend to some very great extent on what her ends are. If her ends are to develop some talents she has or even to remain a lively and developing person, this may not be an efficient route at all. Nor is the evidence clear that this is the most efficient way for her to raise healthy children; that will depend to some extent on whom she thinks of raising them with, how that is likely to work, and so on.

The argument that the current division of labor and role is in some deep and important sense natural is also beside the point. If these roles are "natural," then persons who are taught that they have a right of self-determination will tend to choose them. There is, then, no need to worry about what it might mean to say that the sex roles are natural, nor to await the empirical evidence about whether they are before we decide whether it is justifiable to encourage them or not. Moreover, taking the perspective of someone committed to the right of self-determination accords nicely with a reasonable suspicion that what is natural for persons is not determinate. Sometimes when people talk about a person being a natural in a role, they have in mind that given the person's background, achievement and current interests, he or she would do well at it and flourish in it. Sometimes, however, they attempt to tie success and satisfaction with a role more closely to a person's genetic heritage. In this sense, a role is natural for persons if because of their genetic endowment, they have certain special capacities which enable them to play the role well, the role does not frustrate some deep need and it provides opportunities for them to express their central interests. In the former sense, it is probably true that the domestic role is a natural for most women now, but it is the latter sense that plays a part in arguments that the current division of labor and role is natural and therefore justifiable. In a modern industrial community, however, there must be at the very least several life styles which could be natural in this sense for most any normal person. That is, there must be several ways of life in which their natural talents could be used and which would provide circumstances for the expression of a range of strong human interests without tending to frustrate deep needs. What the right of self-determination gives people is the title to let their own preferences put together a way of life. If these preferences are properly weighted by themselves and others, then the style they put together is very likely to be one which makes use of their special capacities, does not frustrate and provides opportunities for the expression of central interests.

Unfortunately, it is not clear that the right of self-determination will complete the job Harriet hoped it would; that is, adjudicate in her favor the dispute with John over their daughter's education. John, we may suppose, says that it will not do this because the right of self-determination is a right of adults and not of children. He says that it would be absurd if not impossible and immoral to treat young children as if they had the right to make major choices regarding their futures. Either we would give the children no guidance at all, in which case they may well feel lost and have too little discipline to gain what they will want as adults, or we would be required to use the techniques of rational persuasion that we use with adults. This, too, is likely to have disastrous consequences. At best it leads children to confuse the forms of reasoning with reasonable choosing and tends to make them overrate their capacities and status. Guidance must be given to children for their own sakes, and it will be guidance which inevitably will influence what they want later in life. The question is what kind of guidance to give. John wants to encourage in his daughter the feminine virtues. He wants her to be graceful in figure and movement, he is afraid that too much concentration on competitive athletic games will spoil her development. He thinks the modern dance and figure control programs the school has for girls are all that is important for them. He wants her to remain sweet and coy, affectionate and sensitive, and to develop feminine interests in cooking, sewing and children. Not only does he do what he can to encourage these traits in her, but he wants the school to. He thinks that Harriet and her friends have gone too far in complaining about the fact that only a few exceptionally talented or stubborn women are presented as professionals, and in demanding that the girls be taught the manual arts as well as home economics.

In the following section, I argue that even if the right of self-determination is reserved for adults, John's arguments about his daughter's education do not succeed. Even if the right of self-determination does not itself directly limit the kinds of guidance we may give our children, it does in an indirect way.

III. THE IMPORTANCE OF AUTONOMY

Let us say that parents have the authority to make certain decisions affecting the welfare of their offspring. They have this authority because children lack the know-how and the physical and psychological resources to make it on their own. Typically parents are supposed to exercise this authority in the interests of their children though sometimes they may exercise it for their own peace of mind, especially after nine and on weekends. Even given this picture of legitimate parental authority, there is something wrong with John's educational policies. There are, I think, two objections to teaching girls the traditional feminine virtues and role. First (A), such teaching interferes subtly with their exercise of the right of self-determination as mature women. Second (B), anyone committed to the right of self-determination and its importance has reasons for attaching special significance to the development of the capacity to exercise it autonomously.

(A) To begin with, when we say that mature persons have a right of self-determination, we mean that they are entitled to decide for themselves which career they will attempt, whether or whom to marry, whether to have children, how to spend their leisure time and the like. We all know that deciding for oneself is incompatible with being coerced at the time of choice, but there are subtle influences which may occur earlier and which interfere with the exercise of the right of self-determination.

Let us imagine that a school system has the following practices. First, the system leads girls to take up domestic activities and keeps them from others like competitive games and mechanics. Then, when women reach the age to choose how to spend their time, they have already developed the skills to enjoy cooking and sewing at a high level and discover, not surprisingly, that they like domestic tasks, and not car repair, carpentry or basketball. Surely the possibility that these latter might have been objects of their choice is virtually extinguished. By hypothesis, home economics training for the girls has been successful, that is, many of them really have learned to manage themselves in the kitchen or sewing room so that they are creative and effective, and they have not made similar progress in the workroom. People tend to prefer doing what they are good at, and so women will tend to prefer cooking.

It might be said that at the age of reason, women have the right of self-determination, to choose, for example, to learn carpentry or mechanics, but the right to choose these things will not be worth much if at that time they do not have the possibility of getting satisfaction from these activities at some fairly advanced level because whatever original interest they might have had was never exposed. Not, of course, that everyone should be forced to take home economics, mechanics, and so on, but adults would have a reason to complain if they were systematically deprived of the opportunity to develop some legitimate interest; whereas, if the opportunity had been there and they failed to take it, they would not.

Secondly, the schools do not provide girls with information about women's capacities except for domestic affairs like mothering and cooking. If this occurs, then when the girls become women, they will be unlikely to imagine alternatives and choose intelligently between them. If this were to happen, then women could not even freely choose a domestic life, since they would be likely to see it as the only possibility instead of one among several. Alternatively, suppose that girls are presented with a few examples of women professionals, but these are always presented as rare, extraordinary persons who had to pay a high price for their aspirations. They either gave up the possibility of developing a marriage or they withstood criticism and ostracism for their strange ambitions or both. This makes the cost of choosing another way of life seem so high that most would be unwilling to select it.

Imagine next that girls are rewarded for being patient, sensitive, responsive and obedient, but that displays of ambition and curiosity are met with frowns or silence. The result is that the girls learn to be passive, understanding and sensitive, and not at the same time confident, interested and active. What has happened is that the pattern of traits they develop suits them for domestic life, and when they come to choose between being a housewife and a doctor, they may judge quite correctly that given their current wants and temperament, housewifery is a better prospect for them. If, however, they had been rewarded for curiosity and ambition, the pattern of their personalities would have been different, and it might have been worthwhile for them to develop interests they have in, say, some science, and so to choose another style of life. The difficulty with the training they in fact had is that it has made such a choice unreasonable and done so without attending to the spontaneous and quite legitimate preferences of girls as they developed.

Finally, suppose that certain styles of dress and standards of etiquette are insisted upon for girls and that boys are encouraged to expect girls to meet these and admire those who meet them well. Anyone who deviates from the norm is made to feel uneasy or embarrassed. Imagine, too, that style of dress, while insignificant in itself, is associated with certain career roles and basic life styles. Dress in such a world serves to symbolize the career role and set up important expectations. When the time comes for a woman to choose what she will do, her expectations tend to be fixed not just with regard to the otherwise insignificant matter of dress, but also with regard to what role she will take up. When this happens, it is difficult for her to choose any unexpected role, for any deviation from expectations about her will produce stress and recall the uneasiness she felt upon breaking the dress code.

If the above practices in fact have the effects I envisage, they interfere with the right of self-determination of mature women. To believe that mature persons have a right of self-determination and that such practices are justifiable is rather like believing that Southern Blacks have a right to vote, but that Whites may legitimately ostracize those who exercise it. It would be like believing that Blacks have a right to eat where Whites do and that it would be merely impolite for Whites to stare as if they did not. In some important respects, it would be like a government maintaining that its citizens have a right to travel wherever they choose, but confiscating the passports of those who go to Cuba. If these analogies are acceptable, then even though the educational policies described above do not violate the right of self-determination, they should be changed. Or rather they should be revised unless it can be argued reasonably that each proposed revision would cause disaster or violate some equally important right.

(B) So far Harriet's commitment to the right of self-determination inclines her to prevent and avoid violations and to minimize interferences like those described above. If, however, she is also committed to the importance of the right, she will want those she cares about to exercise it and to exercise it in a worthwhile way. It is not in general true that belief that one has a right means that one cares about having it or exercising it; for example, the right to travel or to marry do not seem to be rights that one need care about exercising or having. The right of self-determination, however, seems importantly different at least when it is accepted for the suggested rationale. The right was granted to persons to enable them to work out their own way of life in response to their own assessment of their situation, interests and capacities because it was thought appropriate and important that persons work out their own way of life believing that they have a right to. We may ask why this is important, but that is beyond the scope of the present inquiry. It would require explaining the advantages of regarding persons in part as creators of their own way of life rather than merely contributors to the general welfare or some other social ideal.

Assuming, then, that Harriet is also committed to the importance of the right of self-determination, she will want those she loves to exercise it and that its exercise be worthwhile for them. The right of self-determination tends to be worth less to mature persons the fewer opportunities and more interferences they are confronted with and the more they have been trained to have personality traits which make them suited for some definite life role. To say further what tends to make the right worth more, it helps to ask what one would want for persons one loves as they exercise the right of self-determination. Using this device, we are blocked from regarding ourselves as proper determiners of their life style. We do, however, want their good, but partly because we cannot properly determine it and partly because we do not know what will confront them, we do not know what in particular will be good or best for them. Still something can be said about what we want for them.

First, talking of our children and not knowing what they will face, we shall want them to develop the kind of personality which will enable them to respond well to their circumstances whatever they are. We shall want them to have what might be called broadly useful traits, that is, traits which will be helpful whatever their interests and circumstances, traits like confidence, intelligence and discipline. Self-confidence is, for example, a trait which it is good to have because it is useful in a wide variety of ways and inevitably satisfying. Broadly useful traits are the kinds which make a wider range of alternatives feasible for those who have them and so are important for exercising the right of self-determination. We should set about teaching these, then, rather than those associated with some culturally variable sex role.

Secondly, given that our children when mature will have a right of self-determination and given our ignorance of what they will face, it is not in general reasonable for us to aim for a particular outcome of our children's choices, but rather to develop their capacity to make choices in a certain way, namely, autonomously. That is, at least we want them to make the selections free from certain kinds of pressure. We do not want their selections to be coerced, threatened or bribed, and we do not want them to succumb easily to seductive advice or the bare weight of tradition. Neither do we want their preferences to be neurotic or self-destructive even though there are admittedly circumstances in which neurotic responses pay. In short, we want them to have certain psychological strengths which will enable them to make sensible use of the right of self-determination.

To want our children's choices to be autonomous is also to want their selections to express genuine interests of theirs which arise spontaneously under certain conditions. These are the circumstances in which they have the above psychological strengths and as they are making rational assessments of their capacities and situation. The selections should be spontaneous under these conditions because those are the choices we think of as expressive of us as individuals, and those in turn are the selections we tend to find most deeply satisfying and with which we feel most comfortable. Although we do not usually know what in particular these interests will be, we do know that there are certain basic human interests which anyone might have regardless of their sex or other peculiarities about them. Basic human interests are those taken in the kinds of activities which typically individuals find satisfying and which are potentially healthy. For example, people are capable of gaining satisfaction directly in their work or indirectly because it provides them with income, they find successful friendships and love relations satisfying, they enjoy play and developing their talents. The capacities to enjoy each of these interests, unlike other human capacities—for example, for self-destruction, enmity, hostility, envy and so on—are potentially healthy. They are potentially healthy in that they can be coordinated in one person to produce a satisfying way of life, and styles of life in which these capacities are exploited (and the others minimized) are styles which can be coordinated together in a smooth way. What we can legitimately want and hope that our children have, then, are the satisfactions associated with each of these kinds of interests, and more rather than less. These are legitimate aspirations for us to have for our children because they are the kinds they would want to build their lives around if they were mature and reasonable and if the background conditions of life were decent. Given that these are legitimate aspirations, we should set about helping children understand these potential satisfactions vividly and not to suiting them for some particular lifetime role. Then when people are of an age to warrant saying they have a right of self-determination, ideally they will have psychological strengths and a vivid appreciation of the range of enjoyments possible for them so that they are able to work out a satisfying way of life which is an expression of their spontaneous preferences. This does not require that each be equally capable of fitting in anywhere, but only that there is for everyone some array of feasible options.

According to the preceding argument, young persons should be treated in whatever ways give them the strength and imagination to make use of their right of self-determination autonomously when they reach maturity. Treating them in ways which are believed to do this is a way of respecting the right they will have when they reach maturity. In addition, if one is to respect someone's right of self-determination fully, one must be willing to allow its exercise even when one believes it is being done badly. This suggests that some importance should be attached to the choices of people simply because they are attempts to arrive at the available alternative most in line with their autonomous preferences. For the most part, this will probably amount to keeping out of others' business. In those we care about and love, however, it will mean valuing and appreciating what they choose simply because it is their choice. This is, perhaps, one way of expressing our love. If so, then Harriet may have taken John's reticence about some of her projects as signs that he did not love her. Equally, of course, he may have believed that Harriet was a bit wacky and irresponsible, or he may not be committed to the right of self-determination or its importance. None of these is likely to sit well with Harriet, who we might imagine really has reached a vision about the moral life which is incompatible with John's view and with which she feels quite comfortable.

Robert Young

In the Interests of Children and Adolescents

Young argues that we ought to reject the paternalistic outlook on children and assert, instead, that children and adolescents are competent to evaluate their own interests. He then claims that though talk of moral rights for children has been tactically effective, we should primarily work towards legal protection of children's rights.

Compare Young's views on paternalism with those of Feinberg's. Whose view do you find most plausible?

In section IV, Young rejects a view similar to the one forwarded by Schrag. Do you think Young has adequately responded to this Schrag-like view?

The language of moral and human 'rights' is increasingly resorted to in discussion of social and political issues. Children and adolescents (and some adult supporters of their cause) have on occasion in recent years made use of such language in drawing attention to what they believe is their unjustifiable subordination to adult discretion. In this paper I consider how we should construe their use of such language and whether it is justified. I argue that the nub of their claim is justified, despite reservations about the particular form in which they have chosen to express it.

This article has not been published previously.

I

Traditionally childhood has been associated with immaturity and vulnerability. Accordingly it has been customary to regard children (and adolescents) as bearers of only a limited range of rights, in particular, rights not to be mistreated. At the same time adults and various institutions such as schools, law courts, and the churches, have been held to have rights over children which permit interference to the extent of providing for their welfare. In addition to protecting children and youths from harm (and also, of course, infants who will not, however, figure again in the present essay), adult discretionary interferences are regarded as promoting the child's or adolescent's development as an autonomous agent. In *On Liberty* John Stuart Mill put the point as follows:

. . . Society has had absolute power over them during all the early portion of their existence: it has had the whole period of childhood and nonage in which to try whether it could make them capable of rational conduct in life . . .[1]

Clearly Mill wanted to deny that children, including those in their nonage (adolescents), had a right to liberty from interference with *self-regarding* behaviour. Freedom from such interference is the right of those in the maturity of their faculties. But Mill nonetheless insisted that interference with the liberty of children had to be for their 'improvement' (or welfare) which for him included development as a self-determining individual. Mill's remarks articulate the well-intentioned paternalism so prevalent in dealings between adults and children in societies like ours. Indeed the very tone of the *United Nations Declaration of the Rights of the Child* is testimony to the point. Consider the seventh principle, which has to do with the 'right to education' but is quite representative:

The child is entitled to receive education, which shall be free and compulsory, at least in the elementary stages. He shall be given an education which will promote his general culture, and enable him on a basis of equal opportunity to develop his abilities, his individual judgment, and his sense of moral and social responsibility, and to become a useful member of society.

The best interests of the child shall be the guiding principle of those responsible for his education and guidance; that responsibility lies in the first place with his parents.

The child shall have full opportunity for play and recreation, which should be directed to the same purposes as education; society and the public authorities shall endeavour to promote the enjoyment of this right.

Well-intentioned as all this is, it nonetheless dovetails with the denial to children of a whole range of freedoms and 'rights' available to adults. Now it is, no doubt, true that according rights to S does not commit one to according S all the rights that there turn out to be. So even if children have certain human rights, others may be denied them. But that is not the issue here. Rather the issue is that even the acknowledgement of all ten rights set forth in the *U.N. Declaration* would not be incompatible with the prerogative parents typically have to determine what will serve the best interests of their children, excepting those occasions where even 'parental rights' are set aside in favour of the state and its appointed agencies. Worse still, however, accepting the *U.N. Declaration* or its like at face value would provide support for such present realities as: children (and youths) being restricted as legal agents, being compelled to attend schools, having little or no freedom of travel or association of their own devising, having little choice over the fundamentals of their life styles and, within some limits, albeit rather broad ones, being dealt with by parents and other parties in ways that would in adult affairs constitute actionable assaults. (The harshness of some of these restrictions is, of course, subject to great variation. For one extreme see the masterly recent portrayal in the Italian film *Padre Padrone* of how harsh life can be for Sardinian shepherd boys.)

When children and adolescents, supported by a few adults, have resorted in recent years to talk of their rights they have not been content to tailor their claims to fit the paternalistic outlook on children common to these dignified pronouncements or to the practice of liberal societies.[2] Their use of rights talk has instead been that adopted by those who believe themselves oppressed or unfairly treated. It is a strong form of advocacy.

Used in this way such talk is decidedly political because it is about justifiably insisting upon one's claims against others (institutions and the state included). It is to urge that these others may properly be forced to give one one's due, not merely to benefit one in a discretionary way. Bearers of rights on this account have a good of their own and so may be advantaged in themselves. The most satisfactory way I know of explicating this idea of having a good of one's own is Feinberg's suggestion that it is a function of having *interests*.[3] That which has interests can itself be benefitted or advantaged in the way that having a right confers benefits or advantages. A bearer of rights is accordingly not merely the object of other beings' interests. (For this reason great works of art, machines and other human contrivances cannot have rights.) This notion of 'interest' has also been helpfully analysed by Feinberg who regards it as the having of a stake in something such that we stand to gain or lose depending on the condition or outcome of that thing.[4] (There is some circularity in this analysis, as Feinberg acknowledges, but it is not vicious and hence does not impair it.) We have interests in particular in matters to do with our welfare (e.g. health) and in the achievement of the ulterior goals that reflect what we want to do in and with our lives. The former constitute indispensable means to the latter but as well are constitutive of our good regardless of our wants.

With this backdrop in place we can now see what is being advocated in claims made by children and adolescents for a recognition of their previously disregarded rights. What these claims amount to is a call for the overthrow of certain presumptions and their replacement by a distinct one. These presumptions are, firstly, that children and youths have no independent interests that have precedence over the interests of parents (teachers, other adults and so on), and, secondly, that they lack the competence to articulate and evaluate their interests for themselves. There are, then, two aspects of the 'traditional' view to which talk of children's (and adolescents') rights stands opposed. First, the general subordination of children and their interests to adult control and protection and, second, the alleged incompetence of children to identify and evaluate their own interests, an incompetence which generates the need for control and protection. These presumptions tend, as I previously suggested, to be *decisive* for a large range of matters and for the vast majority of children. The proposed replacement is, by contrast, *rebuttable*[5] but no less a radical replacement for that. This presumption is that children and adolescents are competent to evaluate whether they have interests separable from adults. Advocates of children's rights recognize the need, in addition, for the establishment in some circumstances of procedural safeguards to ensure that any separable interest cannot just automatically be overriden.

There are at least two grounds on which these claim-rights urged by children and adolescents might be challenged. First, it might be said that the whole movement for 'children's rights' is premised on a mistaken account of the relationship between adults (especially parents) and children. Second, it might be argued that it is inappropriate to couch the claim being made in the 'children's rights movement' in the language of *rights*. I shall consider these contentions in consecutive sections.

II

In Book I, Chapter VI of *Two Treatises of Civil Government* Locke explains why (contrary to what his theory of property rights might have seemed to imply) parents don't own their children. Modern commentators have accepted his conclusion but not found his arguments convincing.[6] Even though the view that parents have property rights in their children is one that has held sway in various societies it is as unlikely to strike responsive chords in readers of this essay as it was for Locke, because few, if any, parents hold that children can be treated simply as the parents see fit.[7] Adult discretion, as Mill and others have insisted, is to be constrained by concern for the welfare of the child. Nonetheless views like the following are reasonably common (in societies like ours as well as others): 'parents have the right to bring their child(ren) up in ways that the parents believe are in the child's interest, however rational or irrational, or however informed or ill-informed, their beliefs may be'. While not an ownership view it is one of superintendence and so falls under the heading of the first of the traditional views on children and youths which talk of children's rights confronts.

Most of us are familiar with the fact that Jehovah's Witnesses are committed to refusing permission for blood transfusions to be administered to their children. In such an event the welfare interests of the child are invaded.[8] Many adults while wanting to repudiate such outrageous invasions of children's interests are no happier with what they see as the permissiveness embodied in talk of children's rights. They take the position that they do because they share the belief that parents are entitled to raise their children in accordance with their own views. They simply don't believe that their own views about the rearing of children are contaminated by the sort of irrationality or ill-informedness displayed by, say, Jehovah's Witnesses. Like Jehovah's Witnesses, though, they consider that they have certain rights *over* their children (and associated duties to them), whether these be born of religious notions of stewardship, or as fitting to the relation of moral caring the strong and wiser allegedly have for the weaker.

There are very many important, albeit perhaps not so dramatic, instances of parents, other adults, and the agencies of the state raising children in accordance with their own mistaken or poorly supported beliefs. Suppose, what is still common, that parents encourage in female children the flowering of 'feminine virtues'. Such parents may believe that traditional female roles are the appropriate ones and hence that the sort of activities in which girls should engage and the sort of character traits which should be cultivated in them are ones that will in reality fit them admirably for an unassertive, subordinate, domestically oriented role.[9] The relevant habits, skills and personality traits which children acquire, especially in the period prior to and then during elementary or primary schooling, will have far-reaching effects upon the realization of future interests. Given this, to be under ill-informed adult superintendence in such matters is hardly to the good or advantage of children.

Nor is this an isolated example. The attitudes established by adults about their bodies and their children's bodies, about nakedness and touching, about the naturalness of bodily functions and about expression of affection will have profound effects on the subsequent development of healthy rather than prurient sexual appetites and interests. And who would doubt that many parents are ill-informed on these counts even though it is frequently urged that such concerns fall almost exclusively within the province of parents and guardians.

Further examples of the way in which parents and other adult parties seek to raise children in accordance with ill-founded beliefs could be drawn from areas like the development of aesthetic sensibilities and creative capacities; intellectual and vocational orientations; racial and ethnic attitudes and a host of others. (With certain of these matters the second of the traditional views previously isolated assumes importance.) Rather than giving detailed consideration to the harm which this ignorance may occasion it is more needful to stress that such authority as parents legitimately have where children do lack knowledge or lack the physical and psychological resources necessary for full autonomy is surely out of place when their own beliefs interfere seriously with the development in others of an exploratory attitude toward talents and aptitudes and an associated awareness of the live options so critical for the achievement of rational self-determination. We can and should be critical of the morality of such 'authority'.[10] Just as we find morally repugnant the notion of children belonging to their parents like pieces of property so too should we find repugnant the exercise of power by those whose beliefs are unsustainable over the range of important matters where such beliefs impinge on the formation of habits, attitudes and norms and hinder the development of an autonomous and fulfilling way of life. A proper recognition of the distinctness of children's and adolescents' interests from those of their parents (and other adult parties) and of the need to take steps to ensure that these interests aren't just overridden is imperative if harmful invasions are to be minimized. While my concern has been to draw attention to an unacceptable style of parenting it is perhaps worth making the point that such a style of parenting can only be combatted by exposing children and adolescents to competing points of view, and the evidence for them, though e.g. school curricula, television[11] and radio programmes and the public contesting of ignorance and prejudice.

Among those disposed to go along with my argument for rejecting the style of parenting that we've seen underlies the subordinate status accorded to the interests of most children, there are still likely to be some who will jib at conceding the second plank in the traditional position on the relation between children and adults. It is one thing, it may be said, to agree that children have distinct and perhaps even precedent interests, but it is quite another to agree that children are competent to determine and evaluate them, especially since it was earlier acknowledged that a person's interests are constitutive of his (or her) good regardless of his wants. According to the traditional standpoint children overrate their present desires (what they are interested in) to the neglect of their future interests. The essential point has been neatly put in another context by Gerald Dworkin in his paper 'Paternalism'.[12] He asserts that:

. . . [children] lack some of the emotional and cognitive capacities required in order to make fully rational decisions. It is an empirical question to just what extent children have an adequate conception of their own present and future interests but there is not much doubt that there are many deficiencies. For example, it is very difficult for a child to defer gratification for any considerable period of time. [p. 76]

I agree with the sentiment that it is an empirical question whether children and adolescents have an adequate conception of their present and future interests. But this is all the more reason for not accepting uncritically the presumption that children lack what parents and other adults have, namely an adequate conception of their deepest interests. Nor does this presumption gain plausibility from Dworkin's point (with which I also agree) that there are undoubtedly many deficiencies in children's and youths' conceptions of their interests. This for the simple reason that there is equally little doubt that this holds true, in each of the regards Dworkin specifies, for many adults. Yet no comparable presumption operates in relation to adults. And even if it were shown that children manifest diminished capacities more frequently than adults it still would not follow that children as a class or as individuals should be *systematically* denied scope for assessing their own interests. We would need to know what, if any, were the *particular* spheres in which diminished capacity was endemic. Just as importantly we would need to know whether any of the deficiencies were occasioned by children having been excluded from developing such capacities because of restrictions placed on their access to the appropriate resources and opportunities.

Lest these observations be taken to license only an agnostic standpoint it needs to be said that we do already have a deal of evidence on which to base at least a provisional response. There is, first, one's own contact with children and adolescents which, I believe, makes clear that children subject, of course, to individual variation do progress toward self-sufficiency in assessing their interests. Take a simple example: very young children do have to be restrained sometimes in the interests of their safety in relation, say, to crossing roads, drinking unlabeled liquids, climbing heights and so on. It in fact takes very little time before children become safety-conscious (though, especially in the initial stages, there are regular reminders by adults). In more complex matters like that of nutrition it may seem that children fare worse by comparison. The problem, though, is to ascertain how much of this is due to the influence of the well-documented ignorance of adults on this score, rather than to the child's peculiar incapacity to make rational decisions about what it would be in his or her interests to eat.

Secondly, even though the lack of serious critical studies on children's capacities to evaluate their own interests is lamentable, some relevant information has been made available through the work of Piaget and Kohlberg. As well, the more informal observations of progressive educationalists like A. S. Neill at Summerhill, of George Dennison in *The Lives of Children* and of John Holt in *Escape from Childhood: the Needs and Rights of Children* lend plausibility to the claim that children are well able to assess and manage *significant* interests and to play in consequence a determinative role in shaping their education.

Thirdly, children and adolescents are increasingly being called upon in the courts to give their own assessment of complex matters affecting their interests in custody suits and other family legal affairs.

This is a sufficient spread of evidence to support the provisional judgment (to which careful, critical studies could profitably be addressed) that children and adolescents are capable in varying and steadily developing degree of assessing their own major interests. Where ignorance on the part of parents or other adults about how the interests of a child or adolescent are to be assessed is establishable, we have all the more reason to reject the model of subordination and the adult discretion associated with it. But it also needs to be said that paternalistic interference in adult-child relations is not ruled out by the stance I have defended. Wherever serious harms are likely to ensue if children's interests aren't protected against their manifest ignorance or lack of care, paternalism will have a place. The harms against which protection is to be afforded may either bear on present interests or future interests but it should be a requirement that the child's incapacity be shown not merely presumed. Removal of this latter presumption would go a long way toward meeting the claims of children and adolescents urging the recognition of their human rights.

III

There are some who would hold both that the promotion of children's interests including those distinct from adult ones and that children and youths may be capable of evaluating what is in

their interest are defensible enough notions, but that resort to
the language of rights to express them is not. There are, in fact,
several distinct objections contained in this suggestion. First,
there is the contention that children cannot be the bearers of
rights because rights are discretionary powers and hence can
only be had by those able to exercise the options of waiving or
enforcing them. Second, it might be objected that introduction
of talk of rights brings with it a note of insistence that is
appropriate only where relationships have broken down and
degenerated into confrontation and is, therefore, out of place
where children are concerned. Thirdly, there is the argument
that since no one has any moral rights children and adolescents
don't either. I take each in turn.

In H. L. A. Hart's (and others') theory of rights as discretionary powers it is idle to use the expression 'a right' in relation to
infants (and presumably even older children) or to animals.[13] If
it be agreed, as it generally is, that legal and moral rights are, *qua*
rights, of a piece because they have the same form and may have
the same content despite differing as to backing, then there can
be no conceptual bar to the possession of (moral) rights by
children and adolescents. This follows straightforwardly from
the fact that representatives of children may enter into contracts
on their behalf, initiate legal proceedings on behalf of children
and entirely properly be said to speak for and on behalf of
children in pressing their claims and even it would seem, in
certain circumstances, waiving them. (In these regards the
position is the same as for mentally incompetent or deranged
adults.)

A different tack has been taken by Neil MacCormick[14] who
has argued that we should see powers of waiver or enforcement
as essentially ancillary to, not constitutive of, rights. He holds,
therefore, that children's (and mental incompetents') legal
rights differ from ordinary adult ones in not having a discretionary element. On his account the actions of courts and welfare
officers in enforcement procedures are to be understood as
protecting, and hence recognizing, otherwise insecure *rights*.
Or, put another way, as preserving advantages to which chil-

dren have rightful claim. There is some reason, though, to doubt the accuracy of MacCormick's view of things as it applies to, for instance, U.S. jurisdictions. In recent years children there have themselves had their legal rights enforced.[15] They are, moreover, as I previously mentioned, nowadays often called upon to give their own assessment of complex questions in custody suits and in trials where it is adult interests that are at stake. So there is reason to believe that children will come to be accorded more legal discretion. But whatever the truth on this score there seems little or no reason to accept either the view that rights are discretionary powers, or that because they are children are excluded from being bearers of them.

IV

Let us consider the second objection. Talk of rights clearly has a political as well as a moral function. When appeal is made by an individual to his rights in order to get or insist on his or her due, a jarring note is introduced into relations between the claimant and those claimed against.[16] Many adherents of rights-talk argue that this very feature, that one doesn't have to grovel or plead or be grateful for one's due, bestows dignity on the right-holder. It is, nonetheless, generally true that appeals to rights are made because there has been a breakdown in the loving or caring relationships between people. When this happens and the interests of others are not cared for in the ordinary course of events, people whose interests are threatened fall back on political advocacy. Witness the recent history of racial minorities and women. For this reason it is sometimes argued that rights-talk should be kept out of the issue of getting a better deal for children. Thus Paul Goodman, a well-known supporter of and campaigner for such a new deal, wrote in 'What Rights Should Children Have' [17] that the unhappy plight of so many children:

. . . is not something to cope with polemically or to understand in terms of 'freedom', 'democracy', 'rights' and 'power', like bringing lawyers into a family quarrel. It has to be solved by wise traditions in organic communities with considerable stability, with equity instead of law, and with love and compassion more than either.

It would be foolish to deny that there is a valuable insight here. Nevertheless, when relations between individuals produce a situation oppressive to some there may be no other recourse than to adopt tough political strategies. In our liberal, individualist society the currently most successful strategy for combatting oppression is to assert one's rights against it. Much, therefore, as we might regret any appeal by children and adolescents to their 'rights' it may be that their distinct interests can only be protected against being overridden by adults or institutions by way of such a strategy.

V

According, however, to the third of the considerations I previously mentioned, the whole enterprise of talking in terms of moral rights is to be called into question. Elsewhere[18] I have argued at length that claims to moral rights suffer (by contrast with claims for legal rights and with other moral concepts) from indeterminacy; that where they are construed objectively they are foundationally dependent on, not prior to, correct moral principles for their validity; and that the supposed greater richness of moral rights talk has not been established. There is scope here only for a brief résumé of the arguments to support these claims.

I assume the common view (mentioned in section III) that moral and human rights have a form comparable to that of legal rights and that the differences between them arise out of, firstly, the distinct rules and procedures for gaining recognition of the respective sorts of rights and, secondly, the appropriate remedies and protections. I assume, too, that it is rights in the sense of claims which may justifiably be insisted upon against other parties, and not mere liberties or privileges, with which we are concerned.

Human and moral rights suffer, in the first place, from a

greater indeterminateness than is the case with legal rights or even other moral concepts (like what one *ought* to do, or what one has a *duty* to do). To begin with, moral and human rights are subject to the exigencies of circumstance in a way that distinguishes them from legal rights. Socio-economic considerations may make it impossible for an alleged nonlegal right to be provided for—as is the case in many impoverished countries regarding e.g. the fourth and fifth rights mentioned in the *U.N. Declaration of the Rights of the Child*, viz., the rights to special pre-natal and post-natal care, to adequate nutrition, housing, recreation and medical services and to special treatment for the handicapped. There is an absurdity in the idea that *human* rights or *moral* rights should vary with one's place of birth which doesn't arise with legal rights. Moreover, for violations of human or moral rights there are no established, determinate remedies—one can, at best, protest. With legal rights there are sanctions which can be brought to bear in the courts. Again, the processes which give rise to new legal rights are reasonably determinate, but this is not the case with moral rights which typically come into being because a consensus is achieved regarding the intolerability of some sort of discrimination, oppression or disqualification. Only when a conventional acceptance is achieved is there no longer need to rely on people's altruism or concern. Generally in law-governed democracies the reaching of such an acceptance heralds legal recognition.

In the second place, when moral rights-talk is understood objectively (as I believe it has to be if it is to be taken seriously), it is foundationally dependent for its validity on, not prior to, correct moral principles. Moral rights are said to be those valid claims, the recognition of which is called for by moral principles or the principles of an enlightened conscience. But the ease with which such an underpinning is offered belies the complexities it introduces. Let us suppose, as seems reasonable, that the reference to an enlightened conscience would have to be cashed out in terms of the (objectively correct) moral principles disjunctively mentioned. It follows that if we need to have the correct moral principles in our possession before we can give adequate recognition to the moral rights they underpin, an additional reason over and above the need for moral principles will be required if we are to be warranted in including moral rights in our conceptual armory.

Supporters of the need for the concept of moral rights have advanced several such additional reasons so before we can comfortably leave moral rights out of our armory we must consider these reasons.

In a world without moral (and hence human) rights, one would, it is said,[19] have to depend on the kindness and goodwill of others, and this would deprive people of self-respect, of personal dignity, and of respect for others (and their rights). Bandman puts it this way in his paper:

Rights enable us to stand with dignity, if necessary, to demand what is our due without having to grovel, plead or bet, or to express gratitude when we are given our due, and to express indignation when what is our due is not forthcoming. [p. 236]

Wasserstrom, who suggests that rights fulfill certain functions that neither duties (even correlative duties) nor any other moral or legal concepts can fulfill, offers in answer to the questions "why ought anyone have a right to anything? or why not have a system in which there are no rights at all?" the following:

Such a system would be a normally impoverished one. It would prevent persons from asserting those kinds of claims, it would preclude persons from having those types of expectations, and it would prohibit persons from making those kinds of judgments which a system of rights makes possible. [p. 636]

I frankly fail to see why a world lacking moral rights would be a morally impoverished world. As I shall later suggest, there is some tactical advantage to be gained from appealing to one's rights. But this is not to say there is significantly greater moral richness in doing so than if one simply relied on forming judgments based on (correct) moral principles (e.g., of the necessity sometimes to incorporate wider considerations of justice as well as just the narrower ones of desert in the achievement of social justice). Given the potential for indeterminacy I have already outlined, and given that even adherents to irreducible rights acknowledge them to be less than absolute and exceptionless, no gain or advantage is achieved over a straightforward appeal to the principles undergirding the supposed rights.

Still, what of Wasserstrom's contention that because it is possible to conceive of duties without conceiving of their correlative rights, people like white Southerners in the United States have been enabled to make mistakes that matter morally? And, he continues, the only way to avoid the white Southerner merely having to live with his own (ill-developed) conscience if he fails to do his duty, is to accord the Negro rights which he is then in a position dignifiedly to claim, *and* to claim in such a way as to lift the matter above the level of requests, privileges, and favours.[20]

The first thing to notice is that, in terms of actually establishing the independence of the Negro's interests from those of the white and of giving to each equal consideration, a failure on the part of the white to do those things that he morally ought (in an objective sense), leaves matters in the same sorry state as a failure on the part of the white to accord the Negro rights. And in the absence of moves to give expression to the Negro's interests not in the rather problematic language of moral or human rights, but in the determinate and enforceable language of legal rights, the evidence is that we should expect oppressors neither to behave morally rightly nor to accord the oppressed equal rights. So any gain of the sort Wasserstrom is appealing to must stem solely from the difference in the manner of expression of the Negro's claim for just treatment. If that be so, I can only reply that there does not seem to be any greater moral dignity in expressing the claim in the language of *rights* than in the language of what (objectively) it would be *right* morally to do. Tactically the matter is perhaps quite different. It is one of the prevailing attitudes in contemporary Western society that talk of what it is objectively morally right to do is *outré*. By contrast, appeals to one's right are in vogue. Let it be noted, though, that

Wasserstrom (and others who hold to similar positions) claim a moral not a merely tactical advantage for the inclusion of rights in our moral conceptual framework.

A. I. Melden has advanced a second reason for the view that we lose something of moral significance if we eliminate rights talk in favour of making moral judgments on the basis of moral principles.[21] He claims that a whole dimension of morality—the moral relations between moral agents which talk of moral rights upholds—is left out of account if we look upon rights-talk merely as a convenient summary of what ought to be done. His basic claim is that where we override someone's rights even on morally justifiable grounds, the bearer of the right has been *morally injured* and we, therefore, still owe him something because of the moral relation in which he stands to us, as one having a right against us. I have to acknowledge that I find Melden's claim obscure. Moreover, I do not accept that one who acts as he or she morally ought and in the process (justifiably) overrides another's rights thereby injures that person *morally* or jeopardizes the moral relations in which they stand. (With this compare *pace* Melden how matters stand when a promise is morally properly broken.) So reliance on moral 'oughts' does not have the effect, as far as I can see, of excessively narrowing or constricting the moral framework.

A third reason commonly advanced for preserving the notion of the reality of nonlegal rights is the charge that, since, according to the alternative conventionalist rendering I have been supporting, rights are established by community consensus, a practice like slavery which has always and everywhere been a violation of people's moral rights, must have only become such from the late eighteenth century onwards, which is morally absurd. Rights, in other words, exist independently of their recognition and, to this extent, are more like desires, which can be unrecognized, than like pains, which cannot. In the same vein, the anti-conventionalist would say of any community which just did not possess the concepts of moral and human rights, that whatever moral and human rights do exist, also exist within such a community, albeit unrecognized.

Even though I do not wish to object to this last sentiment, the mere possibility of such a society should appear as deeply disturbing to those strongly committed to a belief in the existence of nonlegal rights. Likewise it ought to be deeply disturbing that our talent for moral epistemology should apparently have developed so rapidly in recent human history thereby enabling us to detect so many previously unrecognized rights, while throughout the same period our progress in laying bare the correct moral principles which provide their foundation has been so tawdry. More importantly for present purposes, though, I do not believe that the charge can be sustained that a conventionalist rendering of the relevant phenomena cannot also accommodate our conviction that slavery was no more morally justified in ancient Athens, say, than it is today. One can simply point out that those considerations which make actions right were not properly weighed up or were not properly understood to be such by those who did the enslaving. Thus, one can employ the relevant counterfactuals to explain and support the judgment that the practice of keeping slaves was morally wrong though it violated no one's moral rights since these had not been brought into existence by a sufficient consensus. Once again the advantage does not clearly lie with rights.

Whatever its philosophical credentials, there is no doubting the prominence in countries with a liberal, individualist heritage of the idea of human rights. My contention, as I intimated in the previous section, is that the idea occupies this position of prominence because it has proved a successful strategy to appeal to one's rights. For that reason arguing against the tradition is apt to seem futile as far as practice, if not theory, is concerned. But regardless of whether my criticisms of human rights-talk are well-taken what should be stressed is that supporters of such talk are agreed with me that it is in virtue of children's *interests*[22] that our conduct concerning them or toward them may either benefit or wrong them. How morally we ought to treat children turns on facts about them, rather than on facts about their parents (e.g. that they love them and have an interest in their wellbeing) or facts about the state (e.g. that it has an interest in having healthy, productive citizens).

So, for instance, in relation to education, if parents have nonlegal 'rights' they will be rights against the state with respect to the protection or promotion of their children's rights (legitimate interests). These 'rights' thus *depend* on the distinct interests of the children. It is, of course, reasonable to presume that for the most part parents do have the welfare interests of their children at heart in insisting on their having access to *education*. But this, to bring in the second of the elements involved in children's rights, is not by any means incompatible with children and adolescents being acknowledged competent (with due allowance for developmental and individual variation) to assess what is in their own interests in such a context. Where, moreover, parents are themselves ignorant their say (e.g. in choice of curriculum in school-centred curricula programmes) should not automatically override.

VI

In the course of thinking and writing about the subject of this essay I have been conscious of my own failings as a parent and as an adult who has dealings with children. More importantly, *perhaps*, I have also been conscious of the difficulties to be negotiated in transforming other adult and institutionalized attitudes towards children from that of a well-intentioned paternalism to that of a serious recognition of their distinct interests and of their capacity for assessing these interests. In a situation of scarce resources, limited altruism and parental failings, it seems unduly risky to bank on achieving conventional acceptance of these legitimate interests as expressed in the rather problematic language of human and moral rights. Better that the adequate recognition of children's and adolescents' rights be clearly and definitely entrenched in legally protected rights. It would be in their interests.[23]

NOTES

1. Everyman edition, p.139. Cf. too, p.73. For helpful discussion of Mill's views on children see John Kleinig, 'Mill, Children and Rights', *Educational Philosophy and Theory*, 8 (1976), pp.1-16.

2. See e.g. J. Hall (ed.), *Children's Rights* (New York: Praeger Publishers, 1971); J. Holt, *Escape from Childhood: the Needs and Rights of Children* (New York: Ballantine Books, 1974); B. and R. Gross (eds.), *The Children's Rights Movement: Overcoming the Oppression of Young People* (Garden City, N.Y.; Anchor Books, 1977).

3. 'The Rights of Animals and Unborn Generations' in W. T. Blackstone (ed.), *Philosophy and Environmental Crisis* (Athens, Ga.: University of Georgia Press, 1974) pp.43-68, esp. p.49f.

4. 'Harm and Self-Interest' in P. M. S. Hacker and J. Raz (eds.), *Law, Morality and Society* (Oxford: Oxford University Press, 1977) pp.285-308, esp. p.285f.

5. To anticipate a little: this is not merely because paternalism is justified where there is, for example, evidence of recognizable irrationality as regards a clear and direct threat to an important aspect of the child's or adolescent's future welfare, but also because there is development in and individual variation over the capacity to assess interests.

6. See e.g. R. Nozick, *Anarchy, State and Utopia* (New York: Basic Books, 1974) pp.287ff and L. Becker, *Property Rights* (London: Routledge & Kegan Paul, 1977) pp. 37ff. Neither, as it happens, addresses himself to Locke's major argument, namely that without God's infusing of a living soul, human activity produces no person (and hence no product of labour). See Ch.6, paragraphs 53-54.

7. Nan Berger in 'The Child, the Law and the State' in Hall (ed.), *Children's Rights, op.cit.* argues, though, that the laws referring to adoption and fostering are only comprehensible if the child is regarded as the parents' property.

8. In such cases it may be that another of the child's putative ulterior interests—of religious purity—is thereby protected, but it also seems that the religious interests of the parents are part of what is at issue.

9. A fuller account of these matters than would be appropriate here may be found in e.g. Sharon Bishop Hill's, 'Self-Determination and Autonomy' in R. Wasserstrom (ed.), *Today's Moral Problems* (New York: Macmillan Publishing Co., 1975) pp.171-186, esp.

pp.181-186. A slightly different version of this paper is included in this volume, p. 154.

10. Nonetheless my concern is not with the evaluation of parents as parents but with the wrongs occasioned to their children by the adoption of the position on parenthood that I have sketched.

11. And this makes the failure of much children's television to confront serious issues (from prejudices about people of other races or social classes, to role stereotypes to the nature of good eating habits) the more condemnable. In Australia recently there has been some evidence in public hearings about the subject to suggest awakening may be beginning, but a lot of damage has doubtless already been done.

12. *The Monist*, 56 (1972), pp.64-84.

13. 'Are There Any Natural Rights?', *Philosophical Review*, 64 (1955), pp.175-191.

14. 'Children's Rights: A Test-Case for Theories of Right', *Archiv für Rechts—und Sozialphilosophie*, 62 (1976), pp.305-316. For a somewhat different picture see Feinberg, 'The Rights of Animals and Unborn Generations', *op.cit.*

15. Cf. Hilary Rodham, 'Children under the Law', *Harvard Educational Review*, 43 (1973), pp.487-514. The fullest study of children's legal rights remains Andrew Kleinfeld's 'The Balance of Power Among Infants, Their Parents and the State', *Family Law Quarterly*, 4 (1970), pp.319-350, pp.409-443; and 5 (1971), pp.64-107.

16. I have been helped to see this by John Kleinig. Cf., too, Meirlys Owens, 'The Notion of Human Rights: A Reconsideration', *American Philosophical Quarterly*, 6 (1969), pp.240-246, esp. p.244.

17. *New York Review*, September 23, 1971, pp.20-22.

18. 'Dispensing with Moral Rights', *Political Theory*, 6 (1978), pp.63-74.

19. E.g. by Joel Feinberg, *Social Philosophy* (Englewood Cliffs, N.J.: Prentice Hall, Inc., 1973) pp.58, 94; by Richard Wasserstrom in his 'Rights, Human Rights and Racial Discrimination', *Journal of Philosophy*, 61 (1964), pp.628-641; and by Bertram Bandman in 'Do Children Have Natural Rights?', *Philosophy of Education: Proceedings of the 29th Meeting* (1973) pp.234-246.

20. *Ibid.*, p.640f.

21. Cf. 'The Play of Rights', *The Monist*, 56 (1972), pp. 479-502 and *Rights and Persons* (Oxford: Basil Blackwell, 1977).

22. *Rights and Persons*, esp. Chs. 2-3.
23. I am grateful to John Kleinig and to the editors for forcing me to make several points clearer (and, I hope, in the process to enhance the essay's usefulness).

A. I. Melden

Do Infants Have Moral Rights?

*Melden begins by briefly describing the oft-held view that
only adults can have rights. According to this received
view, a creature must be rational and self-controlled to
have any rights. That is, he must be at least rational
enough to recognize that others have rights and mature
enough to respect those rights. If a creature is less rational
or less mature than this standard demands, then moral
agents may have duties to him, but he cannot properly be
said to have any rights.*

*Thus, on this view, children and animals are thought not
to have rights, though moral agents may well have duties
toward them. Melden argues that this view is mistaken.
Although adults are the paradigm moral agents, he claims
that children—even young infants—can have rights. In
particular he tries to show that infants can properly be
said to have rights even though they are not presently
mature enough to enter a wide range of moral activities.*

*Schrag claims that talk of children's rights is illicit since
no one can correctly be identified as the person with the
correlative duty to the child. Whom do you think Melden
would identify as the person with the correlative duty?*

I

There are many things, morally speaking, one ought to do
where, however, there is no issue of any moral right.[1] I ought, for
example, to deal kindly and generously with a stranger who has

---

This article has not been published previously.

no right to the kind of treatment I ought to give him—he is not in need and there is no threat to his integrity or his status as a moral agent posed by my indifferent and ingenerous treatment of him. And however much I may later regret or even feel ashamed of myself, I do not suffer any pangs of guilt or attempt to make any restitution for any damage I have caused him. Nor is he entitled to hold me to account however much he may disapprove of my behaviour. And seeing that I do feel ashamed of myself for the way I treated him, he may indeed attempt to console me by minimizing the importance of the matter and try to get me to put the whole affair out of my mind. But forgive me? There is no place for such talk here. It should be clear, therefore, that no issue of rights and their correlative obligations need arise everytime morally speaking one ought to do anything.

Now no one would deny that the very young infant ought to be given the care it needs for its survival. But many a philosopher has questioned whether the young infant has any right, strictly speaking, to the sorts of treatment parents ought to give it in caring for it as they do and in providing it with the necessities for its proper development. Certainly young infants have legal rights against their parents; the latter are under legal obligations or constraints to provide them with certain minimally necessary conditions of decent life. And there is good moral reason for enacting those statutes by which such legal rights and obligations are established. But is it the case that the young infant has any *moral* rights in the matter? Why not, if the matter is sufficiently important to warrant the establishment of these legalities?

The answer generally given is that moral rights are ascribable only to persons, beings who are morally concerned and accountable and capable therefore of entering into and acting in accordance with the moral relations in which they stand to others. For to have a right is to enjoy a status with respect to others of a rather complex sort. A right may be exercised, asserted, claimed, waived, relinquished or forfeited. Correlatively, others are under a moral obligation to the individual who has the right, an obligation they may meet or discharge by performances or abstentions as the case may be, by which they respect, accord, grant the individual his right, or, failing this, deny, abridge, infringe, or violate his right. Both the possessor of a right and those who are under the correlative duty to him must therefore bear certain moral burdens in their dealings with one another. The person under an obligation is constrained in his thought and action by that obligation that is correlated with the right; but the possessor of a right, as in the case, for example, of rights created by such voluntary acts as the making of promises, bears his moral burden too in being required, as circumstances warrant, to waive or even relinquish the right that he has. And even if justifiably because of the peculiar circumstances that arise in his special case a person under an obligation to another by virtue of the latter's right must infringe that right, that is by no means the end of the matter: he owes the person whose right he has infringed, restitution or reparation and often the explanation that redeems him in the eyes of the person who has suffered the moral damage. And the latter, for his part, is morally required to respond appropriately. And one can go on to spell out other features of that complex moral relation constituted by the right that one person has against others—correlatively, the obligation the latter has to the former—how, for example, each must behave with respect to others when one has been wronged through the violation of one's own right or when wrongfully one has infringed the rights of others. No account of the matter could be complete without mention of such moral emotions as guilt and remorse, of such matters as the assertion of one's rights and the demonstration this affords of one's moral status as the possessor of a right and of one's moral dignity, or, where there is remorse and expiation of guilt, of the forgiveness that is in order. The concept of a right with these complex ramifications applies to beings who are much more than sentient, much more than the subjects of pleasant and unpleasant or painful experiences, and much more even than beings who are self-conscious. It applies, rather, to moral agents who are capable of dealing with each other in the light of their concerns for one another, and able to decide how reasonably they are to bear the moral burdens they have during the course of their endeavors. It is small wonder, when we compare the helpless condition of the very young infant, newly emerged from the womb—whose experiences are as diffuse and inchoate as they are, whose interests, rationality, agency and even recognition of others are virtually non-existent—with persons as we find them in the familiar forum of our every day social life, that philosophers have been led to the view that moral rights lie wholly in the future with respect to the young infant, that at best infants have only potential rights, rights they will but do not actually have, and only if they develop some measure of the maturity as persons they cannot possibly have as infants.

Persuasive as the grounds for this view may be, the denial that infants have any birth rights runs counter to the sensibilities of many or most of us. For we do think that parents are responsible for the care and development of their offspring; but on the view under discussion, when parents act in the interest of their children they are engaged only in a complex exercise that is at best only preliminary to the achievement by their offspring of any rights at all. For on this view, parents may be doing what they ought to be doing, just as they may be doing what they ought to do in acting generously and helpfully towards others; but since their young children do not as such have any rights, they are no more meeting their responsibilities to their offspring than they would be if they dealt helpfully and generously with total strangers. Yet we do think that parents are responsible for the care and the development of their young children, that in acting properly in this way parents are meeting their responsibilities. The notion of responsibility, however, involves the notion of their accountability. But to whom are they accountable? Unless it makes sense to speak of the rights of children, even infants, they are not accountable to the latter, nor would it appear that they are morally accountable to anyone else acting in behalf of their children; for who could this be if it is not the parents? Those to whom parents would appear to be accountable can only be, on this view, the adults-to-be into which, hopefully, their infant children will develop. But since the implementation of the plans and projects that parents have for their young when they act in their interest is a matter that relates to them long before they achieve the moral status requisite for their having any rights, the person who emerges from this process with his or her newly acquired rights has no reason to complain, if this should occur despite the neglect of his parents, that they had failed to meet the obligations they had to him or her as a young child—for qua child how could that being have any right against the parents? Shall we say, then, that the parents have an obligation *qua* parents to the future person who only later emerges as a person with rights of his own? But suppose that for some reason or other no such moral metamorphosis occurs—the child dies before maturity—to whom can the parents be said to be accountable? To the society bereft of the person who might have been but never came into being? Only if that society suffered moral injury by having been denied a member of its society of persons, and surely that that society suffered any injury of any sort, moral or not, is far more problematic than the moral injury suffered by those young children—whether or not they ever reach maturity—who are deprived of the care essential to their survival and development by their negligent parents. And if there is no one, neither the young child nor anyone else acting in behalf of the child, and not even society itself, what sense can there be in our familiar talk about responsible parental behaviour towards their young children? Clearly the responsible behaviour of a parent must be the behaviour that consists in meeting the obligation of the parent to that being who *is* infant or young child, the behaviour of one who accords that offspring the rights the latter has against his or her parent, however insensible that being may be of his or her rights and however deficient that being may be in agency, rationality, interests or moral concerns of any sort. But how is it possible for infants to have any moral rights unless they are endowed with just these features conceptually involved in the notion of a moral right, features that are conspicuously present in all of those cases to whom quite unproblematically we ascribe moral rights? For the more these features are lacking as in the case of animals, and at least the newly fertilized human ovum, the more serious are the doubts we have concerning the possession of moral rights. How does the case of the infant differ from these altogether doubtful cases?

II

In order to make good the claim that an infant has no mere potential or future rights, that its rights are actual, some preliminary observations are in order.

(a) Moral maturity is not an all or none matter, something that suddenly pops into being, in all of its perfection, at a certain point in a child's development. Surely those who deny that an infant has actual moral rights would not want to assert that moral maturity must be complete before moral rights can be ascribed correctly to individuals. For there are many who suffer from arrested moral development—witness the white supremacist in South Africa, Mississippi, or in the lily-white suburbs of large urban centers like Chicago and Detroit. And there are many of us, morally mature as we are, who have our off-days and our off-moments, who are subject to moods, emotions, distress or distempers of various sorts which, while they last, submerge the moral maturity which normally we exhibit in our dealings with others. Yet some philosophers seem to be oblivious to such commonplace matters when they suggest that moral rights go with or somehow depend upon the status of individuals as rational or autonomous beings. But how much rationality, how much ability to act on the basis of relevant considerations that serve and recognizably so by the agent himself, as moral reasons for conduct, can be ascribed to the benighted slave or the smugly self-satisfied slaveholder? Surely those who fall a good deal short of such moral maturity have moral rights even when these go unrecognized by themselves or by others.

Nor should one say that, because moral maturity as it develops during the life of a human being is a matter of degree, the rights that each one has are correspondingly held in various degrees. A young child, generally, is less mature than one who is considerably older and may not be held accountable in the same manner as the latter. But does this mean that the right to life that the older child has is a right to a greater degree than that of the younger child? What indeed does this mean? That if one had to choose between saving their lives, the right of the older child should always prevail because it is a right to a greater degree? Or, that the life of the older child should always be saved because that child has possession to a greater degree of that very same right than does the younger child? It is true of course that as one develops one acquires an ability to enter into new personal relations, and with this often go new rights, e.g., the rights of husbands and wives, fathers and mothers. But this does not warrant this obscure if not altogether unintelligible talk about degrees of rights or degrees of possession of rights. In any case a right is not like, e.g., intelligence or knowledge, which an individual has only more or less, to some greater or lesser degree. And while there may be troublesome borderline cases in the upper animal kingdom who in certain limited respects resemble human beings and about whom the flat-out affirmation, or denial, that they have any moral rights may well be misleading, it is not the case that if a maturing but not yet matured youngster does in fact possess a moral right, he possesses it like the child with its growing intelligence and knowledge, only to a diminished degree.

It is not necessary, therefore, that there be moral maturity for the possession of moral rights. And nowhere is this more evident than in the instance of promises. For there are promises and promises, which confer rights on those to whom they are made and impose obligations on those who make them, even in those cases in which there is absent some of the conceptual features present in those paradigm cases of promises made and accepted by morally mature individuals who are fully aware of the moral implications of the transaction in which they are engaged. For a child's understanding of these moral implications is, to a greater or less extent, a mere shadow of what a morally mature agent understands by a promise: that a right is conferred and an obligation is assumed; that the right may, and in some circumstances, must be waived or even relinquished;

that a right is conferred whether or not one has any intention of making good one's word (finger crossing does not work); that failure to keep a promise is no mere failure to keep a bargain in which a useful exchange of benefits and burdens occurs; that breaking a promise is no mere defeating of an expectation, or the disappointing of a promisee, or the infliction of pain, discomfort or unpleasantness upon him but, rather, doing him moral injury as much so as one would if one were to interfere with his endeavors; that the appropriate emotion for one's wilful failure to keep one's word is not mere regret, something one may feel when a rainstorm plays hob with one's plans for a picnic, but guilt and remorse for the moral injury one has caused; that reparation, restitution or, when the failure is not wilful, explanation is called for in order to repair or preserve one's good moral relations with the person one has let down; and so on and so on. A very young child may play the game of promising, superficially imitating its elders when they make promises or count on those they receive. And in many such cases no rights are conferred or obligations are assumed, for it is all play as we say. But later, as the child matures, the transaction does assume more serious overtones, and while no sharp line may be drawn to mark the boundaries that mark off cases in which moral rights are indeed conferred and obligations assumed it is clear that long before the moral enlightenment of a sensitive, understanding adult is reached, there are rights and there are obligations connected with promise transactions even though some of the features of the paradigm cases I have just indicated are missing. Indeed, for some adults who suffer arrested moral development and who regard a promise as a bargaining device for the useful exchange of benefits and burdens (a view echoed, sadly enough, by some moral philosophers) and who fail to see the conceptual connection between the promise transaction and the rights of agents to pursue their interests as they go about their affairs, or who regard a promise as a sacred matter performed in the sight of the Lord and to be kept no matter what, even at the cost of moral disaster and tragedy, there are promises and they do bind even though there is little or no sense of the complex panoply of moral concepts in which the concept of a promise has its proper place. Yet whether moral development is incomplete or moral ossification has set in, there are rights and obligations, unaware as the parties to the promise transaction may be of the conceptual implications of what they are doing.

In order to understand what a given right is and how it may arise we need, no doubt, to attend to paradigm cases in which the complex conceptual features of the right are present, for it is only by reference to such cases that anything like an adequate understanding may be gained, but even where many of these features are missing or present only in an attenuated manner, as in the case of youngsters who fall far short of moral maturity, there can be, and there are, rights.

The condition of an infant, however, is not at all like that of an older youngster who after all has interests, agency and some measure of moral understanding, limited as it may be. The latter *can* engage in promise transactions supporting by the promises he or she makes the endeavors of those to whom they are given, or relying upon the promises received from others, for the support he or she needs for endeavors in the course of which interests of various sorts are pursued. But an infant hardly has interests that it pursues in any lines of conduct; and while it does need the help of, say, its parents if it is to survive, that help cannot be supplied to it on the basis of any sort of mutual understanding of the kind that exists between promiser and promisee, husband or wife, or wherever it is that the mutual understanding to be given and received by persons who stand in some sort of personal relations to each other involves rights and their correlative obligations. For an infant can scarcely have interests, the agency by which interests are pursued, or moral comprehension of any sort. How is it possible, then, that the young infant can have any right, that its parents are under any moral obligation to it?

(b) Let us look more closely at the nature of a parent's relation to its infant child. This relation, of course, may be good, bad or indifferent. Parents may neglect, or they may protect, plan and care for, their young children. But if we are to exhibit the normative considerations that apply to the relations between parent and child we must attend to those features present in the relations in which parents stand to their offspring when a parent is *not* neglectful of what is in the child's interests and does what is morally required. For it is only if we attend to such cases that we can determine whether the structure in which the concept of a right has its place is in fact exemplified in the relation of parent to child and to a degree sufficient to justify us in ascribing any right to the child which it has then and there against its parent.

Now even before a child is brought into the world, parents often act *in* the interest of the child-to-be, even though there is as yet no child there at all, let alone a child that *has* any interests in any unproblematic sense. But what is *in* the interest of any human being, unlike the interest that a human being *has,* connects essentially with its good. A child may show an interest in something by reaching for it which it would in fact be bad for it to grasp, e.g., a razor sharp knife; children, and adults too, do have interests in things that are bad for them. But problematic as it is that a very young infant *has* any interest, it is surely true that there are things that are in its interest. And further, it is clear that what is *in* an infant's interest is good for it. Now some of the things that are in the interest of an infant are in its future interests. It is in the future interest of the infant that parents now plan for their child's education and regularly set aside funds for this purpose. And it is in the present interest of the infant that parents provide it with food, shelter and elementary comforts. Here it is that the interests that parents have when they now act in the future or present interests of their infant child—a largely passive being completely dependent upon its parents for the most elementary of its needs and for all that it needs in order to insure its normal development into what eventually will be a responsible agent—may be viewed as surrogate interests, interests that parents supply on behalf of their infants. So too with the agency that parents supply when they act on behalf of their infant children too young to act in their own interests—this is a surrogate agency parents supply in order to compensate for the agency deficiency of their offspring. And just as parents provide surrogate interests and agency for their infants in support of their development, so they contribute their own understanding and their own moral response when, acting on behalf of what is in the moral interest of their infants they claim the moral, no less than the legal, rights their offspring have. And parents, not their children, are accountable and in some cases liable for the damage the latter may cause others.

Parents, acting on behalf of their infant offspring in making up the latter's deficiencies in interests, understanding and agency, supply out of their own resources as the responsible agents they are surrogate interests, understanding and agency when, in the various ways, they act on behalf of their offspring and in so doing act in their interest. Generally, as the course of development of an infant proceeds during the years—the end result of which is the emergence of a being with interests, agency, moral understanding and competence of his own—the contributions that parents make in the form of the surrogate interests, agency, and understanding they supply, decreases. But in the course of the life of a family that is as it should be, and in which the lives of parents and children are bound together so that more and more interests are shared and each takes pride and pleasure in the achievements of the others, there remains a high level of agency, interest, moral understanding and response that can be attributed to the group as a whole even though, in the case of the children and in decreasing measure as they develop, they are surrogates supplied by parents and older siblings.

All of this, however, is inconclusive, for it is difficult to see how a parent can alleviate, in the manner I have suggested, those deficiencies present in the case of an infant. It is intelligible that a parent should be accountable and liable for the damage children may cause; but children are considerably removed from the passive and helpless condition of newly born infants. For they, unlike the latter, are agents who pursue their interests, and, limited as these are, however incomplete their understanding may be, they do have some sense of the things that are permissible and forbidden. So too with what parents do in acting on behalf of their minor offspring when they lay claim to the rights the latter have. And if, as I have suggested, we regard a promise transaction as a paradigm case of an act by means of which an obligation is assumed and a right is conferred, we shall have good reason to question whether the considerations I have presented can allay the doubts that have been expressed concerning the rights of infants. For in a bona fide promise transaction a mutual understanding is established between the persons involved concerning an act—whether it be a performance or abstention is of no matter here—which the promisor is to supply and which the promisee requires for the success of some line of endeavor in which he intends to engage, and the right of promisee depends, as I have argued elsewhere,[2] upon the right that he has as a human being to pursue his interests. Indeed, there is not only this fact about the right that operates in the background of the promise transaction, but a common moral understanding without which there could not be the complex moral requirements imposed upon both parties to the promise transaction. But in the case of young infants in their relation to their parents what sort of mutual understanding exists between them, what sort of common moral background operates in the background, what agency and what interests does the young infant have that would enable us even to make sense of the remark that it has a right to pursue its interests? We have, it would appear, a complete moral blank in the case of the young infant: no agency, no interests, no understanding of any sort and not even the experiences and mental life of any of us. It is not deficiencies in these matters, but their complete absence, that marks the newly born infant. How then can we speak of supplying surrogate agency, interests and understanding for a being who does not exhibit any of these features to begin with? One might as well talk of supplying such surrogates for the koi swimming about in one's garden pool. So the argument might go.

III

It is an old thought that, wholly devoid as the young infant is of the requisite features of moral agents, it has the potentiality of acquiring them. But this potentiality, present as it is in the young infant cannot confer present or actual rights. Indeed, what is meant by a present potentiality? The contingent matter of fact that some time in the future it will come to have those features of moral agency that will enable it to establish with others the mutual understandings essential to rights and their correlative obligations? But if this is all that is intended, it does not follow that there is anything in its present condition to warrant our ascribing moral agency and rights to it, any more than the fact that it is true of a person that he will later acquire the skills of one who rides a bicycle establishes that he is now a bicycle rider. The problem with this talk about present potentiality is that it leaves us at a loss to understand what difference the presence of a potentiality makes to the *present* condition of the infant. This present condition is, we are told, big with its future moral agency, but unless we invoke entelechies and suppose that they are somehow involved in the present state of infants, we seem to be at a loss to make out a plausible case for the possession by them of moral rights. And even present entelechies cannot be the possessors of rights unless, somehow, we invest them with the features of persons—but how is this possible?

Yet this search for something that is present in any being at the time the ascription of rights is made—something with a measure of those features that persons manifest when they engage in promise transactions with others, or when they conduct their affairs with others on the basis of the mutual support they are to offer each other during the course of their endeavors as in the relation between friends or spouses—is misguided. We use the present tense in the sentences we employ in ascribing rights to individuals, but shall we assume that if we look to the condition or state of those individuals at those times that we shall discover them to be agents, having interests and moral understanding? For suppose someone is fast asleep, an individual who in an earlier waking period clearly manifested all of the features of moral agency. Are we to say that he has no rights now because, being fast asleep, he lies wholly passive, displays no interests and manifests no understanding of himself or anyone else during his present condition? Surely not. Why then do we regard him as a person with rights? Because he had already developed into a person with all of these features and displayed them during an earlier waking period? But all that this would appear to show is that he has been a person with rights, not that in his present condition of deep sleep he is now the possessor of any rights. Or is it that we ascribe rights to him even though he lies there fast asleep because he will awaken and resume his condition of moral agency? But suppose that he never awakens—he suffers a fatal heart attack—shall we then reject as false our idea that the being fast asleep is a person with rights? Or, is it that in attributing agency, interests and moral understanding to that wholly inert individual, we are not ascribing features to him that can be displayed by him in his present condition of deep sleep in the way in which colors and shapes are displayed by objects, to be read off by looking at them, but, rather, asserting conditionals about him, e.g., that if awake he would behave in such and such ways with interests of this or that kind and with a moral understanding of what it is that he would be doing? But conditionals can also be asserted about the young infant: that given maturation, and the requisite moral training and education, he or she would behave in such and such ways with interests of this or that kind. There is of course a difference between the young infant and the man who is fast asleep. For we do say that the latter *has* interests, understanding and agency whereas the former does not, that the latter *has* certain capacities of moral agency whereas the young infant has not yet acquired them. But what this shows is that the features and capacities of moral agency are not to be identified with those features and capacities that are present in every segment of a person's life. For the man in a deep sleep, as long as he remains in that condition, is unable to act and reflect with moral understanding. So too is the man who has suffered a blow on the head that renders him unconscious or comatose; we do not, because of his present incapacities and oblivion to everything that is going on in and about him, remove him from the lists of those whom we take to be persons with rights of whatever sorts these may be.

We do not, then, ascribe rights to the members of our species only if they are able, in their condition at the times in question, to enter into moral relations with others, relations for which the possession of interests, moral agency and understanding are requisite. We do not wait for the human being in deep sleep to awaken, for the comatose victim of an automobile accident to regain his senses, in order to confirm our conviction that the person there possesses rights. And in the case of someone lying in a hospital bed in a deep coma, whose impending death is beyond any possible doubt, we do not on that account cease to regard him as a person, one whose death one might hasten without any moral compunction. For even in this case, it is no mere lump of flesh that lies there.

What sort of being we have at any given moment is determined by the nature of the concepts we apply to it. The being now fast asleep or comatose is not, on that account, a being to be viewed solely in biological terms. For the being there is a being who has made and received promises, fulfilled and unfulfilled, and even if death should shortly ensue, that being is a father, a son or a daughter, devoid as that being may be of the least flicker of consciousness and completely incapable, too, of any moral agency or understanding. The concepts we apply to human beings whether they are awake now and capable of moral intercourse with others or fast asleep or even comatose, refer essentially to periods in their lives that extend back into the past. And so too with the conceptual connection between the present and the future segments of a person's life. For just as a person may be remorseful or engage in activities by which he atones for what lies in the past and no longer exists, so he may now act prudently even though his life may unexpectedly come to an end in a few moments and all of his careful planning and forethought prove to have been in vain. But whether or not lives are cut short, the future, realized or not as it may be, is conceptually linked with the present as shown by some of the practical and moral concepts including that of personhood which we now apply to individuals and their activities. They now promise, plan with foresight, and resolve with determination to carry forward with their endeavors, yet these and many other notions refer us to a future that may or may not come to pass even though they focus our attention upon present thoughts and actions. The moral here is or should be a familiar one, that individuals living as they do in the present are beings whose lives extend back into the past and forward into the future in ways that provide significance to what they now are, no less than to what they now do, think and feel.

IV

I want now to turn to the relation between the present and the future segments of the lives of those now in their infancy.

We think of the acquisition of a skill like that involved in riding a bicycle as a matter that not only lies wholly in the future of an infant but as one that is dependent upon a variety of quite contingent factors—the accidents of its later fortune—which may or may not come to pass in later life. But we do not as parents, when we nurse and care for an infant during the long extended period of its maturation and moral development, regard the gradual emergence, in the later life of what is now an infant, of moral agency and understanding as a matter that is as contingent upon the accidents of fortune as the acquisition of the skill of bicycle riding is upon the accidents of circumstance. For the infant is, as such, a developing being. The later periods of its life in which its moral agency and understanding make their appearance are not merely temporal successors; they are also periods in the life of some being and they follow earlier periods in accordance with its nature as the human being it is. The concept of an infant, therefore, is the concept of a being in whom these changes take place in accordance with the expectations of those who act on its behalf—in its interests—as a matter of its natural development as the human being—the person—it is. This, one might think, is only a definitional matter pertaining to how we are to think of the word ''infant'', just as it is a definitional matter that we apply the word ''combustible'' only to things capable of undergoing combustion, given the application of heat. Yet the analogy suggested that in a similar way we apply the term "infant" only to those beings capable of undergoing transformation into responsible moral agents, given the application of certain conditions of nurture, is at best only superficial. For a combustible remains a combustible even if it never burns, whereas the idea of an infant that continues unchanged in its condition of infancy throughout the years during which, normally, substantial moral development occurs, strikes one as incoherent. It would in fact be as inaccurate to apply the term "infant" to such imaginable creatures as it would be to those extremely rare and deviant living organisms that issue from the womb for which special terms are employed in order to make clear how extreme is the deviation in their condition from that of normal beings to whom the word "infant" is commonly and correctly applied.

The point is that the concept of an infant is the concept of a human being in its infancy. But the notion of a human being is not merely that of a member of the biological species, but the familiar and normative notion of a being endowed with moral agency and understanding and capable of entering into those personal relations with others in which rights and obligations have their place. And the notion of a human being in its infancy is therefore the notion of a being at the beginning of a life in which such moral agency and understanding are as much a part of its nature as appetition, conation and sentience. We do not when we attribute purpose, intention and foresight to human beings at any given time, consider those present segments of their lives in independence of what lies ahead for them later on; and we do not when we consider human beings in their infancy regard their status in their infancy in independence of the lives that lie ahead for them and which gives the infant segments of their lives their significance. An infant that dies before any substantial development takes place is not merely a being whose life has been cut short in the way in which this happens to adults whose lives are terminated before middle or old age has set in, it is a being that is deprived of the life of a human being by whatever accident it is that has brought about its early demise.

It is not my purpose here to enter into an extended

metaphysical enquiry concerning the status of human beings as persons, for that would carry us beyond the scope of this essay. But lest there be misunderstanding I must observe that my preceding remarks are not designed to prepare the way for the endorsement of the view that persons are Aristotelian substances with an ever present essence that renders secure their normative status as human beings, any more than they are intended to endorse the view that infants (also adults and perhaps even newly fertilized ova) enjoy a normative status because of some occult and somehow ever present connection with transcendent egos or souls. For both of these doctrines create more problems than those they are designed to solve, including among others that of explaining how essences or transcendent egos provide any explanation of the normative status for which they are, allegedly, a basis. In any case they assume without question the view I have been at pains to expose and question, namely, that if any moral status is to be accorded to any human being, infant or adult, that status must be capable of being manifested in every segment of the life of that being. Mill once remarked, in the course of his discussion of one objection to his utilitarianism that a happy life is not one of continuous rapture, but that it contains "moments of such, in an existence made up of few and transitory pains".[3] In a similar fashion it must be recognized that the normative status of human beings which is marked by agency, interests and understanding, and without which they could not possess human rights, need not be present in every segment of their lives. To resort to Aristotelian essences or transcendent egos or everlasting souls in order to attempt to render intelligible this normative status of infants—and adults who are in deep sleep, unconscious or comatose—would be like insisting that despite the occasional distresses and pains of the man who admittedly is happy, there must be something present throughout his life, even during the transitory periods of his pains and discomforts, that constitutes the real kernel of his happiness. The members of our species (and perhaps others too) are beings who have moral rights, not because they have moral capabilities that enable them to join their lives with others on the basis of mutual understanding in *every* segment of their lives, but because increasingly as they mature, and in normal circumstances and in their normal conditions, they are able to respond appropriately to others as the responsible human beings they are. To understand, therefore, the normative status of an infant as a being with rights, we need to understand that the infant is at the beginning of a life that is, in characteristic ways, marked by agency, moral understanding and the possession of interests of various sorts. For an infant is a human being in its infancy, and to see it for what it is is to see what it is, not merely in its condition during the infant segment of its life, but as a being at the beginning of a life that is marked normally by developments in which, increasingly, agency, perceptions, interests and moral understanding play their characteristic roles in the lives of maturing and matured human beings. It is, therefore, by virtue of what lies ahead for it in the life that it has begun to live, and which hopefully it will complete, just as it is in virtue of what has occurred before in the life of the man now in deep sleep, unconscious or even comatose, that we count that being as a human being—a person—despite the radical deficiencies in agency, interests, moral understanding and perceptions in the present segments of that being's life.

When, therefore, parents provide surrogate interests, agency and moral understanding when they act as they do in the interests of their infant children, the latter must not be regarded as moral blanks. Their condition is not like that of the koi in a garden pond whose eager response to their owner's approach should not be viewed as a manifestation of affection or friendship. In the world in which we live—and our concepts are tailored to the way things are—that being who now is an infant and that being who twenty years later is a normal responsible adult are the same being, changed as the latter is from the former. It makes good sense for an adult, pointing to a picture of an infant lying in its crib, to say, "That is a picture of me in my infancy". But as things are, we should be bewildered if someone were to say this in all seriousness about koi fingerlings in a photograph. It is because of this personal identity that exists between the early infant and the adult that the conception of an infant is the conception of a being at the beginning of a life of a human being—a person. It is this fact that opens the way to the ascription of moral rights to young infants.

The newly born infant, despite its complete lack of agency, interests, moral understanding and even perceptions at that early stage of its life, is not therefore a moral blank for which nothing its parents can do when they act in its interests can possibly supply the conceptual buttressing needed to render intelligible the ascription to it of moral rights. For that infant is the human being who *later,* in that distinctively human, social and moral life of that human being, can hold its parents to account and even forgive them should they have failed to meet their obligations to it. Such a life is not that biological life of the newly fertilized ovum or the young foetus—not yet the human being that will emerge as the necessary biological changes take place.[4] It is rather that distinctively human form of life of a being at first passive but from the very beginning involved in the lives of its parents, responding very soon to, and increasingly reciprocating, the love and affection its parents lavish upon it, depending, and decreasingly so as it develops as the human being it is during its infancy, childhood and adolescence, upon its parents for the surrogate agency, interests and moral understanding they (and its older siblings too) supply in its behalf during the course of its life within the life of the family. In the case of the infant we have therefore not an entity cut off as it were from the social and moral lives of others, but one that is increasingly involved in those lives as it lives its own life within the common life of the family. To see an infant in this way is to see a being to whom the ascription of moral rights makes good moral sense despite the enormous differences that there are between early infancy and substantial maturity.

Someone might object that the consideration of personal identity, if relevant, would also show that infants are under a moral obligation to their parents; but this, surely, is queer to say the least. Why then the asymmetry between rights and obligation talk about infants?

Is it that in the case of any infant A, it is both meaningful and true that A has a moral obligation to his (or her) parents, but queer or linguistically odd or incorrect to assert the proposition? But surely what it makes sense to think of as true it also makes sense to assert.

We do not need to take such a paradoxical step. For it is apparent, as soon as we reflect on the matter, that there are substantial differences between rights and obligation talk about infants. Parents, I have argued, provide surrogate interests, agency and understanding for their infants, thus providing some sort of conceptual context for the ascription of moral rights to infants. But what analogous conceptual buttressing can there be for any possible moral obligation in the case of a young infant? Consider too the essentially and conspicuously practical character of our discourse about the moral rights and obligations of persons. To understand such discourse is to understand the sorts of appropriate responses in thought and action such discourse calls for. We can understand, easily enough, the sorts of response appropriate to the ascription of moral rights to infants; these, clearly, are the responses of parents sensitive to the moral status of the infants they have brought into the world as they plan and care for them. But what sorts of response can there be for any declarations of the obligations of infants? None, surely, by the infants themselves; and none by their parents. Or, are we to imagine parents saying to themselves; *sotto voce,* as they attend to the needs of their infant children that the latter are under obligations to them of which, only much later in their lives, they will be capable of recognizing and heeding. But what earthly difference can such mouthings make to any morally reasonable response the *parents* might make to their infants—what practical role would such *sotto voce* declarations play in the absence of which their own moral response might fail to occur?

The bearers of the truth or falsity of our moral utterances are not sentences or propositions cut off as it were from the ways in which they are employed in moral communication. The moral points served by the use of such utterances is essential to their meaning. It is conceptually incoherent, therefore, to speak of the moral obligations of infants even though at a much later period in each of their lives, and as morally mature and responsible human beings, they will recognize and respond appropriately to the moral obligations they have because, much earlier in their lives, they were brought into the world by their parents and nursed and cared for by them during their infancy.

NOTES

1. Some of the ideas presented here are explored in greater detail in my *Rights and Persons* (Oxford: Basil Blackwell, 1977 and Los Angeles and Berkeley: University of California Press, 1977).
2. See my *Rights and Persons,* Chapters II and VI.
3. *Utilitarianism,* Chapter I.
4. Does it make any unproblematic sense to say of any ovum in any possible picture medical science of the future may make possible, ''That is a picture of me at the beginning of my life''. *Me,* and *what* life?

Laurence D. Houlgate

The Child as a Person: Recent Supreme Court Decisions

Houlgate examines several recent Supreme Court deci-sions and finds that even that wise body is confused about which moral principles should guide decision making in cases involving children. The court wavers between granting children full legal status as "persons" and regarding them paternalistically.

Would the Supreme Court's confusions be cleared up by considering the arguments forwarded by Schrag or Pal-meri? Would Feinberg's advocacy of the child's right to an open future give them any guidance? Houlgate claims that the court needs a general normative theory of juvenile rights. What might such a theory look like?

In reflecting on the vast differences in treatment accorded children and adults under U.S. law, one is soon brought to inquire about the rationales that have persuaded legislators to distribute legal rights in these ways. What arguments have compelled them to grant certain legal rights to competent adults while withholding them from children (and visa versa?)This is an empirical question that might be easily answered if we had

From *The Child and the State: A Normative Theory of Juvenile Rights*. Copyright © 1980 by Laurence D. Houlgate. Reprinted by permission of the publisher, The Johns Hopkins University Press.

some record of the reasons given by each legislator for voting as he did on a particular law. Unfortunately, there are few such records. Although we sometimes know from newspaper accounts and other sources why a particular legislator voted as he did, we do not know if *his* reasons were *the* reasons persuading his colleagues to vote as they did. We are usually left to make more or less reasonable conjectures in each case.

However, there is one branch of government that does not disappoint us in the search for existing rationales of decisions that have been made about the rights of children. This is the judicial branch. The various court reporters give us a comprehensive account of the majority and minority decisions and the reasons for reaching these decisions in at least those cases that are believed to be sufficiently important for purposes of reporting.

Accordingly, in this paper I shall provide an account of some of the recent decisions on children's rights that have been reached by the United States Supreme Court. I do this not only to illustrate existing rationales, but to show that the Supreme Court makes certain important but unproved assumptions about the way in which the interests of children are to be weighed or balanced against those of the state, school, and parents. Second, I show that the fact that the Court is making these normative assumptions in reaching decisions about the rights of children is obscured by the Court's oft-stated but highly misleading claim that "children are persons" and thus have the full range of constitutional rights. Third, I argue that the Court is still in the process of discovering a set of rational moral principles to guide it in considering cases involving issues of children's rights. Hence, there is as much a need for a normative theory of juvenile rights[1] at the level of judicial decision-making as there is at the legislative.

THE FIRST AMENDMENT: *Tinker and Ginsberg*

A case that is often appealed to by those arguing for granting more rights to liberty to children is *Tinker v. Des Moines*

Independent Community School District.[2] The facts of the case are simple. The petitioners, three school children, decided to publicize their objections to the hostilities in Vietnam and their support for a truce by wearing black armbands to school. The principals of the Des Moines schools became aware of the plan and adopted a policy that any student wearing an armband to school would be asked to remove it, and if he refused he would be suspended until he returned without the armband. The children were aware of the regulation, but went ahead and wore their armbands. They were all suspended from school until they would come back without their armbands.

The Supreme Court held the regulation of the school district unconstitutional. Justice Fortas, who delivered the opinion, argued first, "that the wearing of an armband for the purpose of expressing certain views is the type of symbolic act that is within the Free Speech Clause of the First Amendment"; second, that First Amendment rights are available to teachers and students: ". . . students in school as well as out of school are 'persons' under our Constitution. They are possessed of fundamental rights which the State must respect." Third, that although the Court recognizes the "comprehensive authority of the State and of school officials . . . to prescribe and control conduct in the schools," they cannot prohibit a particular expression of opinion without showing that engaging in the forbidden conduct would "materially and substantially interfere with the requirements of appropriate discipline in the operation of the school."[3] Finally, in the instant case, Fortas held that there is no such showing.

There is no mention of paternalism in the argument of the Court and the school district did not attempt to support its case by arguing that it was protecting the petitioners from doing harm to themselves. However, in a concurring opinion Justice Stewart raises the possibility that the Court is here inconsistent given the fact that in the preceding term it had held that First Amendment rights of children are *not* coextensive with those of adults. The point is well taken. In *Ginsberg v. State of New York*[4] the Court considered the question whether it was constitutionally impermissible for New York to accord minors under the age of 17 a more restricted right than that assured adults to judge and determine for themselves what sex material they read and see. Their answer was that it was not and in their argument the Court relied on a line of reasoning developed much earlier in the case of *Prince v. Commonwealth of Massachusetts* where it had stipulated that "the power of the state to control the conduct of children reaches beyond the scope of authority over adults."[5] In *Ginsberg* the Court tells us how far beyond this scope of authority the state may go. First, the state may design laws restricting the liberty of a child more severely than that of an adult if this will support those who have the responsibility for his well-being (parents, teachers) in the discharge of that responsibility. Second, the state may design laws restricting children's liberty if it can show that these laws will protect the children's welfare and will see that they are "safeguarded from abuses" which might prevent their "growth into free and independent, well-developed men."

Justice Stewart's doubts momentarily aside, it might be argued that *Tinker* does not conflict with the reasoning in *Ginsberg*. There is no plausible reason for thinking that school children would be "safeguarded from abuses" which would prevent them from growing into "free and independent, well-developed men" by the policy of the school board preventing them from wearing armbands. That is, *Tinker* does not represent an abandonment by the Court of the paternalism it had applied in *Ginsberg:* there was simply no occasion to apply it in this case.

The conflict which undoubtedly troubled Justice Stewart was instead on a point that he had developed in his concurring opinion in *Ginsberg*. He had there argued that although the Constitution guarantees a society of free choice, "such a society presupposes the capacity of its members to choose":

When expression occurs in a setting where the capacity to make a choice is absent, government regulation of that expression may coexist with and even implement First Amendment guarantees . . .

I think a State may permissibly determine that, at least in some precisely delineated areas, a child—like someone in a captive audience—is not possessed of that full capacity for individual choice which is the presupposition of First Amendment guarantees. It is only upon such a premise, I should suppose, that a State may deprive children of other rights—the right to marry, for example, or the right to vote—deprivations that would be constitutionally intolerable for adults.[6]

It is not difficult to understand Justice Stewart's misgivings about concurring with the majority in *Tinker*. If a child does not have adequate capacity to make the sort of choice relevant to reading certain magazines, then he surely cannot be said to have the capacity needed to choose whether or not to symbolically express a political opinion.

And yet one is left wondering what Stewart meant by "full capacity for individual choice"? Under what conditions does someone lack it? A three-year-old child can choose between a red ball and a green ball; thus, in one sense of "capacity to choose," he can be said to have this capacity. This is clearly not what Stewart means. Given his examples, I suspect that what he means is that children do not have the capacity to make *rational* choices in a certain range of situations, e.g. marriage and voting. If this is so, then although one sort of problem is avoided, Stewart runs directly into another. Thus, one wants the answer to such questions as: "What is meant by the phrase 'rational choice'?" "What empirical evidence is there to support the claim that children generally lack the ability to make rational choices (in the relevant cases)?" "Why is it important anyway to decide whether a class of beings possesses the ability to make rational choices before deciding whether to grant or deny that being or class a particular legal right?"

This is not to disagree with Stewart's contention that there is a problem in reconciling the decision in *Tinker* with those in *Ginsberg* and *Prince*. However, I think that the problem has a different source than that described by Stewart. In *Tinker* a child is declared to be a "person" and (therefore) a possessor of "fundamental rights which the State must respect." In other words, the *Tinker* court has declared that since children are to be included under the category of "persons" for constitutional purposes, then they are similar to adults at least in the respect that they too possess "fundamental rights." If this declaration had been used in *Ginsberg,* then that decision might have been quite different. If a child has fundamental rights, then he cannot be denied the exercise of these rights on grounds that could not be used in the case of an adult. In particular, a child, possessing First Amendment rights, could not be denied access to books or films on the ground that reading or viewing them would prevent his growth into a "free and independent, well developed" man. It is at least incumbent upon the Court to explain how a child can possess fundamental rights and yet be justifiably denied the exercise of these rights. In what sense of "possess" does a child possess First Amendment rights if it is possible to justify a decision to prevent him from reading or viewing the material he chooses to read or view on grounds that would never be given justificatory weight in the case of adults? The *Tinker* court does not address this question.

THE RIGHT OF PRIVACY: *Danforth and Carey*

The Supreme Court continued to place emphasis on the theme that children are persons and possess constitutional rights in two recent cases involving the right of privacy. In *Planned Parenthood of Central Missouri v. Danforth,*[7] the Court declared unconstitutional part of a Missouri abortion statute requiring an unmarried minor female to acquire the consent of her parent(s) or guardian(s) in order to have an abortion performed (unless the abortion is certified by a physician as necessary to preserve her life). Justice Blackmun, delivering the majority opinion, held that "constitutional rights do not mature and come into being magically only when one attains the state-defined age of majority. Minors, as well as adults, are protected by the Constitution and possess constitutional rights." In this case the relevant right is the "right of personal privacy, or a guarantee of certain areas or zones of privacy . . . (which) encompass a woman's decision whether or not to terminate her pregnancy." Blackmun conceded that although the Court "long has recognized that the State has somewhat broader authority to regulate the activities of children than of adults," upon examining whether there is any "significant state interest" in conditioning an abortion on the consent of a parent, he found that there is none. Parental interest in the termination of a child's pregnancy "is no more weighty than the right of privacy of the competent minor mature enough to have become pregnant."[8]

Second, the right of privacy was again invoked in *Carey v. Population Services International.*[9] In this case, which reached the Supreme Court in 1977, the Court overturned a New York law prohibiting the distribution of non-prescriptive contraceptives to minors under the age of 16 years. Justice Brennan, writing for the majority, declared that "In a field that by definition concerns the most intimate of human activities and relationships, decisions whether to accomplish or to prevent conception are among the most private and sensitive." The Court rejected the Attorney General's argument that the state had a legitimate interest in protecting morality by doubting whether limiting minors' access to contraceptives substantially discourages early sexual behavior. Moreover, the Court concluded, "It would be plainly unreasonable to assume that the state has prescribed pregnancy and the birth of an unwanted child or the physical and psychological dangers of an abortion as punishment for fornication."

Carey did not leave much room for a clash between constitutional rights and "legitimate state interests." Only one justice (Rehnquist) argued that the state had a legitimate interest to promote (deterring sexual activity among minors). However, there was a much stronger basis for dissent in *Danforth.* Several justices argued that there was one significant interest not considered by the majority that deserves serious consideration. The interest is the same as that cited in *Ginsberg:* the child's own welfare. Thus, Justice White protested that:

Missouri is entitled to protect the minor unmarried woman from making the (abortion) decision in a way which is not in her own best interests, and it seeks to achieve this goal by requiring parental consultation and consent. This is the traditional way by which States have sought to protect children from their own immature and improvident decision; and there is absolutely no reason expressed by the majority why the State may not utilize that method here.[10]

In other remarks, Justice White refers us to the dissenting statement of his colleague Justice Stevens who advances the strongest argument for the justification of paternalistic interferences with the liberty of the child:

The State's interest in the welfare of its young citizens justifies a variety or protective measures. Because he may not foresee the consequences of his decision, a minor may not make an enforceable bargain. He may not lawfully work or travel as he pleases, or even attend exhibitions of constitutionally protected adult motion pictures . . . The State's interest in protecting a young person from harm justifies the imposition of restraints on his or her freedom even though comparable restraints on adults would be constitutionally impermissible.[11]

My concern about the remarks of Stevens and White is similar to that expressed in my response to the difficulty of reconciling the decision in *Tinker* with that in *Ginsberg*. If it is an unconstitutional abridgment of the privacy right of an adult female to prohibit her from acquiring an abortion on the grounds that this is necessary to protect her from harm, then *once it is granted* that a *minor* female also has a constitutional right of privacy we cannot consistently prohibit her from acquiring an abortion on paternalistic grounds. In the seminal 1973 case of *Roe v. Wade,* the Supreme Court ruled that the decision to abort one's pregnancy comes within the scope of the constitutional right of privacy. But once having pronounced abortion to be within the area of constitutional protection it is no longer open to the Court to "weigh" that protection against other considerations (e.g. strengthening the family unit, protecting the female from harm). The Constitution says that its guaranteed rights, once correctly determined, "always have more weight than any possible combination of opposing interests, private or public."[12] If the Court proclaims that a child has the right of privacy, it cannot "weigh" or "balance" this right against family or other interests any more than it can do this in the case of the adult female. I would argue, then, that the real focus of the debate between Stevens, White, and the Court majority is not over the question whether in the case of children the right of privacy is to be outweighed by the State's interest in protecting them from harm (this makes no sense), but over the question whether children ought to be granted the constitutional right of privacy *at all*. It is only to the latter question that it is relevant to bring to bear considerations about state paternalism. The Court is barred from raising the issue of the child's welfare if it has already granted that children, like adults, *have* the right of privacy.

THE RIGHT TO DUE PROCESS: *In re Gault*

The Supreme Court has decided five cases dealing in some way or other with procedure in the juvenile court. The most important of these decisions was in the case of *In re Gault*.[13] Put simply, the Court held that fact-finding (adjudicatory) hearings in the juvenile court "must measure up to the essentials of due process and fair treatment." This means that juveniles, in all cases, must be given adequate, timely, written notice of the allegations against them, and in cases in which they are in danger of losing their liberty because of commitment, they are to be accorded the right to counsel, to nonself-incrimination, and the right to confront and cross-examine opposing witnesses under oath.

Beginning with the assertion that "neither the Fourteenth Amendment nor the Bill of Rights is for adults alone," Justice Fortas (speaking for the majority) critically examined the following argument for the proposition that juveniles should *not* be accorded due process rights: (1) One can only obtain due process rights in criminal proceedings. (2) A juvenile court adjudicatory hearing is not a criminal proceeding. Therefore (3) There is no obligation to accord due process rights to juveniles in juvenile court adjudicatory hearings.

The crucial premise in the preceding argument is (1). Fortas' counter to the claim in (1) was to assert that the functional dividing line for the purpose of the Due Process Clause of the Fourteenth Amendment is whether the proceeding may or may not result *in loss of liberty,* not whether the proceeding is criminal or civil, resulting in confinement to a jail or an institution with a benign sounding name:

A boy is charged with misconduct. The boy is committed to an institution where he may be restrained of liberty for years. It is of no constitutional consequence—and of limited practical meaning—that the institution to which he is committed is called an Industrial School. The fact of the matter is that, however euphemistic the title, a "receiving home" or an "industrial school" for juveniles is an institution of confinement in which the child is incarcerated for a greater or lesser time. His world becomes "a building with white-washed walls, regimented routine and institutional laws . . ." Instead of mother and father and sisters and brothers and friends and classmates, his world is peopled by guards, custodians, state employees, and "delinquents" confined with him for anything from waywardness to rape and homicide.

In view of this, it would be extraordinary if our Constitution did not require the procedural regularity and the exercise of care implied in the phrase "due process." Under our Constitution, the condition of being a boy does not justify a kangaroo court . . . .[14]

In dissent, Justice Stewart ignored the fact that a juvenile proceeding may result in a loss of liberty for the child. What is important, he argued, is that the object of the proceeding is "correction of a condition," not "conviction and punishment for a criminal act." Given this object, a juvenile proceeding is not an adversary one, and the requirements of due process "have no inevitable place" in it. Indeed, to impose such requirements "is to invite a long step backwards into the Nineteenth Century" when children were tried in conventional criminal courts with all the conventions of criminal trials and were punished in much the same manner as were adults.[15]

Although we may doubt that imposition of due process standards in the juvenile court will bring a return to the sort of response accorded the juvenile offender in the nineteenth century, one can sympathize with Stewart's claim that where the purpose of the juvenile court is therapy or rehabilitation of the child, the adversary system is ill suited to the task. Fortas meets this point, however, by arguing that *in fact* the juvenile court has failed in its rehabilitative purpose. Quoting his own words in a case decided one year earlier, Fortas observed that "there is evidence . . . that there may be grounds for concern that the child receives the worst of both worlds: that he gets neither the protections accorded to adults nor the solicitous care and regenerative treatment postulated for children."[16] Part of the evidence that the goal of rehabilitation is not being achieved is the high recidivism rate among adjudicated delinquents. It is estimated that sixty percent of the children appearing in juvenile courts will return another time. Second, there is a great deal of doubt that any real effort can be made by the juvenile court judge to diagnose the causes and prescribe the cure for the individual child. Like the criminal courts,

. . .juvenile courts are enormously overcrowded. Juveniles typically wait for hours for an informal hearing that may take only a few minutes. A juvenile court judge may adjudicate as many as ten or twenty cases a day; assembly line rather than individualized justice is the norm.[17]

Coupled with the low level of training in law and the social sciences, clearly inadequate to make diagnoses, predictions and prescriptions for each offender, it is not surprising that the juvenile court judge cannot and does not provide "individualized" attention to those who appear before him. In sum, since the juvenile gets the worst of one world, namely confinement without the promised solicitous care and regenerative treatment, the Court has decided in *Gault* that the Constitution demands that he be relieved of the burden of the other world and be granted some of the due process protections accorded the adult in the criminal court room.

CONCLUSION

The rhetorical question posed at the outset of this essay was whether the application by the Court of constitutional norms to individual children's rights cases will yield some generalizations. I believe that we can observe some general principles at work, but it seems clear that we are left with large questions about social policy, questions that cannot be answered by taking a harder look at the Constitution.

Consider, to begin with, the decisions reached by the Court in applying the First Amendment rights and the right of privacy to cases involving children. It will simply not do to attempt to sum up these cases with the remark that the Court, having decided that children are "persons," now sees them as possessed of the full range of constitutional rights. If the Court does see children as persons, then it surely sees them as a peculiar sort of person for purposes of constitutional analysis. They are persons who must be "safeguarded from abuses," and the state may continue to design laws that will help their parents and teachers discharge their joint responsibility for their well-being; since they do not have the "full capacity for individual choice," they may be deprived of certain rights (e.g. to marry, to vote); and their activities can be regulated if it can be shown (as it was not shown in *Danforth*) that this will "safeguard the family unit and parental authority." In short, the catch-phrase that children are persons is precisely that: a phrase that lacks the precision of a normative principle. Although we learn from it that children have *some* legal rights under the Constitution (and thus are in a different category than animals or trees), since the Court obviously does not intend by it that children have equal rights with adults, we are left without a principle that will inform us about *which* constitutional rights ought to be extended to children.

In my discussion of *Danforth* I suggested that the Court sometimes obscures the issue before it by implying that the debate about children's rights is over the question whether a child's acknowledged constitutional rights are to be outweighed by the State's interest in protecting them from harm. I argued that this way of phrasing the question makes little sense. The force of saying that a person has a "constitutional right" to do something is that no court may "weigh" that protection against such considerations.[18] For example, to say that an American citizen has the right to express in speech or writing his opinion that a policy of his government is unwise, unjust or otherwise mistaken is to refer to a right that is universally accepted as absolutely unconditional in its central core cases. The guarantee expressed in the First Amendment is not subject to judicial overruling as a result of "interest-balancing" in a given case. Hence, if a child is said to have First Amendment rights, then it is never open to a legislative body to deny it access to certain sorts of reading matter on grounds that it would not use in the case of an adult.

The appropriate question for the Court to ask, then, is "Which constitutional rights ought to be extended to children?" It is only in answering this question, I suggest, that it is relevant to weigh and balance the interests of the State, the child and the parent. And viewed in this light, the Court does indeed seem to be in a quandary. There is the desire to accord certain First Amendment rights to children (because they are "persons"), yet there is a strong pull in the direction of denying them these rights on the dual ground that a child should be protected from the consequences of his own "improvident and immature" decisions and the authority of the child's parent or guardian in supervising his upbringing ought to be given state support. As a result, we are left with normative problems about which the Constitution gives no guidance: "what moral liberty-rights, if any, do children have, *qua* persons?" "Is it permissible to legally deny children the exercise of these rights if this is necessary to promote the child's own good?"

The due process cases also illustrate the point that the Court, despite its own assertions, views children as a different class of person, and that, because of their differences from adults, they ought to be treated differently. Indeed, if the Court did not think this, then it would be hard pressed to find a justification for the practice of responding to juvenile offenders with a system of rehabilitation and therapy rather than punishment. Thus, the opinion in *Gault* sees nothing improper in the early conception of the juvenile court in which "a fatherly judge touched the heart and conscience of the erring youth by talking over his problems, by paternal advice and admonition, and in which, in extreme situations, benevolent and wise institutions of the State provided guidance and help 'to save him from a downward career'." The implication of this is that if reality had matched the rhetoric, if the rehabilitative promise of the juvenile court had been kept, *Gault* would never have been decided.[19] The policy question this presents is one that is never reached by the *Gault* court: Is there an adequate justification for treating juvenile offenders separately through a system of specialized courts whose goal is to rehabilitate the child? If the child is a "person" under the Constitution and/or if the juvenile court system does not keep its promise of therapy, moral education, and rehabilitation, then one wonders what the justification is for treating the juvenile offender differently than the adult. On the other hand, if the child is fundamentally different from the adult, and/or if the rehabilitative promise of the juvenile court is kept, then there may after all be ample ground for re-examining the requirement that standards of due process be applied in the juvenile court setting.

To repeat: none of the preceding questions are going to be answered by further analysis of the Constitution or past decisions of the Supreme Court. They each involve questions of social policy. Such questions can only be settled by attempting to formulate normative principles, in brief, to construct a general theory of juvenile rights.

NOTES

1. I mean by the phrase "normative theory of juvenile rights" a justifiable (set of) normative principle(s) that will allow one to make rational decisions about the legal rights that ought to be granted or denied to minors.
2. 393 U.S. 503 (1969).
3. Ibid., at 509. Mr. Fortas also cites *Meyer v. Nebraska,* 262 U.S. 396 (1922) and *Pierce v. Society of Sisters,* 268 U.S. 510 (1924), to support his argument that students and teachers do not shed their

constitutional rights "at the schoolhouse gate." However, it is certainly arguable that the cases cited can be used to support a constitutional argument for extending a right to liberty to children. Instead, these cases seem to give support to the thesis that *teachers* have the right to teach certain subjects in school and *parents* have certain rights with respect to how they can control the education of their children. Thus, in *Meyer* the Court struck down a Nebraska statute which made it unlawful to "teach any subject to any person in any language other than the English language" (Laws 1919, c. 249). The Court argued that this unduly restricts the liberty of the plaintiff (a teacher of the German language) to teach and the liberty of the parents to engage him to teach their children. Both of these liberties are rights guaranteed by the Fourteenth Amendment. The Court does not discuss the corresponding right of the *child* to choose to be taught a foreign language. If we are to construe this as a genuine case asserting a child's right to liberty then it seems to me that this would be a necessary ingredient. At the most, the right guaranteed the child by the decision in Meyer is the positive right to be provided with instruction in a foreign language, if his parents so choose.

We reach the same result in examining *Pierce*. In this case, the Court held unconstitutional the Oregon Compulsory Education Act of 1922 which required all normal children between the ages of 8 and 16 years to attend public school. This was held a violation of the Fourteenth Amendment in that the Act "unreasonably interferes with the liberty of parents and guardians to direct the upbringing and education of children under their control" (573). No mention is made of the right of a child to choose to attend a public or private school. Instead, the only concern of the Court with children is to stress the judgment that in a conflict between their parents and the state over the general question of who should "nurture and di ect [their] destiny," the parents should prevail.

 4. 390 U.S. 629 (1968).
 5. 321 U.S. 158 (1944), at 168.
 6. Op. cit., at 650.
 7. 428 U.S. 52 (1976).
 8. Ibid., at 75.
 9. 431 U.S. 678 (1977).
10. 425 U.S. 52 (1976), at 95.
11. Ibid., at 102.

12. Feinberg, Joel. *Social Philosophy* (Englewood Cliffs, N.J.: Prentice-Hall, 1973), p. 81.
13. 387 U.S. 1 (1967).
14. Ibid., at 27–28.
15. Ibid., at 79–80.
16. *Kent v. United States,* 383 U.S. 541 (1966), at 556.
17. 387 U.S. 1 (1967) at 22.
18. Feinberg, op. cit. This does not mean that a constitutional right is "absolute" in the sense that its scope is unlimited: "the scope of free speech must necessarily be narrower than the range of all possible speech." However, it does mean that once the boundaries of a constitutional right's domain have become reasonably clear and stable it will be unconditionally obligatory within that domain. "The courts would decide whether a given exercise of free speech, for example, falls *clearly* within the boundaries of First Amendment protection; if it does, then any statute that prohibits it, or any governmental action that restricts it, must be declared unconstitutional." (81) Such rights are absolute, then, in the sense of laying *unconditionally incumbent* duties of respect and enforcement upon the courts.
19. The decision in Parham (see p. 26), which was handed down after this paper was written, confirms this point. It was held in Parham that any adversary proceeding is *not* required prior to the commitment of a minor to a state administered mental health care institution. One of the reasons given for this decision was that although there is a "risk of error inherent in the parental decision to have a child institutionalized for mental health care," the promise of rehabilitation and cure is usually kept by state mental hospitals and current informal procedures prior to admission are adequate to reduce the risk.

Francis Schrag

Children: Their Rights and Needs

Schrag argues that talk of children having rights is misguided. If we grant children rights, we will likely deny them what they need: love and affection.

Do you agree that the recognition of children's rights will make it more difficult for parents to love their children? How might Young and Melden respond to Schrag?

One of the legacies of the Civil Rights movement of the 1960s has been a heightened sensitivity to the plight of other groups or classes whose rights have been traditionally denied, trampled or overlooked. The struggle to secure the legitimate rights of women, of members of minority groups, the mentally ill and the retarded, even of animals continues. Children have their public defenders as well. Bills of rights for children have been drawn up and promulgated and children's advocates and defenders have pressed for the recognition of these rights before legislatures, the judiciary, school boards, welfare agencies, etc. That an alarming number of children are suffering from various kinds of avoidable deprivation is hardly to be denied. Yet the propriety of assimilating their plight to that of other groups whose rights have been denied is less obvious. In this essay I shall advance the following claims: (1) Assuming that children have a right to be cared for and educated, there seems to be no rational

---

This article has not been published previously.

basis for assigning the correlative child-rearing duties to either the biological parents or to someone else. (2) The concept of duty, even of supererogatory duty is not adequate to characterize the affectionate relationship in which some particular adult(s) must stand to every child if the latter is to develop in a healthy way. (3) If we take the child's need for adult love and affection as the crux of the matter then we can see that the children's rights strategy is not only in part unnecessary but that it can be dangerous in that, if seriously pressed, the struggle for certain rights undermines the very parent-child relationship on which the child's growth depends. (4) Social policy ought, therefore, to be directed to fostering those social arrangements which would allow parental concern and affection to flourish. The consideration and enactment of such policies depends on children's interests being adequately represented in the legislative arena and children do have a right to such representation, and finally (5) Without denying the importance of justice and the achievement of basic rights for all, I try to call attention to the connection, so easily overlooked, between participation in the "language-game" of the rights and duties and the character traits induced by such participation.

I

Much recent philosophical discussion has centered on the question of what creatures are suitable candidates for rights holders. In this context, some philosophers have denied that young children are capable of being rights holders. Because my concerns lie elsewhere, I do not intend to speak to this issue but will assume throughout this paper that it is *meaningful* to speak about the rights of children, even of infants.

The intriguing questions arise, I contend, not when we inquire into whether children can have rights but when we inquire into where, if children are said to have rights, the correlative duties lie. A hint of this problem was provided by H.L.A. Hart in his notable essay on natural rights. In cataloging the sources of what he calls special as opposed to general rights, Hart notes cryptically, "There remains a type of situation which may be thought of as creating rights and obligations: where the parties have a special natural relationship, as in the case of parent and child."[1] Hart seems to be suggesting that the natural facts of procreation create rights and obligations between parents and children, but it is not clear how Hart perceives this normative relation to follow from the biological facts, and I don't see how it could.

In a more recent essay, Frederick Olafson argues that the duty of parents follows not from the fact of procreation alone but from this fact together with certain other facts and moral principles.[2] The gist of this argument is this: people are responsible for the predictable and avoidable consequences of their actions. If two adults (recognizing the possibility that a helpless child might be conceived) have sexual relations and such a child is indeed born nine months later they are responsible for its existence and have to care for it. There are two problems here. (1) The argument does not protect the rights of all children: it seems to offer no protection to those children born of parents who failed to realize the possible consequences of their actions (due perhaps to misinformation from others), or to those children whose conception resulted from a defective contraceptive device, or to those conceived when their parents were drunk or otherwise incapable of good judgment; (2) Acknowledging that parents have some duty with respect to their biological offspring whom they have caused to exist, does this duty extend to sacrificing their own interests to the extent required to care for and bring up a child? Why should a perhaps spontaneous act of love and passion which takes but a few minutes give rise to an enormously taxing and complex duty extending over perhaps decades? Of course we must at times bear long-term responsibilities for thoughtless acts but these are normally situations where our failure to take due precautions endangers another's welfare, as when we foolishly get behind the wheel after having consumed a few alcoholic drinks. But in the context of procreation we are not only not endangering another's welfare (for no one exists whose welfare we could be said to be endangering) but are perhaps acting quite selflessly in making the only other person directly involved happy. Even admitting with Sidgwick that parents, "being the cause of the child's existing in a helpless condition, would be indirectly the cause of the suffering and death that would result to it if neglected,"[3] fulfillment of the duty to prevent such consequences would be satisfied by the parent making any provisions for the child, e.g. institutionalization which would prevent death and mitigate physical suffering even if these provisions were not conducive to a normal, healthy development.

If the duties correlative to children's purported rights to care, nurture and education cannot be demonstrated to rest with the biological parents, where else might they rest? Perhaps an argument could be made for assigning such duties to the community collectively? Such an argument could be made on three grounds. The duty could be derived (a) from the duty of gratitude or restitution (b) from principles of justice, or (c) from the duty of mutual assistance to those in distress. Olafson in the article I already cited suggests something like the first when he argues that since most of us have received benefits and subsidies from our parents' generation we have incurred a general debt whose repayment requires that we subsidize the nurture of the subsequent generation. This is a bizarre argument as A. I. Melden points out in his reply for the duty of restitution or gratitude, if we have any, is to our benefactors (the older generation) and not to some third party.[4] Moreover such a duty would involve, at most, providing some share of our resources for the nurture and education of the community's children. It could hardly require us to take one or a group of children into our home at birth and feed, clothe, nurture and assume responsibility for their growth until they are capable of sustaining themselves.

Arguments derived from the notion of equality of opportunity might be made along the following lines: It is unjust for some children to begin life with advantages others do not possess. Indeed in a society in which rewards are distributed according to merit, all children have a right to an equal opportunity to perform meritoriously. Therefore, society as a whole has a duty to minimize the accidental advantages accruing to those born into favorable circumstances. From this it would follow that the community had a collective duty to nurture and educate those children whose parents were not able or willing to provide adequate care and nurture. This argument is flawed in numerous respects not the least of which is that unless carefully qualified it permits a degree of intervention into familial life that most would find intolerable. Moreover, one would think that the recognition of such a duty would be accompanied by a recognition of the right to exert some collective social control over reproductive behavior, which almost everyone shies away from. But what I want mainly to point out is that even this argument does not seem strong enough to *require me* to take on the burden of rearing someone else's child whose own parents are indifferent to its development. At most it would compel me to support a public orphanage. The same point may be made with respect to arguments based on the principle of assistance to those in need. No doubt if someone is helpless and in distress and if I can relieve that distress *at no great cost to myself,* then I have a duty to do so. This duty certainly applies to children who are paradigms of human helplessness. But once again this duty extends at most to making some contribution towards the nurture of such children, not to my assuming the burden of nurturing them myself. My taking on such a burden would be morally praiseworthy but could scarcely be considered a binding duty. My refusal to, say, adopt a baby without parents or given up for adoption by its parents can hardly be conceived of as a failure to do my duty.

Now it might be thought that the duty which is warranted by the previous arguments, the duty to make some contribution to the survival of infants whose parents can't or won't care for them is sufficient to protect the interests of these children. How might this be? An illustration from a somewhat analogous situation will prove illuminating. Consider the right of all to adequate medical care, a right which may be met by each of us allocating a small portion of our income to the creation and maintenance of those institutions and professional services required to care for the sick. We do not have to nurse the sick ourselves, we can pay others to do it. But the sick, even the very sick who may require a round-the-clock care, do not *require* continuous care from the *same* person (or few people) over several years, nor is the job so taxing that the doctor can normally treat at most a handful of such sick patients at a time. Furthermore, the doctor is not *required* to act in such a way that the patient forms a deep emotional attachment to her, an attachment so strong that her departure after several years of treatment would cause a trauma likely to result in severe psychopathological consequences. If the sick required this kind of attention, few would become doctors for offering such care clearly entails a considerable personal sacrifice of the doctor's own projects and aspirations. But it is not merely that such "doctors" would fetch a price on the market place that few of us could afford. It is not likely that anyone who went into such work motivated by the prospect of handsome remuneration or even by the wish to do his or her duty could do even an adequate job, for the qualities needed for the patient to develop a strong emotional bond are difficult to simulate even when a large reward is offered for success. Yet not a few but *all* children require precisely such care. Healthy psychological development requires that every human have in infancy just such a "doctor" (or team of doctors). If the foregoing analysis is correct, we must conclude the following: (1) That there is no basis for arguing that parents have a strict duty to care for and educate their own children except perhaps in those cases where after due deliberation they beget a child knowing full well the care and attention which it will require (2) That there is no basis for arguing that you or I have a duty to care for and educate anyone else's children. The claims of helpless infants and children (provided we are not the cause of their distress) are on a par with the claims of any helpless adults in need and distress. While several lines of argument would show that we are obligated to make some contribution to relieving their distress, any duty to take them into our own homes and bring them up would have to be considered an imperfect duty, a duty of supererogation.

Where does this leave children? The position of children could be characterized in one of two ways: We could say that children have basic rights, rights, however, for which no correlative duties can be shown to exist. Alternatively, we could say that children have certain basic needs if their growth and survival are to be secured but that such needs do not provide the basis for advancing rights claims. Either characterization leaves one uneasy. It seems pointless to clamor for children's rights when no one can be found who has the duty of recognizing them and seeing to it that they are fulfilled. On the other hand, it would be embarrassing if the scope of rights claims (according to Wasserstrom, "the strongest kind of claim that there is") is not sufficiently encompassing to secure one of the most basic human needs.

II

This very uneasiness about the adequacy in this context of a theory of rights and obligations prompts the suggestion that there may be something wrong with this entire approach to the problem of securing for children that which they need to develop into healthy human beings. Consider these sentences from a leading contemporary textbook on child development.

"The child begins to develop his sense of competence, his sense of self-worth, from the way he is treated and evaluated by other members of his family. We have seen that it is not techniques alone that convey to him the attitudes and beliefs his parents hold about him. *The presence of love and his perception of being loved is important.*"[5] The use of the word "love" in this quotation, a use which is so typical in this context (as is the use of "affection") indicates that even the notion of an "imperfect" or "supererogatory" *duty* does not adequately characterize the attitude some adult(s) must assume towards an infant if he is to develop properly. For it does not seem that one can have a *duty* to *love* someone inasmuch as loving someone is not something which one can determine to do or not to do. Despite the fact that affection cannot be a duty it is a universal need of all infants. The satisfaction of this need takes place in most human families and is not in any way dependent on the establishment of a well-defined system of rights and obligations. A similar need is found and met in many other parts of the animal kingdom where of course not even the notions of right and obligation obtain. These facts are nothing if not obvious yet their full appreciation leads us to take a somewhat different attitude towards the children's rights movement and perhaps towards the entire "rights and duties" language game.

Consider some examples illustrative of the demands incorporated in recent bills of rights for children: (1) The right to grow up nurtured by affectionate parents, (2) The right to earn and keep his own earnings, (3) The right to be supported, maintained and educated to the best of parental ability. As the preceding discussion revealed, the good which the first right seeks to secure is not one that can be secured by a system of rights and obligations. But does its enunciation as a right do any *harm?* I believe that it does, for it either detracts from the compelling nature of those rights whose achievement is realizable through the legal and political process; or, if taken literally, it would allow widespread removal of children from their families and even support legal action by children against unaffectionate parents. The second example appears to be of a quite different kind. It extends to children a right which is recognized for all adults. From the point of view of justice there is every justification for recognizing such an extension. But the issue is not quite as straightforward as might be thought. Note that not only the first but the second and third as well are rights which a child (or his representative) may claim against his or her own parents. The parent is placed in the role of a potential adversary. The problem arising here is this: granted that these rights ought to be recognized, what is the likely impact of *pressing for their recognition and enforcement?* In particular, what will this impact be on the quality of the relationships between parents and children in general, which relationships are the source of those goods on which children depend but which cannot be secured by any system of rights and duties?

To help see what is involved here let us imagine a scenario which traces the fight for recognition of the right mentioned in the third example, the right to be educated to the best of parental ability.

(A) In 1979 a citizen files a successful suit against the local school board for failing to provide him with an adequate education. He recovers substantial damages for earnings not received due to an inability to find employment.

(B) In 1980 a woman alleging that her parents consistently favored her brothers over her files suit against the parents basing her claim upon the right to be educated to the best of parental ability. To substantiate her case she adduces evidence showing that her brothers attended private schools, received music lessons, art lessons, and were sent to summer camp while she was sent to public schools, had no extra lessons, and stayed home during the summer. The court sustains her allegations and the parents are required to pay damages. The decision is sustained on appeal to the Supreme Court and is hailed as a major victory by child advocates.

(C) In 1981 the sole child and heir of an oil millionaire and his divorced wife files suit for $1,000,000 damages against the father, charging him with a pattern of neglect with respect to his development and education. His lawyers, calling in child-development experts are able to convince a jury that the father's life style, in particular his long trips away from home at critical periods in the child's development contributed substantially to the complainant's later adjustment problems. [After writing this I found out that a suit charging parental malpractice was filed in Colorado in 1978.]

(D) As a result of a rash of similar suits filed the following year, a California judge orders that whenever a child is born of designated "high risk" parents (primarily single parents) a child development social worker be immediately assigned to the family. The parent(s) is (are) required to make a monthly written report to the social worker on its progress and to submit a monthly education and development plan (EDP), and an annual developmental checkup is provided by the state. The Children's Defense League notes that the dreams of its founders in the 1960's are inexorably becoming a reality.

(E) Finally in 1984 the Federal Child Protection Act is passed. Under the act, a child development social worker is assigned to each child at birth with full authority to monitor the child's development until the age of 3, the age when compulsory school attendance begins in most states. The social worker makes weekly home visits during which he disburses the monthly child care allotment, negotiates the subsequent month's EDP with the parents, makes recommendations to them, and, if not satisfied with the parents' compliance with the previous month's EDP, may initiate action to have the child removed from the home. Child advocates recommend the date of the President's signing of the legislation be declared a national holiday, the Day of the Child.

I have not constructed this scenario merely to demonstrate the way in which the rights of children are dependent on the relinquishing of what parents take to be *their* rights. Rather what I am interested in is the effect that such a "struggle for rights" would have on the relationship between parents and their children. This relationship would be defined increasingly by mutual rights and obligations and the natural affection and sympathy most parents feel for their children would be undermined. Parents would focus more and more on meeting their obligations or if not on meeting them on appearing to meet them in the eyes of the law. Parent would begin to practice "defensive parenting", i.e. the art of meeting the letter of the law to forestall the threat of a future suit. As the threat of removal from the home would be everpresent, and as extreme emotional investment came to be seen as a potential impediment to the proper discharge of parental duty, emotional involvement would diminish. Parents would begin to realize that their children were *theirs* in quite an attenuated sense from those born in previous generations. They would tend to see themselves more and more as sub-contractors to the state performing a definite service in exchange for pay. Of course a generally favorable attitude towards their charges would not be detrimental, but intense emotional involvement would not benefit anyone. The present relationship of a competent nurse to a pediatric patient would be the paradigm for the new relationship. It is, I trust, obvious that children would derive dubious benefits from this series of "reforms" introduced in the name of children's rights.

By way of contrast consider the relatively recent recognition of the right of blacks in the South to eat in restaurants previously reserved for whites only. The patron in a restaurant is engaged in a contractual relationship with the management. If he has the money to pay, he is entitled to be served any of the dishes on the menu. The patron does not care whether the owner has a personal stake in his well-being, so long as the terms of the contract are honored. Courteous service is due him, but whether personal revulsion or distrust, concern or compassion lie behind the waiter's smile is normally a matter of indifference to the patron. He might, in fact, prefer not to eat at a restaurant where the staff displayed an intense interest in his general well-being.

Someone might argue that the deleterious effects I describe derive not from the existence of a system of rights and obligations, but merely from their regular exercise. But no system of rights can be effective unless the rights holders and obligation holders are aware of their respective rights and obligations. Though few patients may be aware of their rights or choose to exercise them, the physician's awareness of the existence of patients' rights is likely, nevertheless, to affect the attitude he or she takes towards all patients.

The scenario just discussed was of course deliberately contrived to cast doubt on what I may call the entire children's rights strategy as a societal response to the suffering and deprivation of some children. I have tried especially to call attention to the more subtle and intangible psychic effects of this strategy. Do the above considerations *prove* that children would be worse off were my scenario to be enacted than they currently are? I admit that they do not. Indeed, many might decide that the benefits of the Federal Child Protection Act outweigh the costs. But costs they are, albeit hidden ones, and my main concern is to bring them into clearer focus.

III

The reader may well wonder whether my critique of the children's rights strategy should be taken as a disguised apology for the *status quo*. If one cannot appeal to duties or to rights how can one hope to exert the leverage needed to alleviate the plight of so many children? Or does one simply throw up one's hands in despair? I think that my analysis does furnish a different approach. I stressed the child's need for love and affection. Now it is not only absurd to require such affection as a duty, it is unnecessary. In most normal circumstances, the parents' affection for and psychological investment in the healthy development of their own children is simply a datum. "Normally the physical facts of having begotten a child or given birth to it have far-reaching psychological meaning for the parents as confirmation of their respective sexual identities, their potency and intactness. Derived from this is the inclusion of the newborn and infant in the parents' self-love."[6]

I will not stop to inquire here whether this parental response to the child is natural, instinctive or cultural, though it seems evident to me that its roots are in some measure biological. The point I want to insist on is that the parents' response to their biological children is *not* impervious to the social structures and arrangements that lie beyond the home. Whether the original parenting impulses are permitted to flourish or are destined to atrophy or to become repressed depends to a large extent on how society is organized, and on the kinds of support and esteem it accords parents and parenting. I do not want to be misunderstood. I do not mean to suggest that love and affection are all that children need, or that parents need not be conscientious and aware of their children. But I do believe that these responsibilities stand the greatest chance of being fulfilled when the healthy growth of the children is a crucial element in the happiness of the parents. And I believe that wider social conditions often determine whether a child will be regarded by parents primarily as an additional and unwanted burden or as a source of joy and satisfaction. So far as meeting the needs of children, then, the community's focus should not be on raising parents' consciousness of their *duties* towards their own children, nor of merely urging its members to meet their *obligations* towards all children for such obligations are not as we saw adequate to meeting children's needs. Rather in my view the focus should be on fashioning and strengthening those social arrangements and services that will enable parents "natural" ties to their children to flourish.

How is the latter approach different? There are two kinds of differences, I believe. On the one hand this approach is a good deal broader than one which focuses exclusively on children. Innumerable social arrangements and decisions affect the quantity and quality of parent-child interactions, but when we focus on children directly our view is usually limited to a few areas of social decision making such as the provision of pediatric services, public schooling and the like. On the other hand the second approach offers a way of protecting the interests of children without pitting children and parents as potential adversaries, which the children's rights strategy, if taken seriously, inevitably must. Let me illustrate what this means in more concrete terms by contrasting two specific social policies which might be derived from them. One policy is based on the premise that children are entitled to quality child care which many parents are unable to provide. Although children of the poor, those from homes where both parents work, and those who have only one parent are the worst off, this position advocates the establishment of comprehensive child development programs for all children. Women's movement spokesmen have been among the leading supporters of such a position, calling for "free twenty-four hour child-care centers."[7] One of the founders of the Liberation Nursery in New York City is quoted as follows, "Just as education from six up was taken out of the home, education from birth to six should be too.''[8] Advocates of this approach look towards the creation of programs and centers which would,

. . . address the total needs of the child, physical, social, emotional, and intellectual—and his family in order to enable him to realize his fullest potential. They have a small child-staff ratio, parent involvement, well trained and well-paid personnel, and good facilities. Developmental programs must be comprehensive programs that not only watch over and educate the children involved but provide them and their parents with medical, nutritional and social services.[9]

(The distance between such rhetoric and my scenario does not loom very large here.)

In contrast another social policy focuses on a reorganization of work to enlarge the possibilities for men and women to combine parenting with participation in the work force. The notion here is that the demand for professionally staffed day-care centers by mothers who want to work is premised on the assumption that the father also will have a full-time job. But just as many women are seeking and finding fulfillment in the world of work, so, the argument goes, more men might find fulfillment in parenting if *fathers* could be relieved of full-time work responsibilities when their children are young. A few of the specific policies favoring such a development would be those increasing the earnings and fringe benefits of part-time employees, providing leave for fathers as well as mothers after childbirth, and encouraging job *sharing* in which husband and wife (or any two people) would share a single full-time job. Such policies would not offer much to single-parent families, though even here an idea like job sharing could enable two single mothers or fathers to team up and share bread-winning and childrearing roles.[10] Such policies would of course have to be preceded or accompanied by attitudinal changes regarding the proper roles of men and women.

Now I do not mean to imply that the latter approach offers a panacea or that it is necessarily incompatible with the former. All the illustration was meant to point out was this: (1) that the

welfare of children can be enhanced in perhaps more imaginative and more effective ways if the focus is not directly on
"according them their rights," (2) that such indirect policies
could contribute to the welfare of the young without weakening
or undermining the parent-child bond which is crucial to their
well-being especially in their early years, whereas the children's
rights strategy runs a great risk in that regard.

IV

Although the discussion so far has avoided some of the more
general issues taken up by philosophers interested in the notion
of "rights" (and "duties"), I think it is capable of throwing
some fresh light on one of those issues, namely the question of
the value of rights in human society. According to Joel Feinberg
there are two distinct kinds of moral transaction,

> On the one hand there are gifts and services and favors motivated by
> love or pity or mercy and for which gratitude is the sole fitting response.
> On the other hand there are dutiful actions and omissions called for by
> the rights of other people. These can be demanded, claimed, insisted
> upon, without embarrassment or shame. A world without loving favors
> would be cold and dangerous; a world full of kindness but without
> universal rights, would be one in which self-respect would be rare and
> difficult.[11]

This analytical classification of moral transactions seems to
be an adequate characterization of adult, human interaction.
But the distinction is difficult to apply to the process of
becoming a human adult. As we saw a child has in a sense a
legitimate *claim* to "loving favors" even though this claim is
no one's duty and indeed the very notion of duty is out of place
here. Moreover, in the process of socialization there exists a
causal connection between parental *love* and the development
of *self-esteem*. "Only a child who has at least one person whom
he can love, and who also feels loved, valued, and wanted by
that person, will develop a healthy self-esteem."[12]
In the philosophical tradition and indeed in common sense

morality, the notion of right is closely connected with justice, that is with obtaining and protecting "those things which all men are entitled to have and enjoy."[13] Benevolence and love are thought normally to begin where justice ends. Hence right and duty are thought to have a priority over benevolence and love. In the context of socialization, however, one can legitimately argue that love is the primary value for in its absence human development itself is placed in jeopardy. Now what I think is easily overlooked in discussions which are based on the distinction between justice and benevolence is that in its effect on human character, the struggle for rights and justice may have a detrimental impact on the ability to give and receive love and affection. In a commentary on Feinberg's paper, Jan Narveson characterizes those who are always fighting for their rights as "crabby, thin skinned, cantankerous, touchy, and quite possibly bitchy."[14] This is a caricature, of course, but not a totally invalid one. The person concerned primarily with his rights is focused primarily on what is owed him; in return he is prepared to give others their due, but why give them more. Similarly the person who is being pressed hard to recognize another's rights is not likely to give an iota more than he is required to. Does a person who becomes oriented primarily to what is *due* him, one whose concern for others is limited to what he believes he owes them, maintain the capacity to give freely and selflessly of him or herself to another? This is an especially important question in those contexts in which trust, good will and human caring are essential. The medical and educational contexts come most immediately to mind. But it is an absolutely *crucial* question in the context of parenting. The point I am stressing in this paper is that we must be watchful lest our pervasive preoccupation with rights, even children's rights, impair our ability to give our children what they need.

NOTES

1. H. L. A. Hart, "Are There Any Natural Rights?" in A. I. Melden, ed., *Human Rights* (Belmont, California: Wadsworth, 1970), p. 71.

2. Frederick A. Olafson, "Rights and Duties in Education," in James F. Doyle, ed., *Educational Judgments: Papers in the Philosophy of Education* (London: Routledge & Kegan Paul, 1973), 173–195.
3. Henry Sidgwick, *The Methods of Ethics*, 7th ed. (Chicago: University of Chicago, 1962), p. 249.
4. A. I. Melden, "Olafson on the Right to Education," in Doyle, op. cit., pp. 196–206.
5. Ira J. Gordon, *Human Development: A Transactional Perspective* (New York: Harper & Row, 1975), p. 49 (emphasis added).
6. Joseph Goldstein, Anna Freud, Albert J. Solnit, *Beyond the Best Interests of the Child* (New York: Free Press, 1973), pp. 16–17.
7. Elizabeth Hagen, "Child Care and Women's Liberation," in Pamela Roby, ed., *Child Care—Who Cares* (New York: Harper Torchbooks, 1975), p. 284.
8. Ibid.
9. Pamela Roby, "Young Children: Priorities or Problems? Issues and Goals for the Next Decade," in Roby, pp. 137–138.
10. See e.g. Pamela Roby, "Shared Parenting: Perspectives from Other Nations," *School Review* 83 (May, 1975), pp. 415–432.
11. Joel Feinberg, "Duties, Rights and Claims," *American Philosophical Quarterly* 3 (April, 1966), p. 144.
12. Goldstein et al, op. cit., p. 20.
13. Richard Wasserstrom, "Rights, Human Rights, and Racial Discrimination," in Melden, ed., op. cit., p. 100.
14. Jan Narveson, "Commentary," *Journal of Value Inquiry* 4 (Winter, 1970), p. 158.

Victor L. Worsfold

Students' Rights: Education in the Just Society

Worsfold argues that teachers have both authority over students and specified duties to them. Students, in turn, have legitimate rights against their teachers. Notice that Worsfold grounds the teachers' duties and students' rights in the "just institutions" arising from a hypothetical (Rawlsian) contract. Schrag argues that children do not have rights against their parents; however, do you think Schrag would object to Worsfold's arguments that children (students) have rights against their teachers? If Worsfold's argument were accepted, how, if at all, would it alter present educational practice in elementary schools, high schools, and universities?

At a time when enthusiasm for allowing students a share in the decisions concerning the conduct of education is on the wane, it may seem importunate to offer an argument on behalf of students' rights. The contemporary cry of 'back to basics' and the preoccupation with the cost of student vandalism appear to have replaced the romantic idea of a general deschooling of society, or at least the provision of some alternative forms of schooling within society's existing educational framework. The idea that students might have some interests of their own that they might themselves defend or, indeed, hold their

This article has not been published previously.

teachers accountable for addressing, may by now have lost currency in all but the most radical of schools. Teachers must be in charge of the educational process, once more. The idea of students being guaranteed a say in the determination of that process appears as dead as the sixties which spawned it.

Now, at the center of this kind of talk is the place of the teachers' authority in relation to their students. For what was proclaimed in the days of radical school reform was the freedom of students to participate on an equal basis with their teachers in the matter and manner of their education. Thus egalitarianism was perceived to be the answer to the undemocratic tendency of schools to ignore what students felt their needs to be, so that what teachers knew to be in students' interest would prevail. Underlying this egalitarian thinking was the idea that matters of truth and morality are matters of individual taste so that each individual's opinion is as valid as the next's.[1] Teachers being authorities on what to teach and how to teach it, in this view, bred an elitism in the educational process, characterized by such features as the passive acceptance on the part of students of the teacher's ideas, the valuing of the teacher's authority over the student's independent judgements, and, worst of all, the notion that there are right answers to intellectually justifiable questions. Thus a plea for the anti-rational was spawned by what was perceived as an anti-authority stance. In other words, the egalitarianism of irrationality was the answer to a supposed authoritarianism. But need it have been so? Cannot authority, properly legitimated, be restored to teachers without denying students the kind of rights which the radical reform movement sought by its notion of egalitarianism to guarantee?

It will be the purpose of this essay to attempt to answer this last question in the affirmative. By investigating the source of the teachers' authority in the just society we shall discover the way in which students' rights can be achieved. By grounding teachers' authority in the philosophical framework of John Rawls's theory of justice it will be argued that students have valid claims against their teachers that give rise to rights. What the nature of these rights might be and what might constitute their content in the process of education will also be discussed. Finally, the significance for the nature of education of conceiving the relation between teacher and student in terms of rights will require attention. For it is by construing education with a specific purpose in the ideal just society, namely, the perpetuation of that society, that students acquire certain kinds of rights which structure the engagement of teachers and students in the process of education. But too much of the argument is anticipated. It must begin with a consideration of the legitimate grounds for the teacher's authority.

THE AUTHORITY OF TEACHERS

The authority of teachers, like the authority of governments, is most often represented by their critics in terms of the exercise of power. Characteristically, power is the ability to bring something about; it is coercive. In contexts involving relations between individuals such as education, power can be identified, then, with the ability to make others do what one wishes. And it is precisely in misusing this ability that teachers can become liable to charges of the authoritarianism which so riled the reformers of the 'sixties. Yet it cannot be doubted that the exercise of teachers' authority in so far as they are in authority over their students amounts to the exercise of their ability to influence the actions of these students. But the teacher's power is not necessarily commensurate with the teacher's authority.

The relationship between the teacher's power and his or her authority is derivative, surely; that is, the power of a teacher is a consequence of the acknowledgment of the teacher's authority by his or her students. For without an agreement on the part of students—normally taken to be implicit in their relationship to teachers—to honor the authority of their teachers, teachers' authority would not find a foothold. It is this acknowledgment, thus, which points to there being some kind of legitimacy to the exercise of authority on the part of teachers which the mere exercise of power on their part lacks. Exercising authority, while it may cause some to act on the will of others, does not depend on the mere influence of power but rather on the acceptance, as Winch[2] has pointed out, of there being a right and a wrong way of making decisions, and such a decision can never depend, again as Winch says, "completely on one's own caprice"[3]—or we might add, on another's. This argument has important consequences for authority in the context of the relations between teachers and students.

For, if Winch is correct, the relation between teachers and students so far from being the kind of causal relation which the exercise of power denotes (teachers making students do their bidding), is, rather, an "indirect"[4] relation, involving as an intermediate link the right way of pursuing the activities in which both are engaged. It is this indirectness of relation which ultimately differentiates authority relationships from those based upon the exercise of power which depend on the direct force of coercion. More importantly, it is also this connection between authority and the notion of the right way of doing things which begins to lend legitimacy to those having authority. For by insisting on such a connection, there is built-in a basis for testing the legitimate exercise of authority. Unless the exercise of authority can be demonstrably connected with what is taken to be the right way of doing things, it is not legitimate.

Now by linking the notion of the legitimate exercise of authority to the notion of there being a right way of doing things in the society, there is implied by such a connection the further notion of a rule-governed way of life for this society. A society which adopts this way of life will either generate rules about who has the authority about what, or someone, either from within or without the society, will emerge as the authority in this society's particular way of life. Rules authorize the authority; that is, declare that the individual is entitled to be "in authority." But because the individual acting in authority must be acting under the right way of doing things, the individual entitled by the rules to be in such a position must also be "an authority" on what constitutes the right way to proceed in the situation in which the individual has authority. Thus an individual who is "in authority" must always be "an authority" on the situation in which he finds himself. It is this idea, incidentally, which gives the lie to the egalitarianism notion of education discussed earlier. Students are rarely authorities in this latter sense on what constitutes the subject matter of their education. If they were, one wonders what the purpose of the pursuit of education might be—good conversation, perhaps? Yet, we must establish what rules do constitute the legitimate authority of teachers if we are to avoid such thoughts.

AUTHORITY AND RULES

If a rule-governed context is necessary to an understanding of the exercise of teachers' authority, then the notion of legitimacy can begin to be explicated by asking what it is for a rule to be legitimate. In answering this question, it must be remembered that the issue of legitimacy can arise with respect to the existence of an entire system of rules, the legal-rational system of republicanism, for example, or over the existence of specific rules within a system such as the rules of parliamentary procedure. As Downie has written, it might be argued that "a given system of government was morally illegitimate in that it imposed itself on the bulk of the people against their wishes, or we might say that a given rule of law was morally wrong within a system which was in general morally approved."[5] What is important here is that Downie's concern is with what makes rules morally, as distinct from legally, legitimate and in the context of this essay this seems appropriate since it is not the legal justification for a system of rules that is desired, but rather that which makes rules morally binding so that those who are established as authorities by these rules—in our case teachers—are obeyed.

Traditionally, political theorists have wanted to argue for the moral legitimacy of governmental authority in one of two ways. Either legitimacy is conferred on governments when the exercise of their authority is perceived to be directed to the good of the governed; or governmental authority is legitimated by its being at the behest of a contract with the governed. The second legitimating method attempts to address the major problem of the first, namely, the paternalism implied by the inability of individuals to influence governmental policies by right. For social contract theorists stress that the authority exercised by a government is at the behest of the will of the people. It is easy to lampoon these social contract theorists of the seventeenth and eighteenth centuries, however. Members of society never met in the forest to make a contract with each other or to authorize a ruler by such a contract. Even if they had it seems hardly likely that contemporary men should regard themselves bound by such contracts. But to concentrate on these details is to miss the bite of the theory, which is the demand that some sort of rational justification be given for the exercise of authority in the society. If we regard the social contract analogically, however, then there is real point to it, namely, that government can exercise authority, not simply exert power, so long as society *consents* to the ends pursued by the government and the means by which these ends are pursued. Thus, "it is in consent and not in contract that we must look for the theory of what makes government morally legitimate in . . . society."[6]

Yet the idea that consent is central to the notion of legitimate government requires careful thought. For, as Plamenatz[7] has pointed out, the impression cannot be left that a government governs by consent simply because it, in fact, carries out the wishes of the people. Rather, a government rules by consent, surely, if and only if, it is a necessary condition of its being entitled to do so that those governed have expressed their acceptance of that entitlement. Thus the notion of consent is, essentially, granting to individuals who constitute the government a right of action they otherwise would not have. It is consent which creates this right and thereby makes the exercise of authority legitimate.

Now, it may appear that the argument has strayed far into political theory to find the answer to our initial concern about the justification for the legitimate exercise of the teacher's authority. This is hardly surprising, however, when one re-members that it is the function of education to help create the personal and social lives of those who are in the process of becoming citizens of the state. In addition, it is this state which, if it is ideal in character, will allocate the resources, both human and non-human, for the education of all those in that process. What has been argued here is that it is the consent of the governed that legitimates the exercise of governmental authority with respect to education, so that it is the consent of the governed that creates the set of rules by which this enterprise is conducted. What must now be discovered is how, precisely, the authority of the teacher can be derived from such a set of rules which the social contract creates.

TEACHERS AND STUDENTS IN THE RAWLSIAN SYSTEM OF JUSTICE

1. Rawls's Theory

The theory of justice recently presented by John Rawls[8] provides a framework within which the exercise of the teacher's authority can be legitimated. Briefly, Rawls's theory concerns principles of justice which might form the basic structure of a just society. Subsequently, these principles, which constitute Rawls's notion of justice come to be applied to individuals' dealings with one another in the just society through the principle of fairness. Rawls grounds his theory of the just society on a particular kind of social contract. A system of justice, for Rawls, requires that individuals "understand the need for, and they are prepared to affirm a characteristic set of principles for assigning basic rights and duties and for determining what they take to be the proper distribution of the benefits and burdens of social cooperation."[9] Rawls's goal is to permit each individual to act according to a personal conception of his or her own best interests, but not at one another's expense.

In order to achieve Rawls's just society, individuals engage, hypothetically, in a mutual process of evolving principles of fair treatment for everyone, present and future. His central idea is that everyone in the society must participate in choosing these principles, and that the principles are to be selected in an imagined state, or "original position," in which the individuals are ignorant of their own specific interests and circumstances in real life. All the participants in this society are self-interested in making their decisions. But ignorance of their station in life and of the particular configuration of their society guarantees for Rawls that the individuals will choose principles of justice impartially, with equality in mind, so that no one is made to serve as an instrument of the interests of others.

In the Rawlsian scheme, the only constraints on selfishness in choosing the principles of justice are that the individuals make their choices behind the orginal "veil of ignorance," that they be rational in choosing, and that they understand roughly what might constitute an adequate theory of justice. Assuming these conditions are met, Rawls has argued that only one set of principles of justice will emerge. They will be consented to by everyone, because all individuals in society will see it in their own personal interest to come to the same general conclusions about adequate rules for the conduct of society's institutions—the law, government, health care, education and so on—which the system of justice supports.

In their condition of ignorance and self-interest, the individuals will choose two fundamental principles of justice. The first is that each person should have a personal liberty compatible with a like liberty for all others; no one should be any freer than anyone else in society to pursue his or her own ends. The second is that societal inequalities are to be arranged such that all individuals must share whatever advantages and disadvantages the inequalities bring. This principle is intended to preclude discrimination against those who are born into poverty or natural deformity. Taken together, the two procedural principles provide the basis for an entire system of justice. Individuals agree to the principles because acting on them will best implement the individual's sense of his or her own good, as perceived in the original position of ignorance.

In Rawls's theory, amongst those participating in establishing the initial social contract which creates the set of institutional rules justice supports, are developing persons—those individuals with whom teachers must deal pre-eminently. Such individuals participate to the extent to which they are capable for to participate fully in the formation of the contract one must be rational, and this, for Rawls, means amongst other things that one must have attained the "age of reason." But there is no attempt to define this age rigidly, or to link it with a particular conception of rationality or a particular notion of prerequisite skills and understanding. Instead, Rawls seems to imply that as children's competencies develop, their participation should increase.

Rawls points out that it is the capacity for accepting the principles of justice rather than the capacity's realization which matters when deciding who is to count as a member of society. He has written that "a being that has this capacity, whether or not it is yet developed, is to receive the full protection of the principle of justice."[10] Clearly children are such beings, and therefore qualify as members of the society, with, as a result, just claims to fair treatment by the society. Moreover, the status of children in the just society is further protected when Rawls argues that the principles of justice are chosen not simply by individuals with their own interests in mind but for all individuals to come. Participants to the contract therefore must choose principles without knowing their age or generation as well as not knowing their station in life. Thus they must entertain the possibility of actually being children or, even, of not yet being born. On this argument, then, the conception of children having interests of their own, which may not be synonymous with those of their parents, is taken into account. Children's interests are protected, even if adults must decide on their behalves, by Rawls's insistence that adults must not justify their decisions by finally persuading children of those decisions' correctness. Rather they must base their paternalism on the child's welfare at the time at which the decision is made, taking into account the child's own aims and preferences and demonstrating that the initial presumption of rationality, that is the full ability to decide for one's self, is unwarranted in this particular occasion. The denial of children their own rights, therefore, must be shown to be *just* by those who would deny them. Such a denial cannot ever be taken for granted.[11]

2. *Teachers' Authority*

The implications of Rawls's argument that children share in the establishment of the initial contract to the extent they can will be clear once the applications of the principles of justice to particular individuals as they participate in society's institutions is understood. For Rawls has accounted for all that is required of individuals which, as a result of their adopting the principles of justice, comes to be obligatory, by what he has called the principle of fairness. This principle holds that an individual is required to do his or her part as defined by the rules of an institution provided that two conditions are met; "first that the institution is just (or fair), that is, it satisfies the two principles of justice; and second, one has voluntarily accepted the benefits of the arrangements or taken advantage of the opportunities it offers to further one's own interests."[12] One of Rawls's major assumptions in his theory of justice is embedded here, namely, that when individuals engage in the mutually co-operative business of setting up a just society according to rules, rules which on their agreement restrict the liberty of these individuals for common advantage, those who submit to these rules have a right to expect similar acquiescence from those who benefit thereby. "We are not to gain from the co-operative labor of others without doing our fair share."[13] Thus, obligations are specified by the principles of fairness. Because the principle demands just institutions with established rules, as a *sine qua non* of its existence, obligations presuppose these also.

Just institutions however would not coerce obligations on the part of those who participate in them. Obligations arise as a result of voluntary acts which may be expressly executed or tacitly agreed to. For Rawls, because obligations are owed to those co-operating to maintain the just institutions they have established, those holding office under the rules of these institutions owe obligations to them. The office-holder's voluntary act of accepting office gives rise to the obligation to fulfill the duties of the office. Whatever these duties are defines the content of the obligation.

Teachers, inasmuch as they are entrusted with the process for perpetuating the just society by inculcating its principles in those individuals developing in the society, that is as they educate, clearly hold office at the behest of the agreement amongst individuals participating in the just society. Because children co-operate in the maintenance of the just society in the way lately noted, teachers have an obligation to them (as their students) to fulfill the duties of their office. It is important to understand, however, that such duties in the Rawlsian scheme are not viewed as moral duties, but as "tasks and responsibilities assigned to [the] institutional position."[14] Nevertheless, the teachers' acceptance of the principle of fairness does provide a moral reason for their discharging the obligations their positions of authority involve.

3. Students' Rights

To argue that the teacher has obligations to his or her students means that students have claims to fair treatment against their teacher. That these claims are valid is the result of the system of rules under which the teacher originally accepted his or her position of authority, within the framework of the mutually cooperative venture which is the just society. Failure on the teacher's part to submit to these obligations while enjoying the benefits of his particular office, an office which depends upon the submission to restrictions on the part of others (students) is unfair to the members of society in general and to students in particular. Thus claims of students and the obligations of teachers are, in essence, correlative. The correlation is neither moral or legal but rather logical in nature. For, the rules which give rise to the valid claims of students do not require the obligations of teachers as separate and different. The ascription of valid claims to students logically entails the existence of the teacher with obligations towards students. Claims and obligations on this view, then, are merely different names for the same normative relation, according to the perspective from which the relation is regarded. But by arguing that students have valid claims against their teachers, it can be shown by investigating the definition of what it is to possess valid claims that, in effect, students have rights to fair treatment in the educational process.

By investigating the implications of setting teachers' authority in a Rawlsian framework of justice the relations between teachers and students have come to center upon the students' ability to make justified claims upon their teachers. The rules defining the office of teacher give rise to this ability. But to have this ability is to possess rights, by definition. What else can a right amount to but being in a position to make a valid claim? Rights, on this construction, become a kind of activity which establishes what can be expected in the relations between teachers and students. To exercise rights is to make claims on one's own behalf to what one may justifiably expect. As Fried has recently reminded us, "a claim of right . . . is peremptory" and "rights are peculiarly personal."[15] To talk in this way is hardly to risk leaving rights to be construed as "mystic badges that exist in vacuums,"[16] as Melden has eloquently asserted. Rather, it is to insist that in having rights students can be guaranteed a claim to fair treatment on the part of their teachers.

Exercising rights, then, appears to imply "the right to claim one's rights."[17] It is this implied exercise that the Rawlsian system of justice is designed to honor. For once students actually make claims of right, their claims function as petitions to their teachers to assure their rights: the validity of the claims is the proof of the rights' existence. Acknowledging such rights implies a lack of freedom on the part of teachers to consult their own interests with respect to the matter of the rights. Such acknowledgment, then, demands action based on principle rather than personal interest—precisely what Rawls's theory demands of office-holders. Indeed in an attempt to characterize the theory, Dworkin has said that "its engine is a doctrine of responsibility that requires men to integrate their intuitions and subordinate some of these when necessary to that responsibility."[18] What acknowledging students' rights amounts to for teachers is, in a word, that they become responsible to their students.

Students, then, may justly claim rights to be treated fairly by their teachers. These rights are claim-rights against teachers to that which the process of education entails, namely, morally acceptable treatment and an understanding of knowledge which is deemed worthwhile. In the framework of the just society, teachers effecting less than this are not fulfilling the principles of justice which are the society's basic structure. Teachers must not treat their students as so many empty vessels to be topped up with knowledge, or as putty to be moulded into shape, or even as plants to be gardened until they flower. Students, for their part, however, must be prepared to accept such treatment as education necessitates; that is, they must be prepared to play the role of learner, acquiring the information and skills required to make informed judgements about the subject matter at hand, accepting the discipline of criticism about their work in their chosen subjects.

In virtue of their role, thus, students can be said to have "option rights."[19] Students have a 'sphere of autonomy' or a 'range of action' in deciding how their teachers may act towards them. These notions can be derived from the moral point of view teachers are to take in the conduct of the education of their students. Identifying students' rights is a question of the extent of freedom students are to possess. This position can lead to freedom in two directions, namely rights to do certain things or rights over individuals, teachers, in this case. Clearly the Rawlsian framework within which students' rights have been discussed encourages the moral value of the individual's freedom. Indeed, were freedom not as highly valued as it is by the just society, it is hard to see how students' rights could find a place in the scheme of things.

Yet there are those who would argue caution in the matter of students' rights. Golding has pointed out that the practical problem presented by option rights is "the extent to which they should exist and the areas in which they should exist.''[20] Thus there is a major risk in students asserting option rights, namely that the students will do what is wrong, harmful or foolish. But this is true of any who have such rights to assert, not merely of students. It must be remembered that the decision for the possession of option rights on the part of students is made within the context of a social ideal. That ideal subsumes a particular conduct for the possession of rights so that students are permitted to do what is wrong, harmful or foolish within the sphere of autonomy the social ideal allows. Without the context of the social ideal, however, it must be admitted that to opt for option rights is "to opt for *laissez-faire* morality.''[21]

More recently, Sutton has argued that children, that is, those who are normally students, are to be denied option rights on the ground that they lack the mature intellectual faculties presupposed by the ascriptions of option rights. "It is the exercise of free rational choice and not non-rational choice which option-rights are designed to protect.''[22] Following Schrag's[23] thinking, Sutton has concluded that because rational choice occupies such a fundamental place in the development of a fully human life, option rights cannot be ascribed to "young children who lack the fully developed prerequisite intellectual capacities the right to do what they please.''[24] Clearly, Sutton's objections to ascribing option rights to students, even young students, can be met by reminding him that the framework within which such rights are established is based on the capacity for rationality and not its realization and, moreover, the framework, as lately noted, constitutes a social ideal characterized by mutuality of restrictions on those who would participate in it. No one doubts the fact that a young student may attempt to do that which is harmful to himself or to others. But surely this is the price for students learning the extent to which they may assert their rights within the social framework. Indeed, this may be perhaps the very way students learn how principles of justice function in a community and the fact that under such principles they have rights at all.

Students may also be said, somewhat less controversially,[25] to possess welfare rights, that is, rights to "the goods" of their predicament, namely, an understanding of the particular subject matters which the teacher is obligated to teach for the maintenance of the just society. Because the development of individuals for life in the just society is neither a process of growth by which an individual's potential is simply actualized nor a process in which the individual's general makeup simply interacts with its environment but rather a process enabling individuals to development so that they are able to participate in the maintenance of the just society, central to the practice of education is the initiating of students into appropriate subject matters. To be educated, in this view, is to have chosen to master what Oakeshott has called "historic languages of feelings, sentiments, imaginings, fancies, desires, recognitions, moral and religious beliefs, intellectual and practical enterprise, customs, principles of conduct,"[26] and, a Rawlsian would add, the rules which denote the rights and obligations of the institution in which the individual student is a participant. If the inheritance of these languages were merely states of mind, then education might be accomplished by therapy of some sort. But because the subject-matter of education is the pursuit of that which is deemed worthwhile, nothing short of an understanding of what constitutes this notion of worthwhileness will do for students. Students have welfare rights to such an understanding so that the reasons teachers give for purveying this or that in the name of the worthwhile become subject to student evaluation and criticism by claim of right.

From the teachers' point of view the implementation of their obligations to students can best be approached by further developing the idea that students' rights begin where teachers' acceptance of their responsibility towards their students begins. Implied by the notion of responsibility, here, is the teacher's sympathetic awareness of his or her students and not simply an imaginative construction of their desires. It is possible to imagine the desires of others and remain unmoved. What is involved on the part of teachers is in Raphael's words "The sympathetic representation in imagination of another's interests which we (teachers) can help satisfy."[27] Teachers' obligations to students depend on the thought that students have ends which they have chosen for themselves. Teachers are to think of themselves as obligated to their students not simply by the thought of the students having rights against them but by representing students' ends to themselves as if they were their own. Thus teachers' obligations are essentially altruistic in nature. At once one is reminded of the prescription from Leviticus "to love they neighbor as thyself" (Lev. 19 v. 18). In education the point of such altruism is patent. Because teachers take their students to have experiences similar to their own—or to have the capacity for such experiences—teachers can and, indeed, must feel for their students with sympathetic understanding, coming to view their students as persons like themselves.

THE SIGNIFICANCE OF STUDENTS' RIGHTS

By drawing on the Rawlsian institutional conception of authority with its constitutent rules for acceptable conduct, the argument presented here has attempted to derive a non-ideal scheme of teachers' obligations and students' rights from an ideal conception of the place of education and teacher in the just society. What this amounts to is a conception of the relation between teachers and students which teachers are to achieve if they can. By arguing that it is from the purpose of education in the just society, namely, the propagation of principles of justice in the conduct of that society, rather than from the nature of education itself, that these rights and obligations stem, the interests of students in living justly are, hopefully, vouchsafed. Thus students are not trapped, on this conception of education, into learning merely to survive but rather are encouraged to join the ability to perpetuate justice and flourish in the society. Had the concept of education alone been the context for the argument, then the notion of purpose which provided the form and content of the relation between teachers and students would have been lost. For it is the need of those participating in the just society to make provision for the society's continuance that creates the institutional rules which establish the office of teacher with its concomitant obligations. In short, it is the purpose of education which provides the content of the students' rights which, in turn, gives substance to these obligations.

Some will argue, however, that the conception of the relation between teachers and students presented here in terms of obligations and rights may put teachers and students somewhat in the position of adversaries. Those who oppose this conception[28] will say that the attempt to state in advance the ways in which education should take place, or the degree to which students should accept their teachers' authority, by spelling out students' rights, is wrongheaded. Rather, they will argue that conduct in the educational process is properly guided by mutual trust, dedication and respect, according to the discipline of the work engaged in and the disposition of the students engaged in it. "To introduce the harsh. . .language of rights could only be detrimental to the relationship between pupil and teacher."[29] Perhaps such alarm can be reduced to the deceptively simple query—why is it so important for students to have rights?

An easy answer, in terms of the justification for rights already set out, is to remind the alarmists that there seems no reason to suppose that the interests of students and teachers should never clash. Teachers have aims, interests and desires, or may be subject to pressure or requirements of holding down their own jobs that are not necessarily conducive to the educational interests of their students; while students, for their part, might have goals which, on account of such requirements and pressures, get neglected by teachers. In these litigious days, students' insistence on due process in disciplinary matters, on equal access to facilities, and on a reasonable correspondence between course descriptions and course content must surely be honored. It is precisely in these kinds of areas where teachers and students can choose to pursue opposing interests with respect to both the method of pursuit and the content of the interest that the point of teachers' obligations and students' rights becomes most clear. Hopefully, students' rights can guarantee them a morally acceptable process of initiation into a worthwhile course of study, rather than a recurrence to indoctrinative or other similarly miseducative, but expedient, conduct on the part of teachers. When their students make claims against them, teachers become more accountable to students in the execution of their tasks as educators.

Perhaps this notion of accountability will become clearer, however, if the nature of the world without rights were comtemplated. Mill along with many more recent philosophers thought that "the rights and interests of every and any person are only secure from being disregarded when the person interested is himself able and habitually disposed to stand up for them."[30] While for older individuals Mill's thinking seems patently sound, for developing persons, involved in the process of learning to be interested in themselves and acquiring habits of self-esteem, securing their rights on Mill's thinking may not be so straightforward. Suppose a teacher is not disposed to fulfill his or her obligation to teach children self-esteem and its connection with rights for fear that the students will exercise these rights against him or her. What can be said to such a teacher who fails to fulfill his obligations to students in this (or any other) way?

Such teachers must be reminded of the context within which they perform the tasks of education. That context is the rules defining the office of teacher to which they agreed in the original position. In agreeing to these rules, they were, in effect, agreeing to doing the right thing by them, as they accepted the office. To default in their obligations of office by denying students the exercise of their rights is to controvert the demands of justice, and thereby to lose the advantages which their original agreement to the social contract gained them. Such teachers put themselves outside society.

In maintaining the just society, then, the rules defining the office of teacher create the obligations of teacher and thereby the rights of students. Although teachers can only asymptotically approach the problem of making the whole system of students' rights concrete, their attempt to fulfill the obligations of their office cannot but enhance the educative experience of their students.

NOTES

1. Cf. Mary Warnock, *Schools of Thought* (London: Faber and Faber 1977), pp. 62–77.
2. Peter Winch, "Authority," in *Political Philosophy,* Ed., by Anthony Quinton (London: Oxford University Press, 1967), p. 99,
3. Ibid.
4. Ibid., p. 101
5. R. S. Downie, *Roles and Values: An Introduction to Social Ethics* (London: Methuen & Co., 1971), p. 82.
6. Ibid., p. 85.
7. J. P. Plamenatz, *Consent, Freedom and Political Obligation,* (2nd Edition), (London, Oxford University Press, 1968), pp. 1–25.
8. John Rawls, *A Theory of Justice,* (Cambridge: Harvard University Press, 1971).
9. Ibid, p. 5
10. Ibid., p. 509.
11. For further discussion of this idea, cf. Victor L. Worsfold, "A Philosophical Justification for Children's Rights," *Harvard Educational Review,* Vol. 44, No. 1, Feb. 1974.
12. Rawls, *A Theory of Justice,* pp. 111–112.
13. Ibid., p. 112.
14. Ibid., p. 113.
15. Charles Fried, *Right and Wrong,* (Cambridge: Harvard University Press, 1978), p. 85.
16. A. I. Melden, *Rights and Persons,* (Berkeley and Los Angeles: University of California Press, 1977), p. 79.
17. Bertram Bandman, "Is There a Right to Education," in *Philosophy of Education 1977: Proceedings of the Thirty-Third Annual Meeting of the Philosophy of Education Society,* (Worcester, Mass.: Heffernan Press, 1977), p. 292.
18. Ronald Dworkin, *Taking Rights Seriously,* (Cambridge: Harvard University Press, 1977), p. 162.
19. M. P. Golding, "Towards a Theory of Human Rights," *The Monist* Vol. 52, No. 4 (Oct. 1968), pp. 542ff.

20. Ibid., p. 547.
21. Ibid.
22. Thomas L. Sutton, "Human Rights and Children," *Educational Theory,* Vol. 28, No. 2 (Spring 1978), p. 110.
23. Francis Schrag, "From Childhood to Adulthood: Assigning Rights and Responsibilities," quoted by Sutton, "Human Rights and Children," p. 109. The Schrag essay is printed in *Ethics and Educational Policy,* Kenneth A. Strike and Kieran Egan, eds. (London: Routledge & Kegan Paul, 1978).
24. Sutton, "Human Rights and Children," p. 109.
25. Cf. Sutton, "Human Rights and Children," p. 110, on this occasion agreeing with the idea.
26. Michael Oakeshott, "Education: the Engagement and Frustration," in *Education and the Development of Reason,* ed. by R. F. Dearden, P. H. Hirst, and R. S. Peters (London: Routledge & Kegan Paul 1972), pp. 20–21.
27. D. D. Raphael, *Moral Judgement* (London: George Allen and Unwin, 1955), pp. 124–125.
28. C. A. Wringe discusses this view in "Pupils' Rights," *Proceedings of the Philosophy of Education Society of Great Britain,* Vol. VII No. 1 (Jan. 1973). This essay is reprinted in this volume, pp. 274-288.
29. Ibid., p. 282.
30. J. S. Mill, *Utilitarianism, Liberty and Representative Government* (London: J. M. Dent & Sons, 1964), p. 208. Contemporary philosophers holding the same kind of view include A. I. Melden, *Rights and Persons,* Charles Fried, *Right and Wrong,* and Joel Feinberg, *Social Philosophy.*

C. A. Wringe

Pupils' Rights

Wringe addresses the problem of pupil's rights. Perhaps, he suggests, the relationship of trust between teachers and pupils may be jeopardized by granting pupils rights. Nonetheless, students' interests, ends, and purposes should be taken seriously. Granting pupils rights draws attention to the irreducible value of persons.

Notice Wringe's analysis of the various kinds of rights. Also notice his discussion of the "incompetence" argument addressed by Palmeri. If you think students should have (do have) rights, how extensive should they be? Should students' interests dictate curriculum or course content? How, if at all, does the practice of grading fit in with respect for persons? Do students have a right to relevant course material and interesting teachers?

INTRODUCTION

Rights claimed by pupils themselves and by others on their behalf include the following:—

1. The right to freedom in matters of dress and personal appearance (i.e. the abolition of compulsory uniform and regulation hair-styles).

"Pupils' Rights," by C. A. Wringe, *Proceedings of the Philosophy of Education Society of Great Britain* VII, no. 1 (1973). Copyright © by the Philosophy of Education Society of Great Britain. Reprinted by permission of the author and the Society.

2. The right of pupils to opt out of religious worship on their own account (and not merely to be withdrawn by their parents).
3. The right of appeal, representation and redress in decisions concerning them by the school authorities, and the abolition of corporal punishment.
4. The right to participate in the management of schools through school councils and representation at meetings of staff and governors.[1]

One cannot but be aware of the hazards of engaging in discussion of this topic, for merely to seem to take it seriously is to expose oneself to the charge of irresponsibly adding fuel to a debate which, in the eyes of many, is itself disruptive and harmful. Given, furthermore, the prevailing polarization of opinion in this area, one risks, however judicious one's conclusions, being labelled simultaneously a fomentor of agitation and a bastion of reaction. The issues raised by the above rights claims may profitably be discussed without reference to rights at all, in terms either of educational advantage or of more general moral goods. Why, therefore, it may be asked, should we provoke unnecessary acrimony by employing the language of rights, with its overtones of contention and conflict?

The specific tasks that will be attempted in this paper are the following:

1. To remove elementary confusions arising from the failure to distinguish between various kinds of rights claim and their differing modes of justification.
2. To consider whether questions raised by rights claims can be discussed exhaustively without reference to rights.
3. To consider the appropriateness of ascribing certain kinds of rights to the young, and in particular to pupils in an educational situation.

FOUR KINDS OF RIGHTS AND THEIR JUSTIFICATION

(i) General rights of freedom

A man's right to enter or leave his home whenever he chooses might be taken as an example of a general right of freedom. It is implied in having such a right that there is nothing wrong in taking the action concerned (i.e. no unmerited harm is inflicted on others) and that others should desist from hindering one.[2] If asked to justify such a right, we might properly place the onus of demonstrating that the action was wrong on those who challenged it, since what cannot be shown to be wrong is at least morally neutral and may be undertaken. Our freedom to do without hindrance whatever is not wrong may be justified transcendentally. If the would-be interferer possesses freedom, he cannot legitimately deny it to others without grounds.

(ii) General rights to the positive co-operation of others

To claim the right to a decent standard of living or a minimum of medical care is to claim the help of others in preserving vital interests when one is unable to do so unaided. The possibility of such rights (sometimes referred to as welfare rights) is frequently denied[3] and some attempts to justify them are markedly unsatisfactory.[4] If they are to be defended as a category of rights, this must be in terms of justice[5] and of the fundamental nature of the interests they are invoked to protect. The existence of affluence and destitution side by side in the same society, we might argue, is morally outrageous, whether the latter results from natural misfortune or from governmental or commercial decisions voluntarily made. It may be thought that the extreme detriment suffered by those without sustenance, medicine, and perhaps also education might be held to justify some claim on the society by whose rules a man is expected to abide, otherwise there would seem no reason why he should do so.

(iii) Special rights

Unlike the two categories of rights considered so far, special rights are not rights of all men against all men but are typically held by one man or group against another in virtue either of some transaction (such as an undertaking or a service rendered) or of some relationship such as that between parent and child.[6] Claims to special rights are justified by showing that the transaction in question took place or that the relationship exists with no invalidating conditions. We may point to the great disadvantages of not being able to rely on promises being kept or of children not being supported by their parents. It would, furthermore, be illogical to expect to profit from the benefits of society if others could not depend on our respecting the obligations necessary to its functioning.

(iv) Positive rights

Finally, the term "right" is sometimes used to mean, specifically, a positive right which, if not backed by law, is at least enshrined in custom or convention. The authors of the National Council for Civil Liberties discussion document which states that "all children *should have* the right to be taught by a properly qualified and experienced teacher" are using "right" in the sense of a positive right since they presumably think that all children *have* a moral right to be so taught.[7] To substantiate the claim that there exists a right in this sense, it is normally sufficient to point to the relevant law, regulation, charter or custom. Needless to say, apart from any *prima facie* obligation to obey the law, the existence of a positive right does nothing to remove a contemplated action from moral criticism.

The above analysis is intended to avoid certain elementary confusions concerning pupils' rights claims. In demanding to be allowed to wear clothes of their own choosing or to opt out of the daily act of worship, pupils would seem to be claiming general rights of freedom and placing the onus of justification on those who deny them. If the notion of a welfare right can be sustained, and if the right to education is such a right, this would at least dispose of the argument that children receive education as a gratuitous benefaction and thus owe the adults who provide it a duty of gratitude and unquestioned obedience. Special rights are important to our topic less because they are invoked by pupils than because there exists, both among philosophers and in popular opinion, a tendency to assimilate all rights to special rights, particularly to special rights deriving from transactions.[8] The view that pupils can have no rights because they have as yet done nothing to earn any would be an example of this assimilation. The distinction between moral and positive rights takes account of such absurdities as answering by referring to an act of Parliament, the claim that a boy of nineteen surely has the right to decide for himself whether to take part in an act of worship.

CAN THE NOTION OF RIGHTS BE DISPENSED WITH?

The view that the issues raised by rights claims can be settled without reference to rights at all takes for granted that the relationship between the language of rights and other moral discourse is unproblematical. It may, perhaps, be assumed that rights are to be accounted for simply as the correlatives of duties. Alternatively, it may be thought that rights are claims,[9] justified, like individual duties, by rules subordinate in turn to higher order principles, or directly to some highest good such as the maximization of happiness or the advancement of the human race.[10] Such a view of rights is exemplified by the statement that "a right is justified when the action it licenses or requires is itself good or else a means to what is good".[11]

Examples show, however, that the right to do one thing rather than another does not necessarily depend on the moral desirability of the action itself, which may be morally neutral. My right to buy a red car rather than a blue one does not in any way derive from the superiority of one colour over the other. When Melden's would-be theatre-goer asks his acquaintance "What right have you to stop me entering the theatre?'' the issue is not the morality of theatre-going as such, but the proper limits of an individual's autonomy.[12]

Talk of rights, furthermore, seems to function according to a slightly different logic from that of other moral discourse. Though moral rules may sometimes seem to conflict we cannot, in fact, be said to have two opposing duties. Where a man has to decide whether or not to report his friend's crime to the police, his anguish results not from the fact that he has two duties, but from the difficulty of knowing where his duty lies. We might, of course, speak of his duty as a friend conflicting with his duty as a citizen, but this is to use the term in its more descriptive sense of ''role expectation''. If ''duty'' is used in the sense of ''what a man ought to do'' it cannot be his duty both to report the crime and to conceal it for then, whatever he does, he both ought and ought not to do it.

That rights do not cancel each other out in quite the same convenient manner is shown by those harrowing cases of a natural mother reclaiming an adopted child after a number of years. Both the natural mother and the foster parent would seem to have a moral right to the custody of the child. Both cannot enjoy the right nor is it easy to see how the two rights claims can be resolved under some higher order principle. In practice, it is true, such a conflict may often be resolved by having recourse to some other consideration such as the best interests of the child, but this expedient only emphasizes the irreconcilability of rights as such.

If rights do conflict in this way, it follows that one or the other must be overruled and if this is unavoidable it is difficult to see how the decision to do it can be blameworthy. Nor, it seems, would a decision necessarily be morally wrong which set aside a right on such general moral grounds as that of great benefit to the community. In the case of compulsory purchase, for example, the owner of a piece of land seems at least to have the moral right to keep what belongs to him, though we may reluctantly recognize that the decision which deprives him of it is justified by the resulting public benefit. The process of deciding whether or not it is one's duty to overrule or waive a right is, of course, no different from deciding what one's duty is in any situation. Consideration must be given to all aspects of the situation, one of these being the existence of the right which it is proposed to overrule. A corollary of its being sometimes morally legitimate to overrule a right is that in doing so one is in no way obliged to deny that the right exists.

This apparent paradox may to some extent to accounted for by the suggestion that talk of rights and other moral discourse are not in any straightforward way all part of one system, but two different ways of performing the same task. On this view, questions of what should, or may, be done can be settled either by reference to some general moral good or, alternatively, by dividing up the area of human choice and saying who should decide what, without attempting to say what choices should actually be made. In educational matters, for example, we might either, like Plato, lay down a complete educational programme with a supporting rationale, or we might simply say who should decide how this or that individual should be educated. In the first case, issues are decided by referring individual questions to rules and higher principles, and possibly to some ultimate good. In the second, consideration is given to the proper extent of an individual's autonomy and the limits placed upon it by the prerogatives and interests of others.

Like Lamont, we may envisage societies which rely entirely on one of the two procedures outlined above.[13] In our society, however, which regulates its affairs with a mixture of the two, each having its own logic and forms of justification, it would not be surprising if conflicts and dissonances sometimes arose.

If it is objected that the above account of rights separates this concept too drastically from the rest of moral discourse,[14] it must certainly be conceded that various kinds of rights were earlier justified by reference to such general considerations as the principle of freedom, responsibility for one's acts and undertakings and the preservation of basic interests. For present purposes, however, it is sufficient to show that the concept of rights has a peculiar contribution to make to the discussion of our conduct towards each other, and cannot therefore be dispensed with. This contribution, it is maintained, lies in the fact that it draws attention to the irreducible value of individuals, in which all rights claims are rooted. If we recognize the right of a starving man to receive sustenance when this is available, our justification lies not in the value of the man's life to society—this mode of justification would be appropriate if an animal's life were in question—but in the extreme nature of the man's need alone. Where general rights of freedom are at issue, what is being urged is that things should be decided, not according to some overriding criterion such as the will of the ruler, the interests of the state, or even the greatest good of the greatest number, but in consideration of the chosen ends of those most closely concerned. When a right is overruled in the name of some greater good, it is necessary to weigh the benefits not only against the material disadvantage suffered by the right-holder, as if one man's good and another's were morally interchangeable, but against the undesirability of overruling his right, which is something more.

That the demand for pupils' rights likewise asserts the value of the individual and his point of view may perhaps be confirmed by considering the list of rights claims given at the beginning of this paper. Some of these are certainly expressed as claims to general rights of freedom. On further consideration, however, it may be felt that, with their insistence on participation, redress and representation and their rejection of certain undignified sanctions, the advocates of pupils' rights are not simply concerned with freedom from restraint. More importantly, they wish to ensure that even if pupils are not accorded equal status with adults, they will at least be taken seriously and treated as persons whose ends and purposes are of some account. So to be treated is not, of course, a right belonging to any of the four types we have considered but rather a presupposition of any rights claim. To a large extent, the dispute over pupils' rights resolves itself into one of how far and under what circumstances children, and more especially pupils, ought to be taken seriously in this way.

RIGHTS IN AN EDUCATIONAL SITUATION

Before examining the implications of pupils' rights claims in the light of the above analysis, something must be said of the view that such claims are not so much unjustified as misconceived, implying an inappropriate model of the educational situation. Talk of rights, it is sometimes claimed, belongs properly to relationships of an "associative" kind[15] which are entered into by various groups or individuals, each in pursuit of different aims and each making a minimum of concessions to the interests of the others. This, it might be held, is not the case with education, where pupils and teacher share a common purpose—namely the pupils' initiation into a worthwhile form of life. To attempt to state in advance by spelling out pupils' rights either to what degree or in what way this initiation should take place or the extent to which the pupils should accept the teacher's authority would seem not only unnecessary but impossible. Action in such a situation is properly guided by mutual trust, dedication and respect, according to the discipline of the activities being undertaken and the aptitude of the pupils. To introduce the harsh adversary language of rights could only be detrimental to the relationship between pupil and teacher, to such an extent that a situation in which rights were asserted could no longer be described as educational and the terms "teacher" and especially "pupil" no longer properly applied.

Even on this view, however, it is not clear whether the term "pupils' rights" is actually meaningless, or whether there is merely no point in claiming such rights in an educational situation since they would, *ex hypothesi,* already be fully respected by the teacher. Certainly, anyone who wished to deny that there was any point in talking of pupils' rights could argue that rights are normally only claimed on behalf of those seen as wronged or oppressed, but it cannot be argued from this that those who have no reason to see themselves as oppressed, and therefore make no rights claims, do not actually possess rights. Equally, the fact that it would be inexpedient to raise the question of rights in an educational situation provides no justification for saying that pupils possess no rights.

If one gives the word "pupil" the more mundane sense of someone who is in school because he is young and "teacher" that of someone who is appointed to a teaching post by an L.E.A.* or governing body, there seems no reason at all to suppose that interests should not clash. Teachers in this sense may have aims, interests and desires and are subject to inducements, pressures and requirements that do not necessarily coincide with the best educational interests of their pupils, while the latter may well have valid purposes and aspirations unconnected with learning what their teachers think they ought to learn. There would seem to be nothing in the situation of these pupils and teachers which necessarily renders it pointless or meaningless to talk of rights. Whether we are, in fact, justified in speaking of the denial of pupils' rights and thereby assimilating pupils to an oppressed social class is a further question. That the treatment of pupils is such as to warrant our seeing it in this light, however, is the burden of much of the polemical writing on this topic.[16]

Turning to the questions of how the possession of different kinds of right is affected by an individual's youth or status as a pupil, it would at least appear that in Britain the young have certain positive rights, such as the right to an education according to their age, aptitude and ability. Pupils would appear to possess few special rights resulting from transactions such as promises and services rendered, but our understanding of the teacher-pupil relationship in an educational context would seem to imply a special right on the part of pupils to be taught rather than indoctrinated or otherwise abused.

It is not proposed here to consider in detail the right to education which, it was suggested, might be regarded as a welfare right. If the possibility of rights based on fundamental needs is admitted at all, however, it may be conceded that the infant's dependence on food and shelter is scarcely greater than his need for firm guidance in the way of his best interests if he is to survive and achieve a satisfactory existence and under-

*Local Educational Authority. Eds.

standing of the world. Conceivably, therefore, such guidance might be regarded as a welfare right of the child, justified by the basic nature of the interests it protects.

It is frequently denied that the young can possess rights of freedom on the grounds that freedom implies choice and, therefore, rationality. Certainly, the young cannot properly choose whether or not to do something when they cannot foresee the likely consequences or appreciate the implications of their action. On these grounds we might question the view of Ollendorff that children have the right to sexual freedom and to choose for themselves whether or not to attend school.[17] It has also been held that pupils are, by definition, incapable of understanding the point of many of the activities in which they must engage. They cannot, therefore, be said to be able to choose, still less have the right to choose whether to engage in them, nor can they choose, so the argument goes, either the order or the method of their studies, or who shall be their teachers.[18]

Two points must be made. Firstly, it is not entirely clear on this argument whether pupils' lack of rationality means that they do not have the right to order their own actions, or merely that they do not have the power to exercise such a right because they are simply not capable of choice. Secondly, even conceding that their lack of rationality disqualifies them from possessing rights of freedom, this argument is only valid for as long as pupils are in fact incapable of appreciating the implications of the actions they wish to undertake, not for as long as they are in attendance at school. If it is thought that certain pupils are quite aware of what is implied by conformity in hairstyles, wearing socially distinctive uniforms and taking part in an act of worship, their right to freedom in these matters cannot be denied on grounds of their lack of rationality.

Though understanding the implications of an action may be a necessary condition of having the right to choose whether to do it, it is certainly not a sufficient one for, as we saw earlier, it is also a condition of having a right to freedom that the action one wishes to undertake should not be wrong or inflict unmerited harm on others. Clearly, a supposed right to go to school in clothes capable of distracting or offending others could be contested on these grounds. Whether personal appearance which departs from a prescribed pattern but is otherwise unexceptionable can properly be described as distracting or offensive in school, or in some schools, is a further question.

It would appear, therefore, that some, if not all, pupils are capable of possessing rights of freedom. Where such rights are claimed it must always be asked not only, as in the case of adults, whether the action contemplated is wrong, but also whether the pupil is capable of choice in the matter to which the right would relate. If he is not, adults still owe him a duty of discipline and guidance by virtue of his immaturity. Naturally, there exists a danger that considered rejection of the adult point of view will be mistaken for evidence of continued need for control, but it is hard to see how this difficulty can be avoided.

These considerations would seem to provide a satisfactory framework for the discussion of many of the rights of freedom claimed on behalf of pupils which have been mentioned so far. The claim that pupils have a right to self-determination through participation in the management of their schools is something of a special case. It is sometimes held that pupils cannot possess such a right because appreciation of the issues involved in this task is the result of training and long experience. Nevertheless, the mere presence of parties whose interests are affected by matters under discussion is a valuable safeguard against those interests being ignored. The right, at least to be heard or represented when matters seriously affecting one are decided, would seem a normal consequence of being a person whose interests and point of view are of some account.

As we saw, however, a right, even when acknowledged may not automatically be taken as a licence to do or receive something without further argument, since it may sometimes be appropriate to forego or deny a right which conflicts with the independently justified rights of others. Parents might be thought, for example, to have a special right to a say in their child's conduct by virtue of their present and earlier material support. The fact that the implications of any action contemplated by the child were fully understood by him and that the action itself was not wrong, would not affect the parents' right.

Rights may also sometimes have to be set aside in the name of some general good. If it were thought, for example, that the existing head and staff of a school were unable to preserve an educational environment other than on the basis of absolute authority, this might justify delay in establishing a school council, pupil representation and the means of appeal and redress, even though the right to such provision were acknowledged.

CONCLUSION

If rights may be overruled it may be felt that little is gained by showing that pupils, or indeed anyone else, have them. This would be mistaken. Firstly, if rights are admitted, educational or other advantages must be weighed not only against each other but also against the undesirability of overruling individual rights. If this is done, it follows that the latter consideration may sometimes prevail. Secondly, if a right is not invalidated by being overruled, it continues to stand as a pressing argument for working towards a situation where it can be implemented. Thirdly, quite apart from action that follows from the particular rights of pupils, the recognition that in general they have rights establishes unequivocally that they are to be seen in a certain way and that account must be taken both of their interests as seen by adults and of their own purposes and point of view.

NOTES AND REFERENCES

1. These examples are drawn from various sources. See particularly the National Council for Civil Liberties Discussion Paper No. 1, *Children in Schools* in the series 'Children have Rights', National Council for Civil Liberties, London, 1970. See also Berger, N., 'The Child, the Law and the State' in Hall, J., (Ed.) *Children's Rights,* Panther, London, 1972.
2. For discussion of the view that two different kinds of rights are

involved here, see Mayo, B., 'What are Human Rights?', Raphael, D. D., 'Human Rights Old and New' and 'The Rights of Man and the Rights of the Citizen' all in Raphael, D. D., (Ed.) *Political Theory and the Rights of Man,* Macmillan, London, 1967, pp. 56–7, 71–2, and 103–5.

3. See, for example, Cranston, M., 'Human Rights Real and Supposed' in Raphael, D. D., (Ed.) *Political Theory and the Rights of Man,* Macmillan, London, 1967, p. 43.

4. Raphael, D. D., op. cit. pp. 113–4, Cranston, M., op. cit. pp. 97–99, Mayo, B., op. cit. p. 79. Also Friedrichs, C. J., 'Rights, Liberties, Freedoms: a Reappraisal', *American Political Science Review,* Dec. 1963, p. 844. The examples suggested by Raphael and Mayo assimilate welfare rights to special rights derived from transactions. Friedrichs attempts to justify certain rights in terms of Man's capacities.

5. Raphael, D. D., op. cit., p. 63.

6. Hart, H. L. A., 'Are there any Natural Rights?' in Quinton A. (Ed.) *Political Philosophy,* Oxford University Press, Oxford, 1967, p. 60.

7. National Council for Civil Liberties, op. cit. p. 7, my italics.

8. See note 5. The contract theory of political rights and obligations as a whole would also seem to be an example of this tendency.

9. Mayo, B., op. cit., p. 75.

10. Ritchie, D. G., *Natural Rights,* Allen and Unwin, London, 1894, pp. 101–7.

11. Plamenatz, J., 'Rights' in *Proceedings of the Aristotelian Society,* Supplementary Volume XXIV, 1950, p. 77. Plamenatz rejects this view which he had held previously.

12. Melden, A. I., *Rights and Right Conduct,* Blackwell, Oxford, 1959, p. 7.

13. Lamont, W. D., 'Rights' in *Proceedings of the Aristotelian Society,* Supplementary Volume XXIV, 1950, p. 91.

14. Frankena, W. K., 'Natural and Inalienable Rights', *Philosophical Review,* Vol. 64, 1955, pp. 215–7.

15. See Tönnies, F., *Community and Association,* Trans. Loomis, P., Routledge and Kegan Paul, London, 1955, pp. 37–39.

16. Hall, J., (Ed.) *Children's Rights,* Panther, London, 1972. See particularly chapters by Adams, Ollendorff and Duane. See also the current monthly publication *Children's Rights,* Children's Rights Publications, London.

17. Ollendorff, R., 'The Rights of Adolescents' in Hall, J., (Ed.) *Children's Rights,* Panther, London, 1972.
18. This view was put forward by Professor F. A. Olafson in his paper 'Rights and Duties in Education' at the Philosophical Studies Working Conference in Philosophy of Education, Saint Louis, Missouri, February 1971.

Natalie Abrams

Problems in Defining Child Abuse and Neglect

There is great concern over child abuse and neglect. But as Abrams points out, we must be clear about what we mean by 'abuse'. Must a parent intend to harm a child in order for the injury to be considered abuse? Is concentration on consequences (the actual harm done) adequate to define abuse? Abrams thinks not. She suggests that abuse be understood not just in terms of consequences, but also in terms of treating children as ends in themselves— granting them dignity and respect. Within this broader definition of abuse, even loving parents who do not beat their children can nonetheless abuse them by failing to respect them as autonomous individuals. Notice that she plays down the need for state intervention to protect the child and stresses the need for voluntary preventive and therapeutic services. Do you think this is an adequate way to protect children?

The first problem to be confronted in a philosophical consideration of child abuse and neglect is the definition of abusive or neglectful behavior itself. ''The single most telling indicator that the child abuse area is at an extremely primitive level of theory construction is that there is today no widely accepted definition of child abuse. How does one investigate a phenomenon that has no widely accepted definition? Resolving this definitional dilemma must become the first item of business among workers in the child abuse area."[1] In the first two sections of this paper, I shall examine some current definitions of abuse and neglect, and try to clarify some of the possible consequences and implications of each. I shall not consider whether particular acts satisfy or fail to satisfy certain definitions, but rather, will focus on the standards set out in the definitions. In the third section, I shall recommend a new definition. In the fourth and fifth sections, I shall examine some of the implications of the suggested definition.

Abusive or neglectful behavior might be defined in terms of the agent's intentions, the consequences of the act, or the act itself. These definitions would follow traditional approaches in normative ethical theory. I shall discuss each of these definitions and some of the associated difficulties.

1. ABUSE, NEGLECT, AND PARENTS' INTENTIONS

If intentions are thought to be definitive, an act would be abusive or neglectful if the agent's intention was to injure or fail to care for the child, regardless of whether or not harm actually resulted. Given this definition, parental acts would be considered benign, even if harm did result, provided the parent did not intend the consequences. Intentions should not, however, be taken as the sole criterion of whether or not a child has been abused or neglected, since they do not refer to the effect of an act on a child. Parental behavior may harm a child whether or not parents so intend. The reason it may be important to know parents' intentions is to ascertain parental responsibility and decide about possible legal sanctions. However, even when the harm to the child is thought to be intentional, the parents' behavior may manifest forms of psychopathology and be immune from criminal prosecution.[2]

2. ABUSE, NEGLECT,
AND HARM TO CHILDREN

Most definitions of child abuse or neglect are essentially utilitarian in that they view harmful consequences for the child as the critical factor. Only behavior which harms or is likely to harm the child is considered abusive or neglectful. The argument is made that since there is no well-established theory of parenting and no universally accepted standards for child rearing, the only rational approach to evaluating parental behavior is in terms of how the child is affected. The problem which remains for utilitarian definitions of abuse and neglect is how "harm" to the child should be conceived. There are various possibilities.

One approach is to employ the "best interest" standard. According to this standard, a child would be considered harmed, and therefore abused or neglected, if parental behavior was not in the best interest of the child. The "best interest" approach may be justifiable in custody disputes, but it does not seem appropriate in child abuse or neglect determinations. There might always be another environment which would be in some way better for the child. Furthermore, defining abuse or neglect as failure to act in the child's best interest seems to impose unreasonably demanding obligations on all parents and totally disregards competing interests or rights, such as those of parents themselves or of siblings.

Another version of a utilitarian approach is to claim that a child is harmed (and, hence, abused or neglected) if certain minimum needs are not satisfied. With this approach, it is necessary to determine, first, what needs a child has, and second, what would constitute a minimal level of satisfaction of these needs. Again, this approach focuses on consequences for the child. It would be similar to what Joel Feinberg refers to as the "unmet need" analysis of harm,[3] which views an individual as harmed if he has a need which is not met. Once all needs are satisfied, a further provision of goods would constitute unneeded benefit, and if these additional goods are not forthcoming, the individual is not benefitted but has not been harmed. One problem which Feinberg points out is that, given this analysis, a rich man would not be harmed by a small theft which left him above the minimum level. A distinction must therefore be made between actually being harmed and undergoing a change in one's condition in a harmful direction. A rich man's condition, and that of a child, might be altered in a harmful direction without falling below the minimum level—i.e. without ever reaching the state of actual injury. On the minimum needs definition of child abuse and neglect, parental behavior is abusive or neglectful only if the child's condition falls below the minimum level. Failure to realize a child's potential or even inhibiting a child's development would not be abusive, provided the child's status or level of well-being does not fall below a minimal standard.

A third consequentialist approach to defining abuse or neglect is in terms of social or community standards and specified sorts of harm. According to this approach, behavior which falls below the community norm and also results in specifiable harm would be abusive or neglectful. It is this standard which is employed in cases charging negligence. "The tort of negligence is committed when a legally protected interest of the plaintiff is invaded as a result of conduct on the part of the defendant which falls below the standard of care reasonably to be expected from ordinary members of the community, or if the defendant has some special skill or knowledge, from persons possessing such specific qualifications."[4] A physician, for example, who is charged with negligence is accused of providing medical care which results in harm and which falls below the medical community's standards. The issue, then, is whether child neglect and abuse should be conceived of as forms of parental negligence.

On the one hand, both child neglect and abuse are similar to negligence in demanding that some harm or damages result from the questionable behavior. It might be argued, therefore, that child neglect and abuse should be evaluated according to negligence standards. On the other hand, however, negligence implies inadvertence or unintentional harm, whereas the harmful consequences to children which are under discussion are frequently intended.

In addition, a number of arguments can be made against evaluating parental behavior according to community norms. For the most part, these arguments reflect differences between medicine and parenting. First, as noted before, there is no theory of parenting or body of knowledge which is widely accepted among parents, but there is a body of knowledge which is widely accepted among practicing physicians within a given community. Because there is this fairly well accepted body of knowledge, the law permits the medical profession itself, rather than a jury of laymen, to determine what is due care. "In order to prevail in a negligence suit against the doctor, the plaintiff must prove, not that what the defendant did was unreasonable, but that there is no accepted body of medical opinion according to which what the defendant did might be judged reasonable. Neither judge nor jury is entitled to determine that the practice of an 'accepted school of medicine' is itself unreasonably lax."[5]

Second, the provision of care which meets social standards might demand inordinate sacrifices for some parents in particular communities, whereas the physician receives compensation commensurate with the sacrifice. It cannot be argued that parents have necessarily accepted these sacrifices by bearing children with a given community or society, since parents cannot foresee with any degree of certainty either their future circumstances or the future needs of their children.[6]

Third, until and unless all parenthood is voluntarily assumed, and parents accept a set of community standards just as physicians accept a set of medical standards, it is unreasonable to hold them responsible for nonadherence to those standards. Fourth, the standards employed in any community might fall below the satisfaction of minimum needs, and, also, the standards of one community might fall considerably below those of another. An appeal to social norms runs the risk, therefore, of not providing minimal care. (This fourth point, however, seems to be applicable to medical care as well.)

The criteria of best interest, minimum needs, and community standards are all attempts to determine when a child has been culpably harmed. All of these criteria hold that a child is abused or neglected only when harmful consequences are produced, whether they be physical, emotional, or psychological. A wide variety of conditions has been cited as legitimate bases for considering a child to be neglected or abused and for permitting state intervention. They include parental nonconformity (including religious nonconformity), failure to discipline, excessive discipline or cruelty, parental "immorality," failure to authorize medical treatment, excessive use of drugs or alcohol, parent's mental condition, extreme poverty, incarceration in prison or another institution, extremely low intelligence, and abandonment (including lack of financial support and/or lack of attention). In all these cases, it is supposed that the particular condition has harmed or will likely harm the child.

I claim that this emphasis on effects or consequences reflects an unrecognized purpose. These consequentialist definitions of child abuse and neglect are formulated solely to deal with the problem of state intervention.

Parents are assumed to have both the natural and the legal right to raise their children without outside interference. This right, or rather liberty of non-interference, is protected by the Fourteenth Amendment to the Constitution.[7] In certain instances, however, the state may intervene in the parent-child relationship. Specifically, the state may intervene, under the doctrine of *parens patriae*, to protect the interests either of the child or of the state itself.

Generally, state intervention is thought to be justifiable when parents or guardians fail to provide adequate care for the child, though able to do so and when parents are unable to care for the child. Children who fall in the former category are usually termed "neglected"; those in the latter category are usually termed "dependent." To apply these categories requires an interpretation of adequate care or parental behavior. This interpretation invariably refers only to harm done to or risked by the child. "By finding that a child is neglected, the court's sole focus should be whether the child is being hurt or impaired by his parent's actions and whether he is likely to be impaired if these actions continue. If the child is coming to no harm, the state has no right to intervene in the parent-child relationship through the use of neglect statutes, regardless of how despicable a character the parent may be outside of this relationship. To look at parental behavior except as it constitutes a danger to the child is to grossly abuse the *parens patriae* power which should look toward the salvation of the child, not the damnation of the parent."[8]

Since harmful consequences to the child are considered the only legitimate basis for state intervention, and since definitions of abuse and neglect have been formulated solely to permit state intervention, harmful consequences have become, in turn, the standard basis for a definition of abusive or neglectful behavior. Yet, available data demonstrate the failure of state intervention programs and of foster care facilities to improve the condition of the child substantially.[9] As a response to these data, there has been an attempt to limit the situations in which the state can intervene. This has been done by formulating very narrow and limited definitions of abuse and neglect,[10] often restricted to instances of gross physical abuse or severe deprivation.

Although harmful consequences, in particular as defined by the minimum needs criterion, may be both sufficient and necessary to justify state intervention, they do not necessarily exhaust the definition of abuse and neglect, which may be considerably broader. In addition, if harmful effects, as defined by unmet minimum needs, are taken to justify state intervention, then the child's condition is the significant factor, regardless of how or by whom the harm was caused. State intervention would be justified on behalf of any child who displayed certain traits, whether or not the behavior was thought to result from parental abuse or neglect.

3. ABUSE, NEGLECT, AND RESPECT FOR CHILDREN

I suggest that an adequately broad definition of child abuse or neglect must include reference to the kind of behavior which is abusive or neglectful, regardless of the consequences. This is the third alternative mentioned above, besides intentions and consequences, for a definition of abuse or neglect.

Such a definition would be similar to that employed in applying the concept of "battery" to conduct not involving children. "The central concept of battery is the offense to personal dignity which occurs when another impinges on one's bodily integrity without full and valid consent."[11] In order for a charge of battery to be made, it is not necessary for there to have been any damage, physical or otherwise. The affront is to an individual's dignity. It is this concept of an affront to dignity that is totally omitted in the definitions of child abuse or neglect, which focus solely on actual or risked harmful consequences. It is not enough simply to say that the harmful consequences constitute assaults on one's dignity and, therefore, that the child's dignity is indirectly being protected. Although harmful consequences must be prohibited in order to ensure the possibility of the child's development, the prevention of these harms does not amount to respect for the child's dignity, any more than it would amount to respect for adult dignity.

How might it be possible, however, to protect a child's dignity or to know when it is being violated? An affront to the dignity of an adult is protected by use of the concept of consent. Contact or "intermeddling"[12] with an adult person's body can be justified only if the person consents. Furthermore, the necessary consent must be both free and informed. In other words, an affront to the dignity of an adult is not defined by or protected by reference to some objective or social standards, but rather, by reference to that to which the individual has knowingly and freely agreed. Consent, however, does not seem to be an appropriate measure by which to respect the dignity of a child. The consent requirement presupposes the right to liberty—specifically, the right to the liberty to control what happens to and with one's own body. Children, especially young ones, do not have the right to liberty as much as the right to protection, which can often be respected *only* by violating or precluding a right to liberty—specifically, the right to liberty is restricted because it is believed that if the child had the freedom to choose, he would not necessarily choose according to his own best interest. In essence, the child's right to protection would not be respected.

An important point should be noted here. Restrictions are placed on a child's liberty because without these restrictions, the child might harm himself or not act in his own best interest. The child's liberty is not restricted simply because it is believed the child lacks the capacity for informed consent or rational decision making. "Indeed, if a person who lacked this capacity did no more harm to himself or failed to promote his own welfare no more often than a normal adult, the paternalistic justification for denying him certain legal rights to liberty could not be invoked."[13] A conflict, therefore, exists between a desire to respect the dignity of a child and a desire for the child's protection.

4. PROTECTING CHILDREN AND RESPECTING CHILDREN

This conflict is extremely difficult to resolve, but I would like to suggest one possibility. If protection of the child is the sole basis for not recognizing a child's right to liberty,[14] then when protection is not an issue, recognition of this liberty should prevail. Provided the claim cannot be made that a child's welfare or development is in danger of being hindered, the child should have the right to decide matters about his own treatment or care. Parental decisions should control only those aspects of a child's life which are relevant to protecting the child's physical, emotional, and psychological development. It is legitimate to grant rights to children "provided we can predict that in the exercise of the right, the child would not do himself harm or fail to promote his own welfare or good."[15]

If this account of the respect which is due to children is built into a definition of child abuse and neglect, then parental treatment which fails to recognize or respect the child's right to

make autonomous decisions in matters which are neither critical to protecting the child's basic interests, nor make claims on
others, would be abusive or neglectful. These actions would
essentially constitute a form of "battery" in that they would be
an affront to the child's dignity. Certainly, before such an
interpretation could be applied, minimum needs would have to
be established, so that it would be possible to determine when
the child's basic interests were in danger of being violated.
Further, it would be necessary to restrict such a principle to
those instances in which respecting the child's dignity by
recognizing the child's right to make autonomous decisions
would not make parental obligations more burdensome than
would the course of action which the parent would have wanted
to follow. For example, respecting such dignity would not
require that a parent spend additional money on a child. Rather,
it would require that the money be spent as the child wishes,
unless this would risk harming the child's basic physical,
emotional, or psychological interests. The application of such a
principle should therefore not impose additional parental obligations or increase children's claim rights. It should expand the
decision-making jurisdiction of children, provided there is no
increased risk to the child's well-being or development.

Obviously, a broader definition of abuse and neglect which
incorporates this notion of an affront to dignity refers implicitly
to the concept of consent. So, it can be applied only to children
who can express their own wishes. Two points might be noted
here. First, wishes can be expressed by other than verbal
means. Second, it might be possible to establish standards of
treatment which respect dignity, defined without reference to
consent, to protect very young children. These standards
should emanate from a theory of parenting, which, to my
knowledge, has yet to be developed.[16] Such a theory would go
beyond most contemporary writing on parenting, which focuses
solely on establishing what treatment will further the child's
development or the parent-child relationship. It would have to
establish standards which would define violations of a child's
dignity. Basically, it would have to define behavior which fails
to treat children as people or as ends in themselves, rather than

as mere means to their parents' futures. Given such a theory, certain types of treatment of children would be prohibited because of the behavior itself, even though harmful consequences might not result.

5. STATE INTERVENTION AND RESPECT FOR CHILDREN

What is the implication of such a broader definition of abuse and neglect for the role of the state? Whereas a fully adequate definition of child abuse and neglect would have to be based on a theory of parenting and child welfare, an adequate justification for state intervention would have to be based on a social or political theory which explained the state's role in family life and its capacity to substitute for parents. It is quite possible that this definition and justification may coincide, but it does not seem to be necessary that they do. It seems reasonable, therefore, to reject the automatic connection frequently made, and discussed previously, between definitions of abuse and neglect and grounds for coercive state intervention.

Also, as noted previously, there is considerable empirical evidence of the ineffectiveness of state intervention into family life. "There is substantial evidence that, except in cases involving very seriously harmed children, we are unable to improve a child's situation through coercive state intervention. In fact, under current practice, coercive intervention frequently results in placing a child in a more detrimental situation than he would be in without intervention. This is true whether intervention results in removal of the child from his home or 'only' in mandating that his parents accept services as a condition of continued custody."[17] Increasing state intervention to protect children against parental behavior which would constitute affronts to their dignity, therefore, would certainly not be desirable. Except in extreme cases, the net effect of intervention, taking into account the child's emotional attachment even to a psychologically unfit parent, is frequently damaging.

Based on this evidence, only failure to protect minimum interests should justify coercive state interference. Inclusion of the concept of battery or an affront to a child's dignity in a broader definition of child abuse or neglect would have no implications for the state's role. Most behavior which would produce harmful consequences for the child by not protecting minimum needs, and which would consequently justify state intervention, would also constitute abuse or neglect in this broader definition. Harmful consequences, defined by minimum needs, would therefore be a sufficient but not a necessary condition for behavior to be a violation of good parenting—i.e., abusive or neglectful.

This broader definition of abuse and neglect, which incorporates a concept of dignity and is not tailor made for justifying state intervention, could serve important functions. Using such a definition, a child might be judged abused or neglected, even if, through luck or resilience, he was able to compensate for the treatment he was receiving from his parents. A definition which emphasizes only effects classifies children with unusual capacities for resistance or compensation as neither abused nor neglected, even though treated in ways which would be considered abusive or neglectful for less resourceful children. This possibility would be eliminated by including reference to the parental behavior itself.

Furthermore, such a broader definition of abuse and neglect would help current efforts to identify potentially abusive or neglectful parents. At present, various attempts are being made to identify potential child abusers by factors such as family history, personality traits, attitude during pregnancy, and even attitude and behavior in the delivery room.[18] The hope is that if potential child abusers can be identified before abusive behavior occurs, preventive measures can be instituted. An adequate understanding of what should count as abusive behavior is essential to its prediction. Attempts at such prediction admittedly must focus on those parents who have had "unfortunate childhood experiences that could manifest as unusual child rearing practices."[19] It is not possible now, nor is there any real hope of ever identifying, potential physical abusers. These attempts at early identification must therefore be based on a broad view of what should constitute normal or acceptable child-rearing practices, one which might incorporate reference to a child's dignity. They cannot be related solely to severe physical abuse or extreme neglect.

Because these attempts at prediction cannot be related solely to severe physical abuse or extreme neglect, and hence to deprivation of minimum needs, they should not be used as a justification for coercive state intervention. By separating attempts at prediction from coercive state intervention, a number of ethical problems are precluded. The right to privacy of those labeled potential child abusers could not be invaded by state-mandated investigations. Since psychiatric attempts at predicting violent behavior do not have a high degree of accuracy, state intervention should not be permitted on this basis.

On the view which I have outlined, the traditional presumption of parental autonomy would be maintained. The state would have the right to intervene coercively only to protect minimum needs. But this limited state role would not fully define abusive or neglectful behavior. A broader definition of abuse and neglect, which incorporates respect for a child's dignity, could form the basis for provision of voluntary services, such as preventive and therapeutic parenting programs. Such voluntary programs would not socially stigmatize or threaten their participants, but rather, would attempt to teach them proper parenting and respect for children. There need be no risk that excessive interference would follow, for the state's role in such a relationship would not be as potential guardian of children or as a threat to interfere in family life, but as educator and provider of voluntary services to promote the care of children.

NOTES

I would like to thank Onora O'Neill and William Ruddick for very valuable comments on an earlier draft. The work on this essay was done while I was a Fellow of the Institute on Human Values in Medicine of the Society for Health and Human Values under National Endowment for the Humanities grant #EH–10973–74–365.

1. Edward Zigler, "Controlling Child Abuse in America: An Effort Doomed to Failure," in *Proceedings of the First National Conference on Child Abuse and Neglect,* Jan. 4–7, 1976, DHEW Pub. No. OHD 77–30094, p. 30.

2. See R. Gelles, "Child Abuse as Psychopathology: A Sociological Critique and Reformulation," 43 *American Journal of Orthopsychiatry* 3, 173, for a discussion of this widely accepted interpretation of child abuse.

3. Joel Feinberg, *Social Philosophy,* Prentice-Hall: Englewood Cliffs, N. J., 1973, p. 30.

4. Charles Fried, *Medical Experimentation: Personal Integrity and Social Policy,* American Elsevier Pub. Co.: New York, 1974, p. 14.

5. Ibid., p. 17.

6. Onora O'Neill, "Begetting, Bearing and Rearing," in O'Neill and Ruddick, op. cit., pp. 25–38.

7. "The right of a parent to be free from state interference and to raise his child in the manner that he sees fit has been described as a 'right which transcends property' " (*Denton* v. *Jones,* 107 Kansas 729, 193 Pa. 307, 1920), as an 'inalienable right' (*In re* Agor 10 C.D. 49, 1878), as a 'sacred right' (*In re* Hudson, 13 Wash. 2d 673, 126 Ped 765, 1942), as a 'natural right' (*Anguis* v. *Superior Court,* 6 Ariz. App. 68, 429 p 2d 702, 1967), and most recently as a right that has been established beyond debate as an American tradition (*Wisconsin* v. *Yoder,* 406 U.S. 205 at 232, 1972)." Brian G. Fraser, "The Child and His Parents: A Delicate Balance of Rights," in *Child Abuse and Neglect,* ed. by Ray E. Helfer and C. Henry Kempe, Ballinger Pub. Co.: Mass., 1976, p. 326.

8. Michael Sullivan, "Child Neglect: The Environmental Aspects," *Ohio State Law Journal,* vol. 29, 1968, p. 92.

9. See Michael Wald, "State Intervention on Behalf of 'Neglected' Children: A Search for Realistic Standards," *Stanford Law Review,* vol. 27, 1975, and Stephen W. Bricker, "Testimony on the Child Abuse Prevention and Treatment Act," before the Senate Sub-Committee on Child and Human Development, April 7, 1977.

10. See Theodore J. Clements, "Child Abuse: The Problem of Definition," *Creighton Law Review,* vol. 8, 1975.

11. Fried, op. cit., p. 15.

12. Ibid., p. 19.

13. See Laurence Houlgate, "Children, Paternalism, and Rights to Liberty," in O'Neill and Ruddick, op. cit., pp. 266–78.

14. Ibid.

15. Ibid., p. 14.

16. See William Ruddick, "Parents and Life Prospects," in O'Neill and Ruddick, op. cit., pp. 123–37.

17. Wald, op. cit., p. 993.

18. Ray E. Helfer, "Basic Issues Concerning Prediction," in Helfer and Kempe, op. cit.

19. Ibid., p. 363.

Annotated Bibliography

Berg, Leila, et.al. *Children's Rights: Toward the Liberation of the Child*. New York: Praeger Publishers, 1971.
A collection of six essays discussing the rights of children. One of the included essays, "The Child, The Law, and The State," persuasively argues that our laws basically regard children as possessions.

Chase, Naomi Feigelson. *A Child Is Being Beaten*. New York: McGraw Hill Book Company, 1976.
Briefly describes the history of child abuse. Discusses not only abuse by parents but also what Chase calls "institutional abuse of children."

DeCourcy, Judith and DeCourcy, Peter. *Silent Tragedy*. Sherman Oaks, California: Alfred Publishing Co., 1973.
A moving chronicle of real-life cases of child maltreatment and the inept judicial handling of that maltreatment.

Fontana, Victor. *Somewhere a Child is Crying*. New York: The New American Library, Inc., 1976.
A readable discussion of the scope and causes of child maltreatment. It also offers some concrete suggestions for preventing maltreatment.

Foster, Henry H., Jr. *A "Bill of Rights" for Children*. Springfield, Ill: Charles C. Thomas, 1974.
Foster claims that the legal and social "establishments" are grossly unfair to minors and argues that children should be given a wide range of legal rights.

Gil, David. *Violence Against Children*. Cambridge, Mass: Harvard University Press, 1970.
A detailed study of the scope and seriousness of child abuse. Good source of information.

Goldstein, Joseph, Freud, Anna, and Solnit, Albert J. *Beyond the Best Interests of the Child*. New York: Macmillan Publishing Co., 1973.
A discussion of appropriate guidelines for child placement. Stresses the view that the law should make the child's needs paramount in placement decisions.

Harvard Educational Review. *The Rights of Children*. Cambridge, Mass: Harvard Educational Review, 1974.
A compilation of two issues of this journal. Selections range from discussions of philosophical justification of children's rights to concrete discussions of policy proposals.

Helfer, R., and Kempe, H., eds. *The Battered Child*. Chicago: University of Chicago Press, 1968.
A classic text on the incidence of child abuse. Includes a number of essays on the medical aspects of abuse.

Holt, John. *Escape from Childhood*. New York: Ballantine Books, 1974.
A passionate plea for the liberation of children.

Houlgate, Laurence D. *The Child and the State: A Normative Theory of Juvenile Rights*. Baltimore, MD: The Johns Hopkins University Press, 1980.
A recent book on juvenile rights.

Hunt, William, Ed. *Justice for the Child Within the Family Context: A Loyola Symposium,* forthcoming.
A collection of six articles originally presented at a Loyola University conference. The papers discuss a wide range of problems affecting the child in the family: sex education,

parental unemployment, justification of legal intervention into the family, licensing parents, etc.

Katz, Sanford N. *When Parents Fail*. Boston: Beacon Press, 1971.
A careful, insightful examination of the circumstances, purposes, and means in which the state intervenes into the parent-child relationship.

Kempe, H. and Helfer, R. *Helping the Battered Child and his Family*. Philadelphia: J. B. Lippencott & Co., 1972.
A collection of essays suggesting concrete therapeutic procedures for dealing with child abuse.

Keniston, Kenneth. *All Our Children*. New York: Harcourt Brace Jovanovich, 1977.
Describes the obstacles that our society is creating for parents and children. Argues that more attention should be focused on aspects of the social and economic system which fundamentally affect parents and children.

LaFollette, Hugh. "Licensing Parents." *Philosophy and Public Affairs* 9 (1980).
Argues that the state should license all parents.

Maddux, Rachel. *The Orchard Children*. New York: Avon Books, 1978.
A slightly fictionalized and very moving account of one family's attempt to adopt two children—only to have the children returned by a local court to the biological parents who had repeatedly abandoned them.

Nagi, Saad. *Child Maltreatment in the United States*. New York: Columbia University Press, 1977.
An informative sociological study of the frequency of, and governmental services dealing with, child abuse and neglect.

O'Neill, Onora, and Ruddick, William, eds. *Having Children.* New York: Oxford University Press, 1979.
A collection of philosophical essays on various aspects of the parent-child relationship.

Steiner, Gilbert. *The Children's Cause.* Washington, D.C.: The Brookings Institute, 1976.
Examines the machinery for making children's policy. Also evaluates substantive policy proposals.

Wilkerson, Albert E. *The Rights of Children: Emergent Concepts in Law & Society.* Philadelphia: Temple University Press, 1973.
An anthology principally focusing on the legal rights of children. Many essayists argue that talk of human or moral rights is not enough; children's rights should be legally protected.

Wooden, Kenneth. *Weeping in the Playtime of Others.* New York: McGraw Hill Book Company, 1976.
An impassioned, readable, but sometimes one-sided, study of the juvenile justice system.

Notes on Contributors

NATALIE ABRAMS teaches in the philosophy and medicine program at New York University Medical Center.

SHARON BISHOP is professor of philosophy at California State University, Los Angeles. She is the editor (with Marjorie Weinzweig) of *Philosophy and Women* and author of essays in ethics and political philosophy.

JOEL FEINBERG is professor of philosophy at the University of Arizona. He is the author of *Doing and Deserving, Social Philosophy,* and numerous articles in ethics, social and political philosophy and philosophy of law.

LAURENCE HOULGATE teaches philosophy at California Polytechnic State University. He is the author of *The Child and the State: A Normative Theory of Juvenile Rights* (1980).

A. I. MELDEN is professor of philosophy at the University of California, Irvine. His most recent book is *Rights and Persons*. He is also author of *Rights and Right Conduct* and *Free Action*.

ANN PALMERI is professor of philosophy at Hobart and William Smith Colleges where she teaches political philosophy and the philosophy of the social sciences.

FRANCIS SCHRAG holds joint appointments in the departments of philosophy and Educational Policy Studies at the University of Wisconsin. He is the author of articles on the status of children appearing in a number of professional journals and anthologies.

VICTOR WORSFOLD is professor of philosophy and education at the University of Texas at Dallas; he also serves as the Assistant to the Vice President for Academic Affairs, in charge of undergraduate studies. He is the author of various articles on children's rights, and philosophy of education.

C. A. WRINGE is a professor in the Department of Education, University of Keele, England.

ROBERT YOUNG teaches philosophy at LaTrobe University, Melbourne, Australia. He is the author of *Freedom, Responsibility and God* and of more than thirty articles in ethics, social and political philosophy, philosophy of religion, and metaphysics.

The Editors

WILLIAM AIKEN is assistant professor of philosophy at Chatham College, Pittsburgh, Pennsylvania.

HUGH LAFOLLETTE is assistant professor of philosophy at East Tennessee State University.

They are co-editors of *World Hunger and Moral Obligation* (1977).